THE

EVERYTHING

Saints Book, 2nd Edition

Dear Reader,

Before I began this project, I was more familiar with the "plaster saints" version of some of these lives. I imagined these invincible figures sleeping half a second a night, munching a single locust for dinner, and nursing lepers to health, all the while offering unceasing praise to God.

As I dove headlong into the research and writing of this book, I discovered far more expansive, textured, and human saints than I anticipated. Some of the saints made me laugh, some made me cry—all of them made me hunger to learn more.

I explored questions such as "How did saints respond to the Holocaust?" (see Chapter 15) and "How did the saints navigate relationships?" (see Chapter 7), as well as "What compelled some of the saints to move out to the desert or to devote their lives to caring for the poor?" (see Chapter 10 and Chapter 12).

Not only did I find answers to some of my questions, but I found real people lurking behind them. Hopefully, in *The Everything® Saints Book, 2nd Edition*, you'll find some bread for your own journey. It is my hope that you'll also find a little bit of yourself, tucked into these very human saints who never stopped aching toward eternity.

Jenny Schroedel

The EVERYTHING® Series

THE EVERYTHING® SAINTS BOOK

2ND EDITION

The inspiring lives of martyrs and miracle workers throughout history

Jenny Schroedel

Adams Media
Avon, Massachusetts

To Anna, who rubbed my sore back as I worked; to Natalie, who tickled my womb with her toes; and to John, who never stopped believing this was possible.

An Everything® Series Book.
Everything® and everything.com® are registered trademarks of F+W Publications, Inc.

Published by Adams Media, an F+W Publications Company
57 Littlefield Street, Avon, MA 02322 U.S.A.
www.adamsmedia.com

ISBN-10: 1-59869-265-8
ISBN-13: 978-1-59869-265-5

Printed in the United States of America.

J I H G F E D C B A

Library of Congress Cataloging-in-Publication Data
available from the publisher

Unless otherwise indicated, the Revised Standard Version of the Bible was used for quotations.

Interior illustrations by Michelle Dorenkamp and Brewster Brownville

This book is available at quantity discounts for bulk purchases.
For information, please call 1-800-289-0963.

Contents

20

Acknowledgments

I'd like to thank my editor, Lisa Laing, for her encouraging tone, her help in forming a vision for this book, and her attentive approach as the manuscript developed. I'm also grateful to Katrina Schroeder and Suzanne Goraj for their help with the final phase of this manuscript. I'd also like to thank Jim and Nancy Forest for sharing photos and for their invaluable work on Mother Maria Skobtsova and Fr. Dimitry Klepinin.

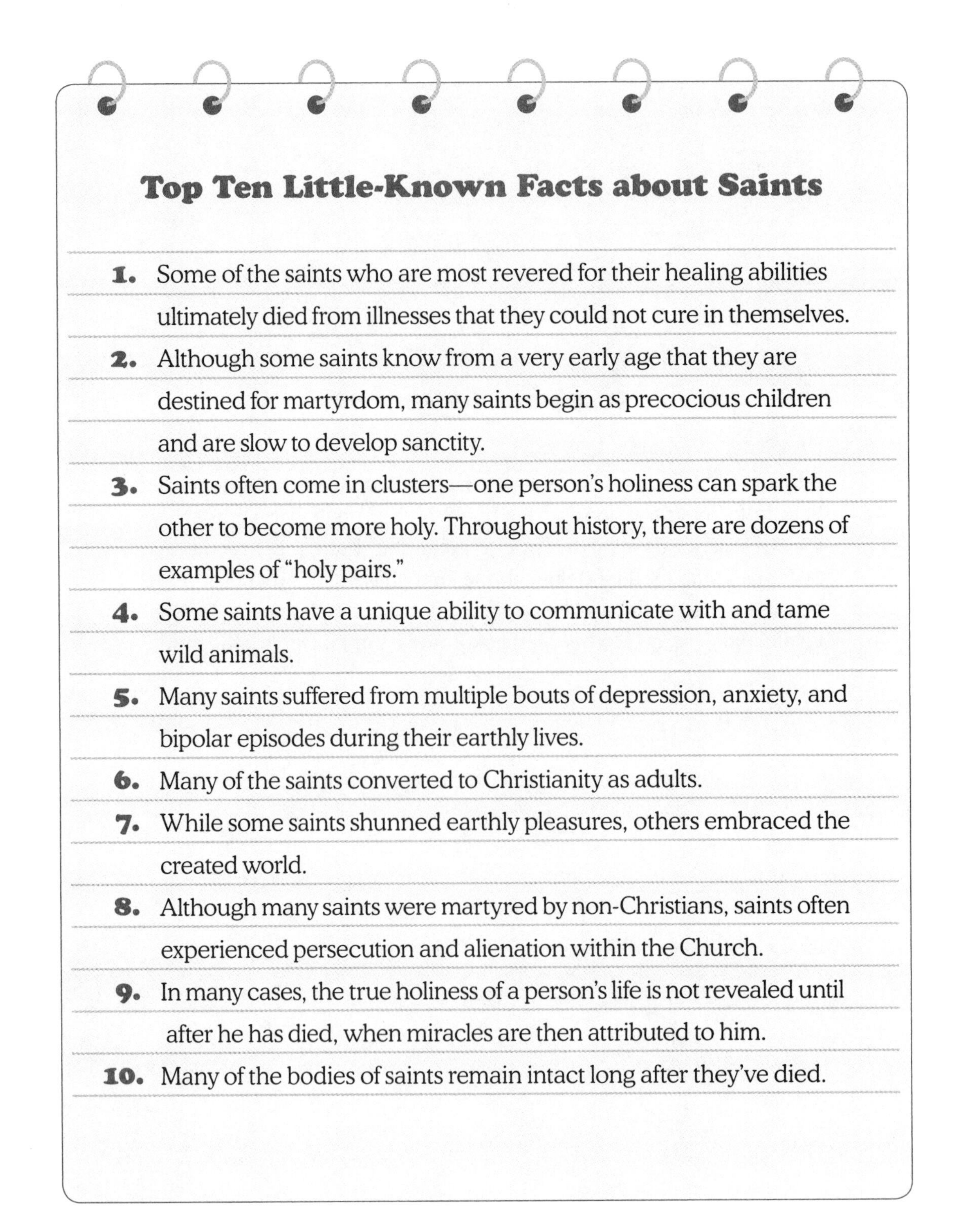

Top Ten Little-Known Facts about Saints

1. Some of the saints who are most revered for their healing abilities ultimately died from illnesses that they could not cure in themselves.
2. Although some saints know from a very early age that they are destined for martyrdom, many saints begin as precocious children and are slow to develop sanctity.
3. Saints often come in clusters—one person's holiness can spark the other to become more holy. Throughout history, there are dozens of examples of "holy pairs."
4. Some saints have a unique ability to communicate with and tame wild animals.
5. Many saints suffered from multiple bouts of depression, anxiety, and bipolar episodes during their earthly lives.
6. Many of the saints converted to Christianity as adults.
7. While some saints shunned earthly pleasures, others embraced the created world.
8. Although many saints were martyred by non-Christians, saints often experienced persecution and alienation within the Church.
9. In many cases, the true holiness of a person's life is not revealed until after he has died, when miracles are then attributed to him.
10. Many of the bodies of saints remain intact long after they've died.

Introduction

▶ AS ST. TERESA OF ÁVILA said in the sixteenth century: "From silly devotions and from sour-faced saints, good Lord, deliver us." People often assume that the more "saintly" a person becomes, the more severe and dull she becomes. Nothing could be further from the truth. The saints scattered throughout these pages were authentic human beings who, as they drew closer to God, only became more and more fascinating and—in some cases—a wee bit more eccentric.

Many led exciting, even dangerous lives. They battled evil people, wild beasts, corrupt governments, bureaucratic processes, savage seas, and persecution. Sometimes they died for their convictions. Some experienced incredible loneliness as they dwelt in the desert or among natives in foreign countries. A few were dissidents, which made life even harder for them.

Many of the saints in this book are also contemporaries who struggled with familiar vices—some lost their faith for a time, some smoked and drank beer (to meet a beer-drinking, cigarette-smoking nun, see Chapter 15), and still others sank to the depths of despair and then dug their way to the light above.

The saints come from every rank of society—princes and queens, peasants and farmers, even former prostitutes, thieves, and murderers found their way to sanctity. The majority of the saints were celibate, but there are also married folk and parents who achieved a celebrated level of holiness.

All of the saints showed charity and mercy to those they served—the poor, the sick, prisoners, and so on. The unfortunate and needy did not have to suffer ill humor from those ministering to them. In fact, the saints were surprisingly cheerful, given all that they endured.

This book will explore the lives of both Western and Eastern saints, as well as some who are on the path to canonization in both churches. It is important to know, before starting out, that until about the year 1054 there was one Christian church, generally united in theology and practice. This church encompassed what is now known as the Roman Catholic and Eastern Orthodox Churches. The separation of the churches in 1054 was tragic for all of Christendom. Some might even say that this great "schism" paved the way for all of the divisions found in the church today—some estimate that there are presently as many as 35,000 denominations.

Many of the saints profiled in this book lived before Christendom was divided. For this reason, some lives offer a glimpse of the shared heritage of the whole, undivided church—preserving a fading memory of what the church was—and still could be. As separate practices have evolved, however, distinctions have emerged. Many of the saints have two different days of commemoration, for example, because the Roman Catholic and Eastern Orthodox Churches follow different calendars.

These types of linguistic, calendar, aesthetic, and theological distinctions can make for some confusion to those new to "saint-watching." That said, a rich tapestry of holiness is wrapped all the way around the globe, and this edition strives to demonstrate this diversity.

These pages offer a glimpse of desert saints, holocaust saints, missionary saints, animal-loving saints, literary saints, healing saints, and companion saints. Do keep in mind that most saints could have been listed in several of these categories—St. Francis, for example, was a companion of humans and wild beasts, a healer, and a writer.

The saints also bore witness to the intrinsic value of life, in every age and circumstance. "Life would be almost unbearable without such people," said Thomas Cahill, famed author of *How the Irish Saved Civilization* (Random House, 1995). "The saints are for everyone—believer, unbeliever, Christian, non-Christian—it doesn't really matter. They are the people who say by their lives that human life is valuable—that my life is valuable—and there is a reason for living. Without them, history would be just one horror after another."

Chapter 1

The Making of a Saint

Over the past 2,000 years, thousands of people have been canonized. But what does it take to become a saint? This chapter will explore the questions related to everyday sanctity—small steps toward holiness that anyone can take—as well as the larger issues involved in the canonization of those who have been (or will be) sainted. The process of canonization, particularly within the Roman Catholic Church, is extremely rigorous. This chapter will explore the phases of canonization and the questions at the heart of the process of "saint making."

Saintly Kids?

Saints are both born and made. In the vast majority of cases, holy people are the fruit of holy parents (especially mothers) who prayed for them even before they were conceived, who carried them under their hearts to church when they were growing in the womb, and who committed themselves to teaching their children the faith. This is certainly the biblical model—think of Abraham and Sarah, Isaac and Rebecca, Mary and Joseph, and Zacharias and Elizabeth—the parents of St. John the Baptist. This model has inspired generation upon generation of parents.

This is not to say that all adult saints were perfect children. Far from it! Many of them were as mischievous as any child. Holocaust martyr St. Maximilian Kolbe was so difficult when he was little that he caused his mother to throw up her hands in exasperation and say "What will become of you?" The young boy was so troubled by his mother's question that he took it to the Virgin Mary, and the rest is history—or, more accurately, hagiography (read more about this remarkable man in Chapter 15).

What made these children different was the way that they were spiritually nurtured from a young age. Even those who strayed from the faith during their teenage years found their way back in adulthood—and went on to become saints. Because the seeds were planted when the soil of their hearts was still soft, those seeds never stopped growing, even if they were dormant for a time.

Wounded Healers

Henri Nouwen popularized the term "wounded healers." The idea of bringing healing to others even while coping with one's own physical and emotional wounds applies to many of the saints. Many of the saints became deathly ill as children, only to be miraculously restored to health. Yet some of them struggled with chronic illnesses all of their lives, while others suffered because of their own extreme ascetic efforts. Many died young.

And while many of the saints were unable to achieve the level of bodily health they might have hoped for in themselves, almost all of them were able to bring health and wholeness to others—if not during the course of their lifetimes, then afterward.

A few of them died after contracting the very illnesses they sought to heal in others. (To learn about Fr. Damien of Molokai, who contracted leprosy while caring for lepers, see Chapter 11.) The saints, despite their boldness and courage, were vulnerable like everyone else to sickness, pain, and sorrow. Their wide-open hearts and lives only increased this vulnerability.

A New Way of Seeing

To become a saint, one must develop a radically different vision of the world. One common mark of saintliness is a willingness to view suffering as an intrinsic part of life that can be embraced and transformed.

A willingness to suffer, however, does not neccessarily make for a gloomy person—the saints are often the most buoyant, radiant people. They are able to remain hopeful and grateful even in the most painful circumstances. Some of the saints were also able to do crazy, playful things—like King David, who scandalized his wife when he danced before God wearing practically nothing (learn more about him in Chapter 4).

Robert Ellsberg, author of All Saints: Daily Reflections on Saints, Prophets, and Witnesses for Our Time, *describes everyday saints as "People whose love, courage and inner balance seem to set them apart—not above ordinary humanity, but as a standard of what human beings ought to be. When we are with such people, we come away feeling gladder, more grateful to be alive, perhaps wishing that we knew the secret of their inner illumination."*

The saints are remarkable for the way they lived (and live), which is rooted in the way they saw the world. Instead of being weighed down by earthly realities, they were able to live with gratitude and hope in every circumstance.

Everyday Saints

During the papacy of Pope John Paul II, he canonized more than 300 people. Not only was the sheer number of canonizations remarkable, however, but it was also obvious that he was seeking to expand the limits of the way that sanctity was understood. Although in the past married people have been canonized, this has been the exception rather than the rule. Pope John Paul II sought to canonize more married people, and he expressed a desire to see more laypeople (those who aren't monks or nuns or clergy) aspire to sanctity.

The Roman Catholic Canonization Process

By the fourth century the veneration of saints was widespread. Holy men and women were declared saints by acclamation until the thirteenth century, when the saint-naming process became more formalized, and Pope Gregory IX decreed that papal canonization would be the only legitimate process. A few centuries later, in 1588, Pope Sixtus V charged the Sacred Congregation of Rites with the duty of processing candidates for canonization.

In 1983, Pope John Paul II simplified many procedures called for in the canonization process, now handled by the Congregation for the Causes of Saints. The congregation is composed of a group of some twenty-five cardinals and bishops.

E-FACT

During Pope John Paul II's papacy, he canonized over 300 men and women. The canonizations that occurred during his papacy added up to more than half of the total amount of Roman Catholic canonizations over the last 500 years.

Pope John Paul was also responsible for officially recognizing the first saints from Nigeria and Papua New Guinea. One of those he beatified in 1995 was Mary MacKillop (1842–1909), cofounder of the Sisters of St. Joseph of the Sacred Heart. When she is canonized, she will become Australia's first saint. Mary MacKillop dedicated her order to providing free education to all those who needed it, particularly in rural areas. The order also spread to include New Zealand. Pope John Paul II was especially interested in conferring sainthood on men and women outside Europe, which has provided such fertile ground for canonization since the early days of Christianity.

Advancing the Cause

It usually takes years—generations—for a canonization to take place after initial interest is shown in a particular holy man or woman. The first requirement, which may seem obvious, is that the person under consideration must be dead. Also, the official canonization process cannot start until five years after an individual's death. That allows time for the possible flood of initial enthusiasm to die down. After the initial enthusiasm fades, it can be easier to determine if serious interest is maintained. This pause also allows for those pushing a particular canonization at the local level to plan the path of their cause.

The canonization process begins in the diocese where the candidate for sainthood lived or worked. A "petitioner" approaches the local bishop to seek permission from Rome to begin the canonization process. The petitioner can be anyone. Perhaps the candidate saint was a member of a religious order. The superior of that order locally—or at a higher level, regionally—might start the ball rolling.

When permission is received, a "postulator of the faith" in that diocese is named. Similar to a defense attorney, he or she can be a member of the clergy or a layperson but must be familiar with the workings of the Congregation for the Causes of Saints. The postulator brings the case to a panel of judges appointed by the local bishop. A "promoter of the faith," similar to a prosecuting attorney, stands up for the church's position and can challenge all evidence with objections. The promoter of the faith replaces what used to be called "the devil's advocate."

The investigative process covers an extensive biography of the person in question, and depositions from those who knew him, if witnesses are still alive. Every facet of the individual's life will be explored, in order to guarentee that canonization is warranted. It is also important to avoid any potential scandals associated with the candidate. Alleged miracles are noted but must be proven in another step in the canonization process, which takes place in Rome. All of the documents, now known as "the Acts of the Cause," are sent to Rome.

When a person's case is accepted in Rome by the Congregation for the Causes of Saints, he is given the title "Venerable." Now, all of the evidence of his life is vetted even more stringently. If there is a reason to, the evidence is challenged by the promoter of the faith.

The Slightly Faster Track

Some potential saints are helped along in their cause by active boosters at the local level or in Rome. For example, some saintly candidates move extremely slowly through the various layers of canonization or may be, in fact, stalled in the process. Their cause languishes in musty files in Rome because there is no group lobbying for their canonization.

Money can also help a would-be saint's cause. While no one who is worthy will be sidelined because of a lack of funds to advance the cause, backers have much to spend their dollars on: fundraisers to bring in more money for their cause; high-quality—and fast—research on their candidate's life; the ability to fly witnesses and supporters to Rome when needed for testimony; publicity, perhaps with a regularly published newsletter that can also bring in word of miracles to be studied; and in general, public relations, never letting the candidate's name drop from sight for too long. If all else is equal, these folks can often steer their saintly candidates to canonization more quickly than those with no public relations effort behind them.

The Miracle Requirement

Within the Roman Catholic context, miracles must be associated with a candidate. This part of the process is extremely rigorous. Potential saints must have at least two posthumous miracles attributed to them.

The miracles must be instantaneous cures; there must be no medical explanation or medical interference, and they must be complete. No partial cures are considered. No remission is accepted, either, so in some instances it can take as long as ten years to be certain that a sufferer claiming a miracle is indeed permanently cured. Medical specialists are consulted for their testimony. However, no evidence of miracles is needed if the one considered for canonization is a martyr.

When it seems—finally—that everything is in place and one miracle has been confirmed, the pope publicly beatifies that individual, with veneration permitted in a particular religious community or geographic area. The candidate is given the title "Blessed."

After the second miracle has been documented, which could be many years after the acceptance of the first one, the pope issues a bull of canonization, declaring the person in question to be a saint and recommended for universal veneration.

This is then followed by an elaborate, solemn liturgy in Rome, attended by the newly canonized's family and friends and, if he was a religious, members of that community and others. It is a day of great joy and celebration, the culmination of many years of study by Rome and by the local diocese—and years of waiting for the cause of the honored holy person to move on to the next level.

Canonization in the Eastern Orthodox Church

Although the Eastern Orthodox Church also has a canonization process, it is not entirely the same as the Catholic one. Most notably, in the East there is no miracle requirement, although in the vast majority of cases, Eastern saints are associated with miracles.

Like the Roman Catholic process, the recognition of a saint begins at the local level. A person exhibits signs of holiness during her lifetime. After she dies, she continues to be vividly remembered by her own local community. Stories related to that person might spread, and strangers might come to visit her gravesite and pray. Sometimes, long before a person is officially canonized, icons (two-dimensional stylized images) will be created—not as an official statement about a person's sanctity, but to be used for private devotions. In some cases, the body of the saintly candidate will begin to emit a sweet aroma, like lilies, roses, or myrrh. This "sign" is interpreted as a confirmation of other markers of holiness that are already present.

As a candidate becomes increasingly well known, bishops will meet to pray and review material and decide together if her life warrants veneration. When it has been decided that a person will be canonized, a full liturgical cycle must be generated in her honor, as well as an icon and hymn.

The cycle of services follows this general pattern lasting several days: first, there will be a final prayer service for the person. Next, there will be a service in which the relics and icons are carried through the church, along with special prayers and hymns related to the saint. Then there will be a Communion service (or liturgy) in which the relics and icons are again brought out, and finally, instead of praying for the candidate, a prayer service will officially offer prayers to the candidate (to read more about a recent Orthodox canonization, see Chapter 15). The most significant shift that occurs during these services is that they begin with prayers *for* the person and they end with prayers *to* the saint.

Canonizations do not "create saints." They are merely the official recognition of a holy life. They are like a marriage in this respect—they recognize, affirm, and bless the good thing that took seed long before the church noticed what was taking place. By recognizing a holy life and incorporating it into the liturgical calendar, the church vows to keep the memory of the saint alive—and the link to that person vital—through stories, imagery, hymns, and prayers.

Chapter 2

New Testament Saints

The saints of the New Testament are most likely the most familiar saints in this book. Although the Bible does not offer a complete biography of any of them, the Bible does offer useful and inspiring glimpses into their lives. In many ways, the earliest Biblical saints provided a model for the later saints—demonstrating with their courageous examples that it is possible to live completely for God, and in some cases, to dramatically transform your own life as well as those around you.

Mary, Mother of Jesus (First Century)

There is no woman in the history of the world who has generated more attention, enthusiasm, and devotion than the Virgin Mary. She has been the subject of thousands of paintings, poems, and prayers. She has captured the hearts of monks, sailors, kings, and knights, and millions of people have claimed that their devotion to her has made them better, wiser, and more pure than they might otherwise have been. Still, there is astonishingly little known about her life, and only a few words attributed to her.

Early Days

According to church tradition, Mary's parents, Joachim and Anne, had to wrestle through a period of infertility before giving birth to her. Their story is preserved in an ancient extrabiblical text, the *Protoevangelium of James*. According to the *Protoevangelium*, Joachim and Anne were a wealthy couple who prayed fervently for a child, but month after month were unable to conceive.

FIGURE 2-1: Mary, Mother of Jesus

One day Joachim went to the temple to pray and was told that he had no children because of his sins. Distraught, he went into the wilderness to pray for forty days. He neglected to tell Anne where he was going, and this omission intensified her grief. Not only was she barren, she thought, but she was also a widow. She went out to her garden and saw a mother bird feeding her babies in a nest. She could only lament with the cry of so many couples who struggle with infertility. "*Everyone* has children but me!"

While she was praying, an angel came to her and told her that she would bear a child. At the same time, an angel came to Joachim with the same message. The two then rushed to the city gates to embrace. Their little Mary was born exactly nine months (less one day) after she was conceived.

When Mary was a teenager, she was visited by the archangel Gabriel, who, according to the

Gospel of Luke, said to her, "Hail, O favored one, the Lord is with you!" (An archangel is an angel of the highest order.) After calming her fears, he went on to tell her that she would conceive and bear a son named Jesus, who would be called "the Son of the Most High."

Gabriel explained that she would conceive by the power of the Holy Spirit. After struggling with the question of how she could have a child when she had not yet known a man, Mary responded, "Let it be done to me according to your word."

When she visited her cousin Elizabeth, who was pregnant with John the Baptist, Mary told Elizabeth her news and offered the exultant prayer of praise known as "The Magnificat," which retains an important place in the liturgies of both the Eastern and Western Churches.

E-QUESTION

What is the Immaculate Conception?

The Immaculate Conception is the belief that from the moment of Mary's conception, she was freed from the stain of original sin, which was passed on to all after the Fall. The Immaculate Conception is a significant belief in the Roman Catholic Church, but has never been subscribed to by the Eastern Orthodox Church.

Little is known about Mary from this point on, although there are a few incidents related to her in the Scriptures. It is believed that she was at the foot of the cross at the Crucifixion, and that Jesus asked his apostle John to look after her. This scripturally based belief gave rise to the legend that Mary lived out the end of her days with St. John in what is now known as Ephesus, Turkey, where a small stone structure is believed by many to be "the house of Mary."

Because so little is known about Mary's life, she has been the subject of much speculation. Each age has imbued her with the qualities most admired at that time. In years past it was her apparent meekness and deference to her son that was most emphasized.

In recent years, however, small details of her life have been reinterpreted. For example, after Jesus's ascension into heaven, Mary was in Jerusalem with the rest of the small band of Christians, waiting for the coming of the Holy Spirit and the beginning of the distillation of Christ's message to the world. Now it is believed that Mary was an integral part of the nucleus of this community of believers.

Marian Devotion

If little was said about the mother of Jesus during her lifetime, the millennia have since propelled her to a position right behind Jesus in interest, study, and devotion. There is no other saint as loved and admired as Mary is.

E-XTRA

Some modern-day scholars do not believe that Mary was the one who actually composed the Magnificat, but that it may have been written by the author of Luke's Gospel or may have had its beginnings in a song composed by early Christians.

Art has also fed the continuing interest in Mary, with hundreds of paintings and sculptures done by masters as well as by unknown artists. Found in churches and museums, these works have been widely reprinted for the public in books and magazines, and also appear on television and the Internet.

Special Marian exercises—such as reciting the rosary—help keep Mary prominent in personal devotions, as the faithful often ask her to intercede for them to Jesus in the hope that he will not deny his mother what she asks of him.

Beliefs

The Church holds to four principal doctrines about the Blessed Mother. From the ancient world there is her virginity before, during, and after the birth of Christ, and her divine maternity that made her the mother of God. According to the Roman Catholic Church, it is important to realize that Mary does perform the miracles that constitute her doctrines, but not by her own power. She merely channels the power that comes from God. In the nineteenth century, the Roman Catholic Church proclaimed a third doctrine: the Immaculate Conception, which states that Mary was conceived without original sin. (The Immaculate Conception has often mistakenly been thought to refer to Jesus.) Finally, the Assumption was officially declared by the Roman Catholic Church in the twentieth century. The Assumption is the belief that Mary was taken, body and soul, into heaven at the end of her years on Earth.

Where and when Mary died is uncertain, although there has been a good deal of speculation. The apostle John is believed to have cared for her after the Crucifixion, but here, too, there is no agreement by religious scholars as to exactly how or where that occurred. The Virgin Mary is commemorated on many different days in both the Roman Catholic and Eastern Orthodox Churches. In the Roman Catholic Church, the entire month of May has often been called "Mary's Month." During this month, Catholic-school children traditionally crown a statue of Mary with flowers.

E-FACT

The belief in the Assumption has been bolstered by the fact that, as with Christ, no bodily relics of the Virgin Mary have ever been discovered. There are relics associated with things that she touched, or wore, however. In particular, her "belt" has been much venerated through the ages.

Seeing Mary

Mary's name will crop up in the next few hundred pages in the context of those saints who have a special devotion to her and those who claim to have seen her in apparitions. Over the centuries these visions have kept Mary alive in the minds and hearts of the faithful.

There have been more apparitions of Mary than of any other saint. According to some sources there have been around 20,000 appearances of Mary from the year A.D. 40 to the present. These apparitions are reported to have occurred in almost every culture in the world. In most cases, Mary comes dressed in the local garb and speaking the local tongue.

Those who directly witness an apparition are called "visionaries." In cases such as Fatima, where the Virgin Mary is said to have appeared multiple times, thousands have gathered to witness the apparitions. Although only the visionaries see Mary, others can often glimpse accompanying phenomena, such as the famed "miracle of the sun" at Fatima, witnessed by an estimated 70,000 people (see Chapter 17).

E-QUESTION

What is "Marian"?

"Marian" is an adjective used to denote special reverence for Mary, in devotions and feasts. A Marian year, for example, is a twelve-month period periodically set aside by popes as a time of renewed devotion to the Blessed Virgin. Marian feasts—the Assumption and the Immaculate Conception—honor Mary.

Apparitions can also come in the form of weeping statues and icons. When statues bleed, the tears and sweat are most often human tears, sweat, or blood. When icons weep, they tend to emit a myrrh-scented olive oil, which is believed to contain healing properties.

Historically, apparitions were sometimes related to building projects—many of the great churches of the world, such as St. Mary Major in Rome, are associated with apparitions. In other ages, apparitions of Mary have offered encouragement or healing. More recently, apparitions have contained frightening warnings about the apocalypse, as well as exhortations to pray and work for peace.

A couple of years ago in Clearwater, Florida, the tinted windows of an office building seemed to be forming a mosaic of the Blessed Mother, attracting believers and the curious. Special parking areas near the building were roped off for the "viewing."

Even when scientists have explanations for those phenomena, the devout are often willing and eager to believe that a link exists between them and Jesus in the form of his mother, Mary, as she visits the faithful on earth.

St. Mary Magdalene (First Century)

Mary Magdalene, often remembered as a former prostitute, was a disciple of Jesus. She was one of several women who believed in him and followed him as he preached. The women did not get as much "press" as the twelve apostles, but they were just as faithful and supportive. The other women remain nameless, but Mary Magdalene is prominent in this gathering.

All four gospels name Mary Magdalene as being among the women who followed Jesus to Calvary, where he was crucified. Then they went to his tomb, hoping to anoint his body, and found it empty. An angel guarding the tomb announced that Jesus had been resurrected.

Witness

The angel instructed the women to tell the apostles to meet Jesus back in Galilee and mentioned Peter by name. The Gospels tell of Mary Magdalene's vivid encounter with the risen Jesus. Mary was weeping outside the tomb when suddenly she saw Jesus, but she did not recognize him.

Figure 2-2: St. Mary Magdalene

Mary then said to the strange man, "Sir, if you have carried him away, tell me where you have laid him, and I will take him away." Jesus answered her with one word: "Mary." She recognized him and cried "Rabboni!" (Rabboni means "teacher"). He instructed her, "Go to my brethren and say to them, I am ascending to my Father and your Father, to my God and your God." Mary went to the apostles and told them she had seen Jesus.

After Mary washed Jesus's feet with her tears, he said, "Her sins, which are many, are forgiven, for she loved much." (Luke 7:47) Through the years the image of Mary Magdalene as a repentent sinner has persisted.

Some religious historians believe that Mary Magdalene is the "Mary" of the two women in the book of Luke: Martha and Mary. Martha tended to household tasks while Jesus preached. Mary, on the other hand, set work aside to sit at his feet and listen to his words. Jesus said, "She has chosen the good part and it will not be taken from her." There is no proof that this Mary and Mary Magdalene are the same person.

Because Mary proclaimed the good news of the Resurrection to the other disciples, Mary Magdalene has been called "Apostle to the Apostles." Her feast day is July 22. She is a patron saint of hair stylists, repentant sinners, and repentant prostitutes.

E-FACT

Mary Magdalene was characterized in the early church as "a woman from whom seven demons had gone out," but scholars in later years debate whether this statement referred to prostitution. She is, however, thought to have been the unnamed repentant "sinner" in the New Testament, who washed Jesus's feet with her tears during the early days of his ministry.

St. Paul of Tarsus (Died c. 64)

Paul, who once persecuted Christians, had a radical conversion experience. He was never the same afterward, and went on to transform the early Christian Church. He was born Saul, in Tarsus, Asia Minor, of Jewish parents. He described that city as a cosmopolitan capital of the Roman province of Cilicia, a crossroads for Asians and Europeans as well as Greeks and Jews.

Saul received both a Greek and a Jewish education, and then went into the trade of a tentmaker. He described himself as a Pharisee and a serious persecutor of Christians. Paul was present at the stoning of St. Stephen, the first martyr. Although Paul was merely part of the crowd of onlookers, it is believed that he was supportive of the stoning. After Stephen's death, Saul went into surrounding houses and dragged Christians off to prison.

But Saul was to have an epiphany, as did so many others. He went to the high priest in Jerusalem asking for permission to seize the Christians of Damascus and bring them back to Jerusalem for punishment. On his way to Damascus he had a vision of Christ, and a flash of light threw him to the ground. A voice asked, "Saul, Saul, why do you persecute me?" (Acts 9)

Figure 2-3: St. Paul of Tarsus

When Saul asked who spoke, he heard, "I am Jesus whom you are persecuting." Blinded at the time of the incident, Saul was led into Damascus. He spent several days there, unable to eat or drink. Then he met Ananias, a disciple of Jesus who seemed to know the enormous task Saul would be taking on. Ananias laid his hands on him and his eyesight was immediately restored and new strength surged through his body.

Saul had now experienced two miracles: a vision and a cure. Not surprisingly, he asked to be baptized and set about preaching Christianity with the same zeal he had once channeled into persecutions.

He headed first to Jerusalem to meet with the apostles. It took some convincing for them to believe that their persecutor was now their ally, but eventually they accepted him, directing him to join the apostle Barnabas in three missionary journeys.

When entering a new community, Paul—he had now taken the Hellenic name Paul in place of Saul—tried a strategy of first making contact with the local synagogue. He was saddened to discover that they wanted nothing to do with him as Jewish convert to Christianity. So he turned to the gentile community, which was more receptive. Over the years Paul became known as "the apostle to the gentiles."

E-QUESTION

Was Paul on a horse or donkey when he was knocked to the ground?
Possibly neither—the scriptural account does not say. Generations of artists, however, have portrayed Paul as thrown from his horse or donkey, and this extrabiblical image has become fixed in the minds of believers.

He was apparently not too skilled in social graces. He was intense and did not always work well with others. Yet he got along with the apostle Luke, who was an educated, sophisticated man. And he got along with Peter as well, perhaps because Peter had known Jesus and been appointed head of the new church. Peter and Paul complemented each other. According to some scolars, Peter was a large, rather easygoing man who meant well but was unschooled and not great on follow-through. Paul was smaller, angular, and well educated.

Travels

Paul's missionary endeavors did not always run smoothly. He was often met with hostility, suffering imprisonment and stoning. He endured shipwreck and hunger, fear and anxiety, and countless sleepless nights. He was also not well some of the time, suffering from what he described as "a thorn in the flesh." (2 Corinthians 12:7).

His travels were long and lonely. He sent letter after letter back to the Christian communities he had established. These epistles—to the Thessalonians, Galatians, Corinthians, Philippians, Philemon, and Romans—are read in churches to this day. His letters covered problems of the new Christians, interpreting the faith and observing Mosaic law (the law of the Jews attributed to Moses). The letters covered a period from about A.D. 50 to 65 and are the earliest New Testament writings.

Paul established Christian communities around the eastern Mediterranean. The aim for his second missionary journey was Corinth in Greece, and the third took him to Ephesus in Asia Minor.

Paul's Lasting Impact

Back in Jerusalem sometime around A.D. 50, Paul, with Peter supporting him, convinced the other apostles that gentile Christians did not need to be circumcised and have Jewish law forced upon them. That important decision ensured the universality of Christianity.

Eventually, around the year 57, Paul returned to Jerusalem, where he was arrested as a Christian and spent the next two years in prison. Exercising his right as a Roman citizen to appeal his case to Caesar, he was sent to

Rome and was held under arrest there for about two years. Finally, he was beheaded, when St. Peter was crucified.

One of St. Paul's most famous sayings, from 1 Corinthians 13:4–7 "Love is patient and kind; love is not jealous or boastful; it is not arrogant or rude. Love does not insist on its own way; it is not irritable or resentful; it does not rejoice at wrong, but rejoices at right. Love bears all things, believes all things, hopes all things, endures all things."

On his way to Rome to what he knew would be his death, Paul was still writing to the communities he had visited and converted. At the end, he said, "I have fought the good fight, I have finished the race, I have kept the faith." (2 Timothy 4:7) He is buried in Rome, in the major basilica St. Paul's Outside the Walls. He has been called "the second founder of Christianity." Paul's feast day is June 29, which he shares with St. Peter. He is the patron saint of Malta.

St. Peter (Died c. 64)

In Roman Catholic teaching, Peter was the first pope, appointed by Jesus. Yet despite the best of intentions, he denied his master and was not to be found near the Crucifixion. Peter has also been described as uneducated; yet once Peter came to believe in Jesus, he spent the remainder of his years preaching, advancing the cause of Christianity, and establishing the new church.

He was said to have been a large man, bold and sometimes speaking without thinking, yet in other instances fearful. He seemed to spend his years stumbling over one mistake or another, then getting up, tripping again, dusting himself off, and trying once more. When one thinks of Peter, one can't help but think of a story from an ancient monastery in which a monk was asked what they did there all day and he replied, "We fall and get up, fall and get back up again."

Early Years

Peter was born in a small village near Lake Tiberias and was called Simon. He lived and worked as a fisherman on Lake Genesareth, alongside his brother, who was the apostle Andrew. Andrew introduced Peter to Jesus, who called him "Cephas," the Aramaic version of the word rock. Aramaic is a language closely related to Hebrew; a form of it is thought to be the language spoken by Jesus. In Greek, "rock" translates as Peter. Peter was told by Christ, "Come with me and I will make you a fisher of men."

Although there were twelve apostles, the trio of Peter, James, and John were closest to Jesus. Peter was reportedly in attendance at Jesus's first miracle: at the marriage feast at Cana, when Mary told her son the guests had no wine. Jesus said to her, "My time has not yet come," but added "What would you have me do?" although he must have known what she was requesting. Soon water that had magically become wine materialized, enough to see the wedding guests happily through the day's festivities.

Peter was married, and his wife often traveled with him. He was with Jesus throughout his public life, making his boat and home available to him. Jesus stayed with the apostle on a few occasions and once while at his home healed Peter's mother-in-law.

Figure 2-4: St. Peter

At the Last Supper, Peter made the dangerous statement to Jesus, "Even though they all fall away, I will not." (Mark 14:29) When Jesus was held prisoner at Pontius Pilate's palace, Peter denied him three times. Peter wept after his betrayal. Later, when he heard that Jesus had risen, he went to the empty tomb to see for himself. An angel had told Mary Magdalene and the other women to take the news that Jesus had risen "to the disciples and to Peter," mentioning him by name.

It is apparent from all of Peter's too-human faults that Jesus intended his message to be more important than the messenger. Jesus emphasized the importance of love. He was forgiving to those who showed their love in service to others, in love of God, and in self-sacrifice. As Jesus said about Mary Magdalene, "Her sins, which are many, are forgiven, for she loved much."

The risen Christ asked Peter three times: "Do you love me?" And, of course, Peter, who had three times denied him, now said three times, "Yes, Lord, you know that I love you." Then Jesus commanded him, "Feed my sheep." (John 21:15–17)

E-FACT

Christ said, "You are Peter, and upon this rock I will build my church" and "I will give you the keys of the kingdom of heaven." (Matthew 16:18–19) Roman Catholics believe that this statement established Peter as the first pope, and helped give rise to the larger concept of authority centered in the papacy.

The Early Church

Peter took the helm of the small band of Christians after the Crucifixion and was the first apostle to perform a miracle. In Jerusalem and in later travels, he combined preaching the news about Jesus with defending the faith in courts and settling squabbles among individuals and groups of believers. An especially important move for Peter was authorizing a missionary outreach to the gentiles.

He did not stay in Jerusalem for the rest of his life, although most of the other apostles did. He went on to Lydda in Palestine, and beyond. In Antioch he met with St. Paul and worked closely with him.

Peter was arrested and imprisoned more than once during those years, and then, miraculously, was set free. Eventually he became the first bishop of Rome. During the reign of Nero (c. 54–68), he was martyred. He died by crucifixion, although Peter insisted that he be hanged upside down on the cross, saying that he was not fit to die in the same way as his master.

Peter is still considered the first bishop of Rome. To this day the pope carries the title of bishop of Rome. Peter's tomb is presumed to be under St. Peter's Basilica. Bones found there, however, are still being studied. His feast day is June 29, which he shares with St. Paul. He is the patron saint of longevity and fishermen.

Chapter 3

The Gospel Writers

They are known as the four men who wrote the Gospels of the New Testament. Two names are recognizable as apostles, but what about the other two? Who were these four whose work has endured for millennia as God's message to the faithful? Perhaps the first question here should be: What are the Gospels? This chapter will explore the lives of the writers of the Gospels as well as the documents they produced.

The Gospels

Four books make up the Gospels. These books captured the life of Jesus, his teachings, miracles, and, most important, his Crucifixion and Resurrection and the message he sought to impart. They are attributed to Matthew, Mark, Luke, and John, who wrote from their own perspectives in different times and different places. The Gospel accounts work together as a mosaic, each offering pieces of the puzzle that made up the life of Christ.

St. Matthew

Matthew was one of the twelve Apostles. He was a tax collector before he left that work at Jesus's directive. Matthew wrote his gospel, probably somewhere in Syria, for a community of Christians who had been Jewish. He stressed how Jesus came to the Jews as a new Moses and thereby fulfilled the Old Testament prophetic texts. He also emphasized Christians growing together in faith, in a community of love.

Interestingly, many scholars debate whether the first gospel as we know it today is in fact Matthew's original work. It is now believed to have been written by Matthew in Hebrew, and then translated into Greek by a well-educated Grecian Jew knowledgeable in rabbinic scholarship. Matthew's feast day is September 21. He is the patron saint of accountants and bankers.

St. Mark

Mark was not one of the original apostles, although he probably was a disciple of Jesus. Mark's gospel is the clearest and the shortest of the four. Written somewhere around A.D. 65–70, it contains more miracles and less teaching than the others. Broadly speaking, Mark's gospel emphasizes Christianity in times of persecution (which was true of Rome in the year 64) amid feelings of abandonment. Mark notes the words of Jesus on the cross: "My God, my God, why have you forsaken me?" Mark tells readers that the way to be a Christian is by imitating the self-emptying love of Christ on the cross. It is here, according to Mark, that hope lies.

Figure 3-1: Saints Matthew, Mark, Luke, and John

Mark is said to have been the first to bring Christianity to Egypt, taking along the gospel he had written and establishing churches in Alexandria. His feast day is April 25, and he is the patron saint of Egypt.

St. Luke

Saint-watchers, and even many people who are not, are likely to know Luke's profession: he was a physician. He was not one of the apostles. In fact, Luke never met Jesus. He was from Antioch (although some say Greece), and wrote the Third Gospel there around the year 85.

Luke's gospel was directed at Christians who had been pagans. The work was marked by concern for those who needed words of hope and were often overlooked: women, the poor, and so on. It is Luke who gives an account of the Nativity, stressing how humble the birth of Jesus was.

Because he wrote for those in the Hellenic world, with their ideals of Greek humanism, Luke endeavored to show those people that the ideal for the people's lives now was not the heroes of Greek culture, but Jesus. He redirects his readers toward Christ, saying that it is in him that one finds healing and forgiveness.

Not having known Jesus, Luke was able to maintain a certain distance from the Passion and Resurrection, taking a long view of Christianity and its impact. His gospel goes beyond the Resurrection and Pentecost.

A companion of St. Paul's, Luke went along with him on his second and third missionary journeys to Macedonia and Greece, on his final journey to Jerusalem, and then on with him to Rome. In one of Paul's letters to the Colossians, he calls this gospel writer "Luke, the beloved physician," which seems to confirm Luke's profession.

After Paul's death, Luke is said to have gone to Greece, where he lived to be eighty-four. It is uncertain where and when he wrote his gospel, but it is thought to have been written either in Greece or what is now Ephesus, Turkey, A.D. 70–85. His feast day is October 18, and he is the patron saint of doctors, artists, and butchers.

St. John

John often carries appellations to his name: St. John the Evangelist or St. John the Divine (for his theological vision). His was the last gospel, written around the year 95, although it may have been as late as the first decade of the second century.

John was one of Jesus's twelve apostles. Born in Galilee, he was the brother of James the Greater, another apostle. John was a fisherman until, like James and Matthew and the others, he was called by Jesus to follow him.

One of the three apostles closest to Jesus (the others were James and Peter), John was, along with Peter, the first apostle at the tomb after the Resurrection. John was the only apostle at the Crucifixion, and it was there that Jesus placed his mother, Mary, into John's care.

E-FACT

The Gospels have been a continual source for inspiration for the saints. As St. Thérèse of Lisieux wrote, "Above all, it's the gospels that occupy my mind when I'm at prayer. My poor soul has so many needs, and yet this is the one thing needful. I'm always finding fresh lights there, hidden and enthralling meanings."

John is thought to have gone to Rome during the reign of the Emperor Domitian, and barely escaped being martyred there. In Ephesus (a sizable Greek city and prominent center of early Christianity, now part of modern Turkey), after the death of Domitian, he wrote the Fourth Gospel and three epistles. John is also the author of the book of Revelation, which opens with, "In the beginning was the Word. . . ."

John's gospel was directed at a Christian community around Ephesus. It contains only a bit in common with the synoptic Gospels. What stands out in John's words is how few miracles by Jesus are mentioned. Highlighted are Jesus's claims to divinity, but John also stresses Jesus's humanity, such as when he weeps over the death of his friend Lazarus.

John died in Ephesus, the only apostle who was not martyred. John's feast day is December 27. He is the patron saint of Asia Minor (the Near East).

Chapter 4

The Righteous of the Old Testament

The great figures of the Old Testament were willing to act boldly and to struggle out of love for God. Like the holy people featured in the other chapters of this book, these people weren't perfect—some of them, such as King David, were particularly far from perfection—but they never stopped seeking God. This chapter will explore the stories of a selection of the men and women from the Old Testament.

Old Testament Figures in the Roman Catholic and Eastern Orthodox Churches

Although all Christians share an admiration for the great characters of the Old Testament, there have been some historical differences of perspective on this subject, particularly between Eastern Orthodox and Roman Catholics.

Both churches are rooted in the teachings of the Old Testament, as well as the witnesses of the prophets and patriarchs (and matriarchs). Often, typography—a form of Biblical interpretation that views the Old and New Testaments as one seamless work—was used as a way to tie together the Old and New Testaments. Instead of viewing Old Testament stories as standalone accounts, the earliest Christians saw these stories through the lens of Christ.

They believed that the Old Testament stories ultimately culminated in the central figure of the New Testament—Christ. Abraham's near sacrifice of Isaac was seen as an image of God the Father offering his Jesus; Jonah in the belly of the whale was viewed as an image of Christ in the damp darkness of the tomb before he arose to the day again.

The Roman Catholic and Eastern Orthodox Churches have found different ways to integrate the witness of these holy ones into the lives of the faithful. The Eastern Orthodox have historically celebrated many feasts related to figures from the Old Testament. They have also used a term that is classically Christian to refer to these pre-Christian faithful ones—"saints." The hymnography of the Eastern church often calls the forefathers and prophets saints, and icons of these figures from the Old Testament have been made and venerated. Although love for the Old Testament runs deep in the Orthodox church, the Orthodox do not regularly read from the Old Testament in their churches on Sunday.

Instead, Old Testament passages are often clustered together and read in succession on the great feasts, such as Theophany, when Christ's baptism is celebrated. On this day, when water is also blessed, multiple passages related to water in the Old Testament are read together. Likewise, on Holy Saturday, which is the day before Easter (or Pascha) is celebrated, multiple passages from the Old Testament related to the themes of death and resurrection are read.

Within the Roman Catholic context, Old Testament figures have played a different role. Before Vatican II, only one Old Testament feast was kept according to the Roman Catholic church calendar. This was the feast of the Maccabees. Since Vatican II, it has been suggested that the church make more of the Old Testament patriarchs and prophets—devoting a feast day to them as has been done in the East for many centuries.

Abraham

Abraham is one of the greatest Old Testament figures. His willingness to obey God and to venture out into a new land—to a place far away from family and friends and all that was familiar—has been inspiring to many throughout the ages.

The story of Abraham is detailed in Genesis. Abraham was called by God to move away from home. His call was accompanied by a promise that he would become the father of a great many nations. But his story, like the story of so many holy people, is marked by sadness.

E-FACT

Abraham was visited by the enigmatic "Melchizedek." Little is known about him, except that he was a priest and king. Abraham, upon meeting him, offered him a tithe—10 percent of all he had. Melchizedek brought out bread and wine. Many Christians see striking parallels between Melchizedek and Christ.

Abraham did exactly what God has asked him, and then discovered that his wife was unable to bear children. It almost seemed as if Abraham had kept his side of the bargain, but that God had forgotten what he had promised to do. Out of desperation, Abraham had a child with one of their servants, Hagar. Although Abraham's wife, Sara, was initially supportive of this plan, she eventually began to envy Hagar and her child, and the two were sent out into the wilderness to fend for themselves.

As with modern-day couples who struggle with infertility, adopt, and then, to their surprise, become pregnant with biological offspring, there is a surprising twist in the story of Abraham and Sara.

E-XTRA

An Orthodox hymn for Abraham: "Thou didst justify the Forefathers by faith, when of old through them Thou didst betroth Thyself to the Church of the nations. The saints rejoice in the glorious fruit of their seed, even in her who bore thee seedlessly. By their prayers, O Christ our God, save our souls."

When Sara was ninety years old, three beings—often interpreted as angels—came to visit and told Sara that she was to bear a child. Because she was so old and had been barren for so long, she was incredulous and laughed in their faces. For this, she was renamed "Sarah," meaning "the one who laughs at God."

Sarah did ultimately bear a biological child and the child's name was Isaac. Abraham loved this child fiercely, but when the child was still young, God called Abraham to sacrifice this child for him. These passages are troubling and difficult to understand. One can't help but wonder why God would fulfill his promise only to ultimately take the child away. Abraham was deeply grieved by God's request, but he chose to obey.

He rose early one morning and took his son to a mountain for sacrifice. As they traveled to the mountain it became clear that Isaac had no idea what his father was planning. At one point, Isaac even said, "I see you have the wood for the fire and the knife, but where is that which you plan to sacrifice?" Abraham responded with these brave words, "The Lord himself will provide a sacrifice."

Figure 4-1: Abraham

And this is exactly what happens. Just before Abraham took Isaac's life, the Lord intervened and told Abraham to stop. He informed him that there was a ram caught in the thicket nearby and that Abraham was to use the ram for the sacrifice instead of his son. Abraham then gratefully sacrificed the ram.

For centuries, Christians have seen this story of a father being asked to sacrifice his only son for God as a "type" or image of what was to come with God and his son, Jesus. The heartbreaking portrayal of the father being asked to do the impossible has often been seen as an image of the heartbreaking decision God made for the sake of humanity. The perfect innocence of Isaac in this account only compounds the sadness.

Although Isaac ultimately survived and did become the father of many nations, Abraham did not get to see the fulfillment of all that God has promised. Instead, he continued to wander in a foreign land for many more years. When Sarah finally died she was 127 years old. One can sense how weary Abraham must have been from all those years of traveling, when he said to the local people, "I am a stranger and a sojourner among you; give me property among you for a burying place that I may bury my dead out of sight." (Genesis 23:4)

E-FACT

Within the religion of Islam, it is believed that Abraham's first son, Ishmael, was nearly sacrificed instead of Isaac. According to Islamic belief, Ishmael, who survived just as Isaac did in the Old Testament account, goes on to become the father of the Arab nations.

Abraham ultimately dies an old man, after many good days. During his life, however, he only saw the seeds of the promises that had been planted in him. He was never able to see them grow to fruition. As it says in Hebrews 11 (about Abraham and many of the other forefathers): "These all died in faith, not having received what was promised, but having seen it and greeted it from afar, and having acknowledged that they were strangers and exiles on the earth. For people who speak thus make it clear that they are seeking a homeland." (Hebrews 11:13–14)

The story of Abraham, Sarah, and Isaac expresses well the lives of the saints, who are willing to take fearful, sometimes even crazy, risks for God. It also expresses the way in which the saints might sometimes appear to be foreigners on the earth, quite unlike everyone else, for they live by promises and always look toward a home that is beyond the edge of the world. Abraham is commemorated in the Eastern Orthodox Church on October 9 and on the Sunday of the Holy Forefathers.

The author Frederick Buechner, on Abraham: "It's true that in the last minute God stepped in and said he'd only wanted to see if the old man's money was where his mouth was, but from that day forward Abraham had a habit of breaking into tears at odd moments, and his relationship with his son Isaac was never close."

Ruth and Naomi

Many people believe that the book of Ruth is one of the most beautiful books in the Bible. This story begins with incredible hardship. Naomi was dealt several rough blows in short succession. Her husband died and then she lost her two sons, who had recently married but had not yet had any children.

Naomi found herself in a desperate situation—she had no offspring to call her own, and two daughters-in-law who are no longer hers to claim as she could not provide them with other men to marry. Her daughters-in-law traveled with her for a short time, but then she tried to send them on their way, knowing that she could do nothing for them. The young women wept when Naomi tried to send them on, but they make very different decisions. Orpah kisses her mother-in-law and goes on her way, but Ruth, "clung to her." (Ruth 1:14)

Still, Naomi was not convinced that it would be the best thing for Ruth to remain with her, so she tried again to send her on. But Ruth won't have it. She bravely promised Naomi, "Entreat me not to leave you or to return from following you; for where you go I will go, and where you lodge I will lodge; your people shall be my people, and your God my God; where you die I will die, and there will I be buried." (Ruth 1:16–17)

Naomi then understood that Ruth had made her decision, and said no more. Together, the two traveled to Bethlehem at the beginning of the barley harvest. Ruth began to work in the fields of Bo'az, a wealthy relative of Naomi. Bo'az was kind to Naomi, allowing her to eat and drink and providing her with protection.

E-XTRA

According to Orthodox writer Patrick Henry Reardon, the sons of Naomi were given names at birth that suggested that they would not live to see old age. The meaning of her son's name "Mahlon" is "sickly," while the meaning of her other son's name, "Chilion," is "wasting away."

Naomi then conspired to seal the deal between Bo'az and Ruth, understanding that if the two should marry, life would ultimately be good for Ruth. In an amazing passage of the Bible, she advises Ruth to wait until Bo'az has feasted and had wine to drink, and then Ruth is to go and "uncover his feet" and lie down there.

This symbolic gesture would show that she wanted to marry into his household. Ruth does just as her mother-in-law has advised her and Bo'az, who was initially startled to find the woman lying at his feet, was delighted by Ruth's attentions. He says, "May you be blessed by the Lord, my daughter; you have made this last kindness greater than the first, in that you have not gone after young men, whether poor or rich. And now, my daughter, do not fear, I will do for you all that you ask." (Ruth 3:10–11)

Bo'az then took Ruth into his home, and, much to Naomi's delight, the two gave birth to a child, named O'bed, whom Naomi took to her breast and nursed. This story, which began in grief and sadness, turns to joy and hope. For not only did Ruth find her place among Naomi's people, but it is through her son, O'bed, that King David will ultimately be born. She has woven herself into the royal line that will ultimately produce Christ. In the Orthodox church, Ruth is referred to as "St. Ruth the Moabitess." The name "Ruth" means companion, friend, or compassion. The friendship between Ruth and Naomi is an image of undying spiritual friendship, overcoming loss and finding hope together.

King David

King David was fatally human in almost every respect. His own lust brought great pain, and ultimately death, to others, and he was often self-serving. But his very grave flaws do not conceal the fact that he was considered one of the greatest Kings of Israel, and that although he sinned boldly, he repented boldly as well.

After King Saul died, David became king. He was a humble man and wanted to please God. One day, however, when he was on a walk, he saw a beautiful woman bathing on the roof of her home. He desired her. Her husband, Uriah, was away at war, and David sent his messenger to retrieve the woman, named Bathsheba. He slept with her and she became pregnant.

His original crime was compounded by another ruthless act—he ordered Uriah to be sent to the frontlines of battle so that he would die and be done away with. David did not see the error of his ways until the prophet Nathan came to him and told him a story of a poor man who had a sheep that he loved very much. The sheep was his only one. He raised it with his own children, shared his meager food with it and let it drink from his cup and sleep leaning against his chest.

Figure 4-2: King David

A rich man who had numerous herds of animals had a visitor. The rich man, however, was unwilling to take from his own herds, so he took the poor man's only lamb.

When David heard this story, he considered it a great outrage. He said, "As the Lord lives the man who has done this deserves to die . . . because he had no pity." (2 Samuel 12:5–6)

Nathan then looked David squarely in the eye and said, "You are the man." David suddenly realized the horror of what he had done and he repented. But although the Lord took away David's sin, the newborn child born of Bathsheba grew sick. David fasted and prayed and wept for the child, but when he was just seven days old the child died.

David comforted his wife, and then the two conceived another child, named Solomon.

David captured Jerusalem and made it the capital of the kingdom. He placed there a new tabernacle. The Lord promised David that "his kingdom would stand forever." And he is often associated with Christ's unending kingdom, as one of his ancestors.

E-FACT

In the mind of the Church, David is connected to the Psalms, which are full of rage, grief, repentance, and hope. These hymns express his life of sin, his repentance, and God's mercy to him.

David's Dance

In one of the most celebrated events from David's life, he brought the Ark of the Covenant back into Jerusalem, detailed in 2 Samuel 6. This act required a good deal of courage on his part, because he had already watched one of his companions on the journey, Uzzah, die because of the Ark. When the oxen stumbled, Uzzah put his hand out and held the Ark, but his action provoked the rage of God and he died instantly. David was angry after watching this unfortunate chain of events and refused to take the Ark any farther. But then he saw the blessings that came from the Ark and he was able to recover some of his courage.

When he and his companions arrived in Jerusalem, they danced before the Lord, rejoicing that they had finally made it. Unfortunately, David, the King of Israel, only wore a small piece of linen, and when his wife caught sight of him dancing in his skivvies she was disgusted and humiliated.

Frederick Buechner on David's Dance: "How they cut loose together, David and Yahweh, whirling around before the Ark in such a passion that they caught fire from each other and blazed up in a single flame of such magnificence that not even the dressing-down David got from Michal afterward could dim the glory of it."

His wife then rebuked him for his act, asking why the King of Israel would dance nearly naked before the Lord. She was never again invited to share the King's bed after her scolding. Still, King David's Dance is remembered to this day as an example of gleeful foolishness before God. His example is suggestive of the many holy ones throughout history who, every now and then, acted a little wild for the sake of their God.

King David's Dance before the Lord is commemorated in the Eastern Orthodox Church on the Sunday following Christmas. David is also referred to as "King David the Psalmist" or "The Prophet." He reigned for forty years and then, while he was still alive, appointed his son Solomon to be his heir. He also entrusted his son with the responsibility of building the temple. In Orthodox hymnography, he is also referred to, despite all his imperfections, as "The Grandparent of God."

Job

The story of Job may be helpful to those who have suffered from extreme losses in life. He expresses the essence of grief—the rage, the tears, the questioning. And he asks a question common amongst those who try to serve God but suffer hardship: "Why did God do this to me when all my life I sought to serve and honor him?"

Job was a wealthy, righteous man. According to the Old Testament account, he had seven sons and three daughters, as well as numerous servants and thousands of animals to serve him. All that he had, however, was taken away in a flash after God and Satan made a pact. God had been pointing out to Satan that he had at least one very righteous servant who feared him and turned away from evil. Satan was unimpressed and said that it is normal for people who have everything to be faithful. What if, Satan suggested, God took everything away from Job? Under these circumstances, Satan predicted that God's "faithful" servant Job would curse God in a heartbeat. So God decided to turn the situation over to Satan to see what would happen.

Satan struck fast and hard. All of Job's servants, his children, and his animals were destroyed through a series of calamities. After hearing that almost everything has been taken away from him, Job tears his robe and shaves his head. Then he does something astonishing. He falls down on the ground and he worships God. Saying, "Naked I came from my mother's womb, and naked shall I return; the Lord gave and the Lord has taken away; blessed be the name of the Lord."

But this was all before Job developed leprosy. And while he sat in a pile of ashes in his yard scraping his wounds with a potsherd, his wife helpfully suggested that he "curse God and die." But Job didn't take the bait. Instead, he said, "How can I take good from the hand of God and not expect bad things to come as well?"

Job's plight was then aggravated by three of his friends who came to offer help. At first they did well by sitting silently with him for seven days. But when they began to speak, they only caused him more pain.

E-FACT

Within Orthodox Judaism there is a wise custom related to grieving. Immediately after the death of a loved one, those that visit the house are not to try to offer words of consolation. Instead, those that visit are expected to sit quietly with the grieving person, as Job's friends did initially.

Job's friends each offered lengthy sermons about why so many hardships had befallen him. All of their theories reflected the widespread belief of the time that God blesses the righteous with good things and punishes those who have committed sins. Although Job is said to be blameless, his friends tried to help him figure out what it was that he had done to offend God. One of his friends also offered the unhelpful suggestion that Job's hardships would build his character and make him stronger. Job's friends so tried his patience that he finally called them "useless physicians" and told them that it would be better for them to keep silent than to offer him their theological ponderings.

Job said many times, "But I didn't do anything to offend God." He knew that he was blameless before God so he struggled intensely with the questions surrounding his afflictions. He wanted to see God so that he could express his complaint and see how God explains things. When God finally spoke to Job, he said, "Where were you when I laid the foundation of the earth? Tell me, if you have understanding. Who determined its measurements—surely you know!" (Job 38:4–5) With a surprising degree of sarcasm, God went on to point out all the things about the creation of the world that Job couldn't possibly know. And Job, awed by the presence of God, responded with humility, saying, "Behold, I am of small account; what shall I answer thee?" (Job 40:4)

Ultimately, everything that had been lost was doubly restored to Job—he had more children and lived to see four generations of them; his wealth was restored, as were his health and servants. The book ends, "And Job died, an old man, and full of days."

Frederick Buechner on Job's encounter with God: "He had seen the great glory so shot through with sheer, fierce light and life and gladness, had heard the great voice raised in song so full of terror and wildness and beauty, that from that moment on, nothing else mattered."

In the Orthodox Church, the prophet Job is commemorated on May 6. Some biblical scholars do not believe that Job actually existed. There are some who posit that the book of Job was written as a parable that was intended to show the errors associated with the idea that all hardship comes because of personal sin. Still, there are many people who believe that Job actually existed, and that his example continues to speak to those who mourn and who struggle with the problem of evil in the world today.

Chapter 5

Saints of Tradition

This chapter turns to the saints who are remembered by Christians with great fondness, although in many cases very little is known about them. Over the years, traditions and legends have grown up around these saints and they have become a vivid part of the living memory of both the Eastern and Western churches. This chapter will explore a few of the great saints known through the traditions of these churches.

St. Joseph

When one thinks of Joseph, one usually pictures a figure in the Nativity scene standing next to Mary and watching over the infant Jesus in the manger. Joseph has been far overshadowed through history by his wife and the Marian devotion accorded her.

Not much is known about his life—he left no words behind for hagiographers to study, and he apparently died before the Crucifixion because he was not at Calvary with Mary.

Still, to this day he continues to attract the faithful in a quiet way, some to churches bearing his name, devoted to him for his fidelity to family and home. In fact, it is said that in the Roman Catholic Church, next to Mary, he and St. Jude are the most popular patrons.

Betrothed

The gospel authors Matthew and Luke agree that Mary and Joseph were to be married at the time that Mary discovered that she was pregnant. Mary was informed that her pregnancy was divine, but Joseph did not know about that part of it. He was, quite understandably, aghast at the news, since the two had not lived together. He decided he would quietly "put her away" and not marry her, which was certainly a kind alternative to having her stoned to death, a common custom at the time with errant girls.

Figure 5-1: St. Joseph

But then an angel appeared to him in his sleep and said, "Joseph, son of David, do not fear to take Mary your wife, for that which is conceived in her is of the Holy Spirit; she will bear a son, and you shall call his name Jesus, for he will save his people from their sins." (Matthew 1:20–21) Joseph awoke with fresh courage and decided to go through with his plans to wed Mary.

Since Mary and Joseph had planned to be married anyway, it is conceivable that Joseph was a young or reasonably young man. When we see paintings of Joseph, or when he is portrayed in films, he is often presented as much older than she. On the other hand, the hypothesis that he was no longer living at the time of the Passion of Christ could lend some credence to the tradition that he was many years older than Mary.

E-FACT

Within the Eastern Orthodox Church, it is believed that Joseph was a widower, which helps to account for the "siblings" of Jesus mentioned in the New Testament. Within the Roman Catholic Church, however, since the time of Jerome, Joseph was rarely cast as a widower. The "siblings" of Jesus are often explained as members of the extended family.

A Worker's Household

Joseph was probably not a poor man, but he was not prosperous, either. Though he was linked to the house of King David, at the time of the Annunciation he was, and remained, a carpenter in a small town.

Whatever his income, when he and Mary brought their infant to the temple on the occasion of Mary's purification after Jesus's birth and the baby's presentation, the couple took with them only two turtledoves as an offering. Doves were gifts of the working class.

A short time after Jesus's birth, Joseph was warned in a dream to take the baby into exile in Egypt because King Herod had called for the slaying of male children under two years of age. Herod had heard that a "king" had been born and wanted no such person eventually threatening him.

So Joseph left. After the death of Herod he brought his little family back to Nazareth. When Jesus was about twelve years old, Joseph and Mary took him to Jerusalem, lost him, and found him talking with the learned men at the temple.

In those times sons worked alongside their fathers, so Joseph taught carpentry (and possibly metalwork) to Jesus. He was known to be a fair and just man and did not stand in Jesus's way when his foster son began a public life at age thirty. Joseph is mentioned later in the Bible when Jesus is scorned for his humble beginnings: "Is not this the carpenter's son?" (Matthew 13:55)

A Rise in Devotion

Devotion to Joseph in the West rose dramatically when his feast day was introduced to the Roman calendar in 1459. Various saints claimed a special interest in him, too, mentioning him in their writings, which further publicized his name and his life. Two of his more notable "fans" were St. Teresa of Ávila and St. Francis de Sales.

Joseph also became an example for fathers. In 1870 Pope Pius IX declared him Patron of the Universal Church. Pope Leo XIII placed him next to the Blessed Mother among all saints. This saint has two feast days, one on March 19 and another on May 1, which was named the Feast of St. Joseph the Worker by Pope Pius XII.

He is the patron saint of carpenters, manual workers, all workers (May 1), fatherhood and families, holy death, social justice, Belgium, Canada, China, Korea, and Peru. Also, priests, brothers, and nuns turn to St. Joseph in particular when praying about financial problems in their communities.

St. Teresa of Ávila, on praying to St. Joseph: "I don't recall up to this day ever having petitioned him for anything that he failed to grant. It is an amazing thing the great many favors God has granted me through the mediation of this blessed saint. . . . For with other saints it seems the Lord has given them grace to be of help in one need, whereas with this glorious saint I have experience that he helps in all our needs."

Those busy revisionists have been at it again. It is thought now that Joseph might have been a *tekton*, a Greek word for a skilled craftsman, because biblical references use that word for him. A tekton works with metal of all kinds and with stone, although Joseph might have been a carpenter, too. Also, small-town Nazareth was within sight of Sepphoris, a large Palestinian city second in size only to Jerusalem. Sepphoris, destroyed by military action around the time of Jesus's birth, was then under reconstruction, providing plenty of work for artisans like Joseph and Jesus.

A curious trend surfaced during the economic recession of the late 1980s. Roman Catholics struggling to sell their homes would "plant" a statue of St. Joseph on the property, head down, and then pray to the saint for success with their venture. The practice continues today with hard-to-sell properties. The Church considers this a superstition.

Still, this custom persists. When some Catholic families move into a new home, they bury a statue of this saint right-side up on their property, as a way of invoking his blessing for their life there. When the family decides to move and hopes to sell their home, they might dig the statue up and bury it upside down.

Sts. Anne and Joachim (First Century)

The mother of Mary is a little-documented saint, though her influence belies her vague history. Churches, shrines, and feast day celebrations attest to our continuing interest in this holy woman. Her husband, Joachim, is just as little known. Anne might have been born in Nazareth, the daughter of a nomad. Actually, even her name is uncertain. That is true of Joachim, too, and he also could have been a Nazarene.

Anne was about twenty when she married Joachim; his age then is unknown. The couple was desolate because they had no children; and when publicly taken to task for that lack, Joachim went into the desert and fasted for forty days. Then, one day while Anne was praying, an angel appeared and told her she would have a child. Anne, who was forty by then, promised to dedicate the child to God's service. That baby was, of course, Mary. Joachim is said to have died about sixteen years later, just after the birth of Jesus.

Figure 5-2: Sts. Anne and Joachim

A Grandparents' Garden

At least one church named after St. Anne has created a spot on its grounds honoring both Anne and Joachim, which it called a grandparents' garden. St. Ann's Church in Lawrenceville, New Jersey, wanted to have a statue of the saint on the premises. She is usually pictured with Mary, seldom with Joachim. "Today, more than ever we need concrete reminders of spousal love," the church said, announcing that it would capture the couple's devotion in two life-size statues.

E-FACT

A procession to celebrate the feast of St. Anne (sometimes spelled Ann) is not uncommon in some ethnic, especially Italian, neighborhoods in this country. Selected faithful carry a 500- to 600-pound statue of the saint through the streets of the community. Often a festival at night closes the day's events.

The church noted that grandparents are strong connectors to the complex family system of which we are all a part. The garden is a place where anyone can come to remember their grandparents. Also, grandparents might come to the statues to pray for their children and grandchildren. In the base of each statue are names of hundreds of grandparents submitted by parishioners.

A Role for Today

Joachim has a feast day, and churches have been named after him. Anne has been viewed as a powerful intercessor. She is the patron saint of Canada, of cabinetmakers, grandmothers, homemakers, pregnancy, and women in labor. In some countries, Anne is prayed to with special fervor by women who want a child. St. Anne and St. Joachim share the feast day of July 26.

St. Jude (First Century)

Jude was one of the original twelve apostles. His name and fame endure far more than the other eleven, most of whom remain fairly unknown today, without much mention outside of church liturgy.

Not that much is known about Jude Thaddeus. It is believed he might have been one of four brothers who were Jesus's first cousins. But this is speculation—albeit educated speculation by scholars and hagiographers. With all the studying of Jude's background, the course of his life with Jesus and after the Crucifixion, little has been passed on that cannot be debated.

Jude is mentioned in the Gospel of John: When Jesus was speaking at the Last Supper, Jude interrupted him, asking, "Lord, how is it that you will manifest yourself to us, and not to the world?" Jesus answered, "If a man loves me, he will keep my word, and my Father will love him, and we will come to him and make our home with him. He who does not love me does not keep my words; and the word which you hear is not mine but the Father's who sent me." This apostle is also said to have written a short book of the New Testament, the Letter of Jude, in which he warned against false prophets. He is also thought to have been martyred in Persia.

E-QUESTION

Why is Jude so well known today?

St. Jude is known well today because he is a patron saint that almost everyone can relate to—the patron saint of lost causes. Catholics will often pray to St. Jude when they feel that all else has failed.

It is not known how Jude came to be the patron saint of lost causes and desperate situations, but many ask for his intercession when life feels hopeless. They ask for his help in finding work when they have been unemployed for many months, to cure a relative with a serious addiction, to cure themselves of severe illness, or to get assistance with any number of other problems that seem to have no solution, or at least not an obvious one.

In *A Book of Saints: True Stories of How They Touch Our Lives* (Random House, 1994), author Anne Gordon tells her favorite St. Jude story. The supplicant was not in desperate circumstance, but her plea was something of an impossible request.

The woman was thirty-six years old, and she and her husband had three sons. Her spouse wanted a daughter very much, but the woman's doctor told her that childbearing was now impossible for her. She prayed to Jude anyway.

One night in a dream her deceased grandmother appeared to her. She said, "I told you if you would pray to Saint Jude he would help you, didn't I?" The woman woke from the dream somewhat confused because she had been praying to that saint. She did not know at the time that she was two months pregnant. It seemed her grandmother had appeared simply to tell her that her dream had come true. The couple named their daughter Mary.

Answered Prayers

Many Catholic churches hold an annual novena to St. Jude, so this is a busy saint, no doubt hearing as many pleas for hopeless causes as St. Anthony does for lost objects.

Traditionally, if St. Jude answers a prayer, the faithful are expected to formally thank him. This can take the form of a special trip to a church or a shrine that carries his name, or some other fitting acknowledgment of gratitude. Many place notices in the classified columns of daily and weekly newspapers that read something like "Thank you, St. Jude, for a favor received." No name goes with the advertisement, although there are sometimes initials at the end of the item. If you look in your paper, you can probably find notices like this from time to time. St. Jude's feast day is October 28.

Chapter 6

Holiday Saints

This chapter features a sampling of familiar, yet surprising, saints. While their names may be recognizable and their holidays are widely celebrated, the details of their lives are often unknown. Likewise, customs surrounding these saints have often become separated from their authentic histories. This chapter will introduce the human lives hidden behind the celebrations, as well as some of the poignant, quaint, and unusual celebrations surrounding these saints.

Remembering the Saints

Although this chapter features some of the most famous saints, all saints are essentially "holiday saints." Each one has a particular day (or set of days) associated with him. In most cases, saints' days are connected to the day that they died. Within the Christian tradition, the day of death is viewed as the greatest "birthday," because it marks the passage into eternal life.

The calendars of the Eastern Orthodox, Roman Catholic, and Anglican Churches are cluttered with the names of saints. These churches are determined to remember the saints, keeping their memories alive by telling their stories year after year. Many saints have particular significance within certain cultures, and some have become deeply connected with nationalities. Other saints' stories are celebrated in countries all over the world, but given a unique spin wherever the stories are told.

The following saints have sprung from the liturgical calendars of their churches, taking on fresh incarnations in secular society. While some of the customs surrounding these saints are quaint and reverent, others would likely make the celebrated saints cringe, as might some of the mythology surrounding these legendary figures. The next few pages will offer a glimpse into the historical roots of these much-loved figures.

Figure 6-1: St. Valentine

St. Valentine (Died c. 269)

St. Valentine was a physician and a priest, perhaps even a bishop, in Rome. During his time, the Emperor Claudius the Goth sought to raise a large army. He felt that single men would make better soldiers. St. Valentine secretly married people who were forbidden to wed under Roman law.

Valentine was arrested for his "misdeeds," imprisoned, and beheaded on February 14.

He was buried on Rome's Flaminian Way, and a basilica was erected there in 350.

The Two Valentines

It seems there was another Roman named Valentine who died on the same day. This man was also a priest and was martyred in Terni, some 60 miles from Rome. This Valentine confessed his faith before the emperor, declaring that the gods Jupiter and Mercury were "shameless and contemptible characters."

While he was in prison, Valentine befriended the blind daughter of his jailer. He cured her and converted his captor to Christianity. When the emperor heard about his deeds, he had Valentine beaten and beheaded. It is now thought that the two Valentines may have been the same man—taken from one city where he was imprisoned, to the other where he was executed.

Valentine's Day

Historically, many Christian holidays have merged with more ancient pagan traditions, allowing new converts to retain some of their beloved customs while finding a new focus for their celebrations. This type of mingling very likely occurred in the creation of what is now known as "Valentine's Day."

Up until 200 years after Valentine's death, the Roman feast of Lupercalia was celebrated on February 15. That day commemorated Faunus, one of many Roman deities. To the Romans, Faunus was the god of flocks and fertility. During the day's celebration, single women placed their names in a large bowl and men drew their names. The man would then be that woman's partner during the festival. Occasionally, love matches resulted from the drawing.

The romantic feast of Lupercalia may have been combined with the feast a day earlier for Juno, the Roman goddess of women and marriage. St. Valentine seems to have become jumbled up in the mix because his martyrdom occurred in proximity to these love feasts and because he seems to have had a tender heart toward lovers.

Love Notes

The medieval tradition of sending Valentine's Day cards may be rooted in the patterns of the natural world. Medieval folk noticed that birds began to pair around the middle of February, and it was thought that lovers might exchange notes around this time as well. Because St. Valentine's feast was celebrated at this time, the cards took his name.

E-XTRA

Legend has it that the very first Valentine may have been sent by this saint. During his time in prison, he befriended a prison guard's daughter. On the day he died, February 14, 264, he is said to have left her a note, thanking her for her friendship. He signed it "Your Valentine."

After the advent of postal systems, Valentine messages grew in popularity—although letters were generally hand-carried, because messages sent through the postal system originally had to be sent "postage due." St. Valentine is the patron saint of lovers. His feast day is February 14, although some religious calendars make no note of it.

St. Nicholas (c. 271–350)

St. Nicholas was most likely born in Asia Minor, to wealthy Christian parents. As a young man, he offered his inheritance to the poor. Many legends bear witness to his generous nature. One involves three young girls. Their father, a nobleman, lost all his money. Without a dowry, the girls were doomed to slavery.

Troubled over their fate, Nicholas devised a plan. One night, while the family slept, he tossed gold through the window of their home. Some of the gold landed in a stocking hung by the hearth to dry, hence the custom of Christmas stockings. The gold became the dowry for the three girls.

Nicholas became a priest, and later bishop of Myra, a rather lowly diocese in that region. He was known for his piety, his hard work, and his miracles. During the persecution of the Christians under the Emperor Diocletian, he was imprisoned. Nicholas was at the Council of Nicaea, where he denounced Arianism.

Several miracles have been attributed to Nicholas. He may have restored to life three children who had been killed by an innkeeper, chopped up, and pickled in brine. Other miracles attest to his care for those at sea.

Figure 6-2: St. Nicholas

When he was a young priest sailing on a boat to Jerusalem, Nicholas warned the sailors of a severe storm approaching. But he added, "Don't be afraid. Trust in God because he will protect you from death." The storm came, and one sailor fell overboard. His body was recovered, but the sailor had died. When Nicholas prayed the stormy waters became smooth. Then, he blessed the dead sailor, who awoke to life, completely uninjured.

E-FACT

Candy canes are a reminder of St. Nicholas, as their shape resembles a bishop's staff. Likewise, gingerbread men used to be made to resemble bishops, and cookie stamps can still be purchased to decorate baked goods with the seal of St. Nicholas.

The exact year of Nicholas's death is unknown. In the eleventh century, Italian soldiers are said to have stolen his body, probably from Turkey, and moved it to Bari, Italy, where his relics remain. Devotion to St. Nicholas remains strong, particularly within Eastern Orthodox churches, which introduced Nicholas to Germany around 980. From there his fame spread throughout Western Europe, where many churches are named after him; in England alone a few hundred churches bore his name before the

Reformation. Celebrations of his December 6 feast day take place in many parts of the world. In the ninth century the first pope to bear his name dedicated a basilica to St. Nicholas.

St. Nicholas is said to be the only saint equally venerated by all Christian denominations. He is a busy patron, as well: of Greece, Russia, brides, children, merchants, dockworkers, travelers, bakers, brewers, prisoners, sailors, as well as pawnbrokers and prostitutes.

E-QUESTION

What was Asia Minor?

Asia Minor was once roughly the size of today's Turkey. It was the site of some of the earliest Christian communities, such as Smyrna and Ephesus. The churches of Asia Minor began to fade in importance in the fourth century, giving way to Antioch, Constantinople, and Alexandria.

Many traditions surround St. Nicholas:

- In Aruba and the Netherlands on the eve of St. Nicholas Day, children leave a bucket of water and a shoe filled with hay for the horse of "Sinterklaas," who arrives with his helper, "Zwarte Piet." If children have been good, the shoes will be filled with gifts in the morning, but if not, Zwarte Piet might load the children into his sack and carry them back to Spain.
- In France, St. Nicholas comes to particular regions on his feast day. The grandparents tell the children stories about the saint, and they leave their shoes out and sing a song to him. Unfortunately, St. Nicholas is followed by Pere Fouettard, who threatens the children with spankings.
- Although Russia has celebrated St. Nicholas Day since at least the eleventh century, under Communism St. Nicholas became known as Grandfather Frost and his attire changed from red to blue. Still, in many pockets of Russia, devotion to the saint has remained strong. According to one Russian proverb, "If anything happens to God, we've always got Saint Nicholas."

- In England, an old tradition of "The Boy of Nicholas Bishop" has been restored to some parishes. A young boy will be selected from the choir. When the choir sings certain words from the Magnificat—"He has brought down the mighty from their thrones and lifted up the lowly"—the young boy, dressed in full bishop regalia, will proceed to the bishop's chair, asking God's blessing for the people.
- In the Czech Republic, St. Nicholas Day remains extremely popular. St. Nicholas is lowered down to earth on a heavy golden cord by the angels. He travels with a devil (who snatches bad children away) and an angel, who pleads on their behalf.
- In Austria, St. Nicholas travels with a frightening creature named Krampus. Krampus comes dressed in fur, adorned with chains and a devilish look, complete with red tongue. He scolds ill-behaved children.
- In Bulgaria, the autumn fishing season ends on the feast of St. Nicholas (or Nikulden). On Nikulden, a special fish dish is baked with two loaves of bread. It is then blessed at home or church before being left out for friends and neighbors to share.
- In Croatia, the children polish their boots and then leave them on windowsills for St. Nicolas to fill. St. Nicholas comes with his strong man, Krampus, who leaves twigs for every child. The largest twigs are reserved for the worst behaved children.

E-XTRA

At the first Ecumenical Council at Nicaea, St. Nicholas apparently became enraged at Arius and punched him in the nose. For this, he temporarily lost his bishopric and was cast into prison. He was released and restored to his bishopric after a vision compelled the other bishops to set him free.

St. Patrick (c. 389–461)

Patrick was born along the west coast of Roman Britain. His father, Calpurnius, was a Roman citizen and a deacon. His mother, Concessa, gave their child the Latin name Patricius. Being the son of a deacon, Patrick was brought up a Christian, with the sense that Rome was the spiritual and cultural center of the universe.

When Patrick was a teenager, a group of Irish raiders attacked his family's estate. His parents were not home at the time, but Patrick, along with many of his family's servants, was taken hostage and forced to live in Ireland as a slave.

According to John Matthews, in Drinking from the Sacred Well (Harper San Francisco, 1998), the names of more than 10,000 Celtic saints have survived: "Some of them recorded only in the land, as place names that summon up long-forgotten events, legends, and miracles that have vanished, along with their owners, back into the mists from which they came."

It can be difficult to appreciate how rugged Ireland was when Patrick was forcefully taken there. The land was wild, travel was extremely difficult, and Christianity existed only in small pockets. Many locals still worshiped the sun. The druids, an ancient Celtic priesthood, practiced rites involving oak and mistletoe, as well as—it is thought—human sacrifice.

Although Patrick must have been profoundly disoriented by all that he saw and experienced in Ireland, his master was kind and Patrick served him for six years.

During that time he experienced profound spiritual transformation. In his sleep, he heard a voice telling him, "Thou doest well to fast; thou shalt soon return to thy native land." Patrick believed the voice and began planning his escape. He made his way safely across the country to the east coast town of Wicklow. Trading vessels were about to set sail. Patrick approached one and was taken aboard as a crewman.

Neither the nationality nor race of the crew is known, but Patrick says they were heathen. After sailing for three days, the ship landed along the

Figure 6-3: St. Patrick

shore of an unnamed country. They then made their way on foot through a "desert" for nearly a month.

The crew ran out of food. One of the men told Patrick that they were going to starve, and asked if Patrick's God could save them. Patrick replied, "Nothing is impossible to the Lord my God. Turn to him truly, that he may send you food in your path this day till ye are filled, for he has plenty in all places." Soon a drove of pigs appeared on the road, and the hungry crewmen killed enough to eat for days.

Scholars believe the boat landed along the southwest coast of Gaul, perhaps at what is now Bordeaux. The group supposedly traversed Gaul and then headed into Italy. It was probably in Italy that Patrick freed himself from the crew. He longed to return home to Britain. Along the way he spent several years at a cloister. When he finally reached home, he was greeted warmly.

He then studied at a monastery in Britain (or Gaul) and was ordained around 417—although some scholars say Patrick never became an "officially" ordained priest. A series of powerful dreams then tugged him back toward the land of his enslavement. In one of the dreams, a man he knew from Ireland named Victoricus appeared to him holding multiple letters. He handed one, entitled "The Voice of the Irish," to Patrick. Patrick opened the letter only to hear voices calling out to him, "Holy boy, we beg you to come and walk among us once more."

E-XTRA

The Chicago River is annually dyed green on St. Patrick's Day, and throughout America on that day, beer is heartily consumed. In Ireland, however, St. Patrick's Day has historically been a religious holiday—until the 1970s the pubs were to remain closed on that day.

About ten years after he became a priest, he may have become a bishop. He eventually surrendered to the dreams and returned to Ireland. Although he sought to bring Christianity to the native people, his approach was respectful. He integrated aspects of the people's native religions into the Christianity he shared with them, superimposing the sun on the cross to create the Celtic cross—a perfect merging of natural symbol and religious faith.

Patrick spent thirty fruitful years in Ireland. He established a network of churches and monasteries throughout the country, all with native clergy. He worked to raise the standards of learning and in general to bring Ireland in line with other "progressive" countries that were allied with Rome. Despite all of his successes, Patrick suffered for his own lack of education, which was likely interrupted by his six years of slavery. He was always aware that his Latin was "rustic" and not quite up to par.

E-FACT

Although much has been made of the legend that Patrick drove all the snakes from Ireland into the sea, there is no historical basis for this story. Still, it is interesting to note that to this day, there are no snakes in Ireland.

No one is quite sure where Patrick died or where he is buried, but his legacy lives on. His feast day of March 17 continues to be celebrated in Ireland, America, Canada, and Australia. Celebrations have also been reported in Singapore, Russia, and Japan. Although St. Patrick's feast day was historically a religious celebration, the feast falls during Lent, and was so significant in Ireland that fasting requirements were lifted for that day, perhaps giving rise to the celebratory character of the feast.

Patrick left two written works: *The Confession*, written when he was close to death and which serves as the chief source of biographical data, and *Letter to the Soldiers of Coroticus*, in which he denounced the killing of a group of Irish Christians by marauding Christian Welshmen.

Figure 6-4: St. Lucy

St. Lucy (Died c. 303)

Lucy was born of Sicilian noble parents. As a young woman, she offered her virginity to God, but her mother pressured her to marry a young pagan. Lucy refused. For several years afterward, her mother suffered from an issue of blood. Lucy urged her to visit the tomb of St. Agatha, believing that Agatha might heal her.

At St. Agatha's tomb, Lucy and her mother spent the entire night praying, until they both became so sleepy that they could no longer stay awake. While Lucy slept, Agatha appeared to her and told her that her mother would be healed and that Lucy would suffer martyrdom, but through her sufferings she would become great. "You will soon be the glory of Syracuse," Agatha told her. Lucy's mother was instantly cured.

Although Lucy's mother allowed her to remain a virgin, Lucy was to experience other pressures. Under Diocletian's persecution, the man Lucy had shunned reported that she was a Christian. As a punishment, she was to be sent to a brothel. But something mysterious happened—the men who tried to move her couldn't. When they tied her to bulls, they were still unable to make her budge. The man responsible for sending her to the brothel became frustrated and said, "How can you, a feeble woman, triumph over a thousand men?" Lucy responded with these strong words: "Bring ten thousand and they won't be able to combat against God!"

At this, a fire was lit, but her body rejected the flames. Finally, she died when a sword was plunged into her. In her last moments, she predicted peace for the church.

Lucy is patron of those with eye diseases, perhaps because of her name, meaning "light." Some stories have her eyes torn out by her judge, others say she tore them out to offer them to a suitor she did not like. In both incidents they were mysteriously and miraculously restored.

The Festival of Light

Most countries around the world celebrate a "Festival of Light" during the darkest days of the year. In Sweden, this festival is closely linked to their saint of light, Lucy, who is remembered on December 13.

Historically in Sweden, in each village a young woman was selected to wear a white gown with a red sash and a crown of lingonberry branches. Before the light of dawn, "Lucy" would go from farm to farm, a torch in hand, candles in her crown. She would then wake the families at each farm with fresh baked goods.

E-QUESTION

Is there a connection between "Lucy" and "Lucifer"?
Yes, there is a connection because both names are rooted in the word "light." St. Lucy is the saint of light, while Satan, otherwise known as Lucifer, is said to disguise himself as an angel of light.

Traditions Today

To this day, in Sweden and Norway, a young girl is chosen to wake each family. She bears a crown of lingonberry branches and electric candles. She carries a platter of hot cardamom buns and coffee. Many homes have their own "Lucy," most often the youngest girl, who wakes the family with song.

In another ancient Scandinavian tradition, children wrote "Lussi" on doors, gates, and walls on the eve of her feast day. This custom was intended to announce to the winter demons that St. Lucy's Day would break their power—the sun would soon return, the days would become longer and the nights shorter. This tradition was especially poignant before the calendar was reformed in the 1300s, when St. Lucy's feast day fell on the winter solstice.

All Saints' Day

The Roman Catholic and Anglican All Saints' Day falls on November 1, followed by All Souls' Day on November 2. These feasts offer an opportunity to remember the holy ones who, according to ancient Christian belief, continue to inspire, challenge, and support those on earth.

All Saints' Day was originally created to honor those who had suffered martyrdom for God. Many of their names and stories have been lost, but there was a desire within the church to create a sort of "memorial day" to celebrate all those unnamed holy ones who had died for the faith.

E-XTRA

A prayer for All Saints: "The work of your hands is manifest in your saints, the beauty of your truth is reflected in their faith. May we who aspire to have part in their joy be filled with the spirit that blessed their lives, so that having shared their faith on earth may we also know their peace in your kingdom."

Back in the fourth century, All Saints' Day was called "the Feast of All Martyrs" and was celebrated on the first Sunday after Pentecost (All Saints is still celebrated on this day in the Eastern Orthodox Church). In the Western church, this holiday was later moved to May 13 because of an event that occurred on that day in 610. Pope St. Boniface IV (608–615) transformed an ancient Pagan Temple, which had once been dedicated to "all gods." The Pope reburied the bones of many martyrs there, rebuilt the temple so that it would be suitable for Christian use, and rededicated the space to the Mother of God and all the Holy Martyrs.

A century later, a new chapel was consecrated in the basilica of St. Peter. This chapel was dedicated to "All Saints" on November 1, and Pope Gregory III shifted the feast of "All Saints" to this day, which was eventually celebrated by the entire Western Church.

What about Halloween?

Halloween shares some common heritage with the feast of All Saints. On October 31, the eve of the Celtic New Year, the Celts held a large celebration. They worshiped the sun and believed that during the winter, the sun God was taken captive by Samhain, the Prince of Darkness and Lord of the Dead.

It was believed that on October 31, all the dead people were called together, inhabiting different forms. Cats were especially suspect. By that date, all the crops had been harvested, and the druids, or Celtic priests, gathered on a hilltop and offered sacrifices of crops and animals while dancing around bonfires.

Christianity eventually permeated Europe, and, starting in 835, the feast of All Saints came to be celebrated on November 1. Although many Celtic people enthusiastically embraced Christianity, some of the old ways of celebrating this holiday remained. October 31 was first known as "All Hallow Even," which became "All Hallow's Eve," then "Hallowe'en" and finally "Halloween."

The Day of the Dead

The Day of the Dead is a Mexican holiday honoring the dead. Like Halloween, this feast has both Christian and pre-Christian influences. In Mexico, the Day of the Dead is a great celebration, falling on November 1 and 2.

In some villages, people dress up as ghosts and parade through the streets with an open coffin. Inside, a smiling "corpse" receives the flowers, candy, and fruit that are tossed into it.

At home, families create altars with photos of deceased loved ones. They light all-night vigil candles and adorn their altars with food, flowers, bread, and candy. If the departed loved one was a smoker, they might even add a pack of cigarettes.

The next day, they travel to cemeteries to clean and maintain the graves of loved ones. They scrub and sweep crypts, plant flowers, and light candles. Some families bring a picnic lunch, and some stay beside the grave all night long.

The Mexican Day of the Dead, influenced by many different religious traditions, offers concrete ways to grapple with loss and to be present with departed loved ones. This is not entirely unlike the other feast days related to saints. These feasts are a reminder that relationships transcend the grave and that the work of loving (and the experience of being loved by) another person never comes to an end. The Eastern Orthodox Theologian Fr. Alexander Schmemann said, "To love is to remember." These great feasts offer an opportunity for love through remembrance.

Chapter 7

Companion Saints

The theme of spiritual friendship is woven through both the Old and New Testaments. Although some saints lived solitary lives, others were deeply engaged in communities. These saints were able to form bonds with others that were lasting and intimate. This chapter will explore the relationships of "companion saints"—holy ones who became bolder and more saintly through their close ties with others.

Friendship in the Scriptures

In the book of Genesis, when God created the universe, He affirmed that all was good. But there was one thing that He was not entirely satisfied with—Adam, who was alone. God said, "It is not good that the man should be alone. . . ." (Genesis 2:18) And then God resolved to make Adam a companion. The essential unity between Adam and Eve is expressed by the way that God built Eve from Adam's rib, drawing two from one so that the two could become one again.

E-QUESTION

Where does the phrase "two are better than one" come from?
It comes from Ecclesiastes 4:9–10: "Two are better than one, because they have a good reward for their toil. For if they fall, one will lift up his fellow; but woe to him who is alone when he falls and has not another to lift him up."

When Noah and the animals were called onto the ark, they were called two by two. Likewise, Jesus's disciples were called in pairs, as were many of the saints throughout the ages, such as Sts. Peter and Paul, Sts. Cosmas and Damian, Sts. Clare and Francis, and Sts. Teresa and John. The stories of the saints are full of tender encounters between individuals who were able to draw strength and hope from each other.

Christopher Bamford, editor-in-chief of Steiner Books, on spiritual friendship for Parabola Magazine: "When we speak, even when it is the intimate expression of a deep, personal experience, we are a single voice. We have forgiven each other a thousand times. We have let go of so much that could divide us that we have let go of ourselves. Our relationship seems to exist in and out of the unknown, the ever new."

This chapter will now consider a few of these companion saints, who were able to grow through friendship with each other. In each case, the friendship helped the saint to become more than he originally was, to be challenged toward a deeper experience of life and God.

Sts. Francis (1181–1226) and Clare (1194–1253)

Francis and Claire had a rich, spiritual friendship, despite the fact that their monastic lives prevented them from spending much time together. Still, they were each able to influence the other, and they both drew strength from their friendship, which was not physical but was spiritually intimate.

E-XTRA

When Francis struggled with lust, he would go out into a cold winter's night and make snow figures. When asked what he was doing, he explained that when his desire for a family became too great, the snow family helped him imagine begging for money to feed and clothe his wife and children. This exercise curbed his desire.

When Clare sought to become a Franciscan, Francis cut her hair. When Francis received the stigmata and his wrists and ankles bled painfully, Clare knit slippers for him. At the end of Francis's life, when he was sick, he moved to a small shack beside Clare's monastery so that she and her sisters could care for him.

Francis was born in Assisi, in the Umbrian region of Italy, to a wealthy fabric merchant and his wife. He grew up taking full advantage of his fortunate circumstances. He traveled, spent money freely, and lived a self-indulgent life. He was said to be charming, charismatic, and generous.

Even war did not tame his spirits. He went off to fight in a conflict and was taken prisoner. He spent a year in jail and then succumbed to a serious illness. His recovery was slow. Both experiences brought

Figure 7-1: St. Francis of Assisi

about a spiritual crisis. Francis gave serious thought to the way he had been living, and decided to make a pilgrimage to Rome in 1206.

A different Francis returned home. He resolved to devote his life to serving the poor and the sick. His father thought he was insane—and went so far as to disinherit him. But at least one person did not think he was insane. And that was Clare, twelve years younger than him, also from a wealthy family, but ready to give it all up if she could follow in his footsteps.

There is one event from Francis's life that brings his human characteristics into sharp relief. He misunderstood a directive—though it was from God. One day, after his decision to work with the poor, he was praying in a church just outside Assisi. The crucifix lit up and a voice spoke, telling him, "Francis, repair my church, which has fallen into disrepair, as you can see." So the saint went out and returned with the thirteenth-century equivalent of a tool kit and began to repair that particular church, which had indeed seen better times. Only later did Francis realize the directive was far more cosmic than he originally imagined—he was to repair the Church at large, not just a single building—and bring it back to simplicity and devotion to the poor.

E-FACT

When St. Francis would speak to women, he would not look into their faces. When a fellow monk once asked St. Francis why he was always avoiding the women's eyes, Francis said, "Who must not fear to look upon the Bride of Christ?"

Francis retreated to a small chapel, the Portiuncula, to devote his life to preaching and to the poor. He soon began attracting disciples, who were at first curious about the rich boy who had given everything away. Among those interested in the saint's work were several prominent citizens of Assisi. With all of those willing workers in mind, Francis founded the Franciscan order in 1209. It would be dedicated to absolute poverty, humility, and the love of all created things.

One of his most famous followers was St. Clare (discussed above), who became his friend and confidant. Although she had several offers for marriage, she turned them all down. On Palm Sunday of her eighteenth birthday, she ran away from home. In a secret ceremony, Francis cut Clare's beautiful blond hair and offered her a belt rope. Francis then sent Clare to live at a nearby Benedictine convent, although she would eventually become the founder of her own austere religious order, "The Poor Clares."

E-XTRA

Although Clare's devotion to God and refusal to marry initially horrified her family, her spiritual way of life eventually inspired some of her own family members to pursue the monastic path. Two of Clare's sisters, as well as her mother, eventually joined her at the convent.

St. Bonaventure wrote beautifully of the great love St. Francis had for St. Clare: "Clare was the first flower in Francis's garden, and she shone like a radiant star, fragrant as a flower blossoming white and pure in springtime." Although Francis loved Clare, he was very cautious about her, only visiting her a few times during the course of his life. One day, when Francis was visiting Clare and her sisters at the convent, Francis spoke of the love of God over a simple meal. His words were so sweet that the monks and nuns completely forgot to eat, and flames seemed to cover them all. The flames were visible from several miles away and the people of Assisi rushed to the convent to put out the fire, only to find Francis and Clare having a meal together and deeply engaged in conversation. There was, after all, no fire, just a powerful radiance between them.

In great pain during his final illness, Francis called out, "Welcome, Sister Death." He died in Assisi on October 3, 1226. At the moment of his death a light shone from his body, and the church bells at San Stefano pealed with no assistance from a bell ringer. Giving his blessing to the friars who had gathered around him, he told them, "I have done my part. May Christ teach you to do yours."

Throughout her life Clare fought hard to follow Francis's instructions. She became extremely influential over the years and is credited, next to St. Francis, with being most responsible for the growth of the Franciscans.

Sts. Teresa of Ávila (1515–1582) and John of the Cross (1542–1591)

Teresa was intelligent, charming, and quite witty, even tart. One time a visitor came upon her happily digging into a partridge dinner someone had sent. The visitor was appalled. A woman of God appearing to enjoy her food? What would people think? "Let them think what they please," Teresa responded. "There is a time for partridge and a time for penance." Another time she said, "I could be bribed with a sardine."

Teresa's Life

Teresa was born Teresa Cepeda y Ahumada in 1515, the daughter of a wealthy merchant of Ávila. Teresa expressed interest in religion at an early age, although not in any traditional manner. When she was seven she and her brother ran away from home, wanting to reach land occupied by the Moors—in the hopes of being martyred for Christ! Fortunately, an uncle intercepted the two children and brought them home.

Figure 7-2: St. Teresa of Ávila

Teresa's mother died when she was fourteen, and her father arranged for her to be educated at a local convent, which was typical of the times. At twenty Teresa decided to become a nun, a vocation she later said was due more to a fear of purgatory than a love of God.

Her father was not in favor of Teresa taking vows, whatever her motive, but she was willful and ran off again, this time to the Carmelite convent in Ávila. While there she became ill, and her father had to bring her home. Her health deteriorated further. She became paralyzed from the waist down from an illness that has never completely been explained.

Eventually she rallied, and after a long and painful convalescence returned to the convent. By now her faith, rather than being strengthened by her ordeal, was tepid.

Life in the convent did not help her in finding a path to God. At that time the Carmelites and several other religious congregations led such easy, even pleasant, lives that they might have been living in a resort.

Many wealthy widows and single women would enter a convent. They wore jewelry over their habits. They had special foods brought in. In fact, many women ran to convents for the freedom they provided. Young girls living in convents for schooling had quite a nice life, too. Teresa's winning personality made her quite popular in this busy, social atmosphere.

A Vision

But Teresa was to have her moment of truth. One day when she was in her thirties, she looked upon the image of Christ on the cross as she had done hundreds of times before. This time, however, as she thought of his suffering, she became almost disgusted with her "religious" life. She determined to spend more time in prayer and other spiritual pursuits. Almost immediately after making that decision, Teresa said, she felt God's presence and love within her.

Teresa of Ávila, wrote these words on friendship, from her letters no. 170:1, 450, "What a wonderful thing it is for two souls to understand each other, for they neither lack something to say, nor grow tired."

By now repelled by the ways of the Carmelites, she decided to found a new, reformed Carmelite order. After some difficult groundwork, she finally did, in 1562.

She named her new community the Discalced (shoeless) Carmelites. Actually, the nuns wore sandals, but the word referred to the vow of poverty the sisters would take, making them, figuratively speaking, shoeless. The nuns in the Discalced order lived by hard labor and by alms. They kept strict hours and slept on straw pallets. Food was simple, and there was not much of it. Prayer was the focal point of life. And these nuns did without jewelry, even without visits from friends.

Teresa was full of common sense and had no use for pomposity. Once a young nun came to her with stories of all kinds of temptation and of how she was such a sinner. "Now, Sister," Teresa said, "None of us is perfect. Just make sure those sins of yours don't turn into bad habits."

Teresa Meets Juan de Yepes y Álvarez

After the Ávila convent, Teresa founded another sixteen religious houses throughout Spain, traveling with little or no money and enduring the hardships of the Castilian countryside. While setting up the second convent, at age fifty-two, she met a twenty-five-year-old friar named Juan de Yepes y Álvarez.

Teresa and John were like-minded. They both sought to retain the Carmelites' original simplicity and dedication to prayer. John was in fact considering joining another order, because he was so dissatisfied with the Carmelites. The two joined forces. John began a parallel reform for men to Teresa's Discalced Carmelites movement for women.

Although John was much younger than Teresa, he became her closest friend. In her letters, she said that she "had gone here and there looking for the light and had found it in him" (642). The two of them enjoyed many hours of conversation together and it was said of the two of them that they sometimes even levitated together. What could be more intimate than that?

In the book, *Falling into the Arms of God* (New World Library, 2005), Megan Don said that Teresa believed that close friendships were deeply beneficial. She encouraged nuns and priests to let others know them deeply—to form lasting spiritual bonds. According to Don, some priests were wary of Teresa's open affection; they thought she was a bit reckless. Don wrote, "She would laugh to herself at their fear, since she knew they mistook the purity of her actions for something less elevated."

Teresa loved to tease her friend John, calling him "half a friar" because he was so short. Just as Francis had helped Clare establish the "Poor Clares," Teresa helped John establish the first reform monastery for men, and she placed him in charge of it.

Mystic and Writer

Teresa of Ávila has been called one of the most profound mystics of all time. Besides experiencing ecstasies, it is said that at other times in church she had to hold on to the altar rail to keep from ascending upward. Commenting on her own life, or perhaps the difficult life of the cloistered nun in general, she noted, "The sufferings God inflicts on contemplatives are of so unbearable a kind that, unless He sustained such souls with the manna of divine consolation, they would find their agony unbearable."

This Carmelite was a prolific writer, too, leaving much behind for historians—and anyone who wants to know the Love of God—to ponder. Her autobiography offers insights into her visions and other mystical experiences. Two of her other writings, *Way of Perfection* and *Interior Castles*, guide the reader toward grace and perfection. Teresa also wrote numerous letters that offer insight into her mind and temperament.

Tough Times

Teresa ran afoul of the Spanish Inquisition, just as John of the Cross, Ignatius of Loyola, and so many others did. She eventually endured a formal investigation, although charges against her were dismissed.

Her own order caused grief, too, as she experienced a bitter five-year struggle with the Calced Carmelites. John of the Cross was imprisoned for a time in the Calced Carmelite monastery in Toledo. Finally, Pope Gregory XIII recognized the Discalced Reform Carmelites as a separate order.

Teresa died at Alba de Tormes, Spain, in 1582. As her full life drew to a close, she said "My Saviour, it is time that I set out . . . Let us go." It is said that a marvelous scent emanated from her body, and later, when one of her confessors had her grave opened, her body was still intact and emitted the aroma of lilies. As was the custom of those times with saintly people, the body was cut up and pieces given to various powerful admirers of the nun as relics. Her confessor kept the little finger of the left hand for himself.

Teresa of Ávila was canonized forty years after her death. In 1970 she became the first woman to be named a Doctor of the Church. Her feast day is October 15. She is a patron saint of Spain and of headache sufferers, and is invoked against heart disease.

In her writings, she left behind many insights into the nature of spiritual friendship. As Megan Don wrote, "She said that at times spiritual and sensual love become so intermingled that no one can understand such love. She maintained that this is a completely normal occurrence between souls, whether male or female, and that there should be no torment over this feeling of love."

St. John of the Cross

Among a handful of saints who could be considered the greatest mystics of all time, and one of the greatest Spanish poets as well, is St. John, who was the author of the famed "Dark Night of the Soul." He led a harsh, often criminally rough, life, suffering persecution by his own church, indeed from his own religious order. Yet he remained cheerful in the face of many struggles.

Holy Orders

John was born Juan de Yepes y Álvarez in Fontiveros, Old Castile, Spain. His father died soon after his birth, and Juan grew up in poverty. He became a Carmelite friar at the age of twenty-one, taking the name Juan de Santa María. Dedicated to prayer and solitude, the Carmelite order had become somewhat complacent, even lax, about its mission by the time John joined.

John became prior of the first community of Discalced Carmelite friars, taking the name Juan de la Cruz—John of the Cross. Later, when Teresa became prioress of a convent in Ávila, she asked John to be its spiritual director.

Figure 7-3: St. John of the Cross

Conflict from Within

Differences between the reform movement and the traditionalists plagued the Carmelite order. When he was thirty-five, John was kidnapped and taken to a Carmelite monastery opposed to reform in Toledo, where he was held for nine months, surviving only on bread and water and subjected to regular beatings.

After his release he made his way back to his community, where he was eventually elected to several offices as prior and provincial in different parts of Spain and established several houses for the order. In 1590 conflict among the Discalced broke out, and one year later the Madrid general chapter took away all of John's titles and offices because of his support for the moderates in the order.

Now a mere monk, John was sent to a monastery in Andalusia, where he contracted a fever and died on December 14. He died alone and almost forgotten in the very congregation he had helped to found.

E-QUESTION

How did St. John feel about love?

St. John of the Cross said this of love: "An instant of pure love is more precious to God and the soul, and more profitable to the church, than all other good works together, though it may seem as if nothing were done."

Writings from the Soul

This powerful mystic was able to explain and analyze what he called "the dark night of the soul," when God cannot be seen and the soul suffers the desolation of abandonment. In John's view, that suffering, if courageously borne, can lead a soul into union with God. John carefully discusses how stripping away our imperfections, especially our ego, can lead us closer to God and his love. Although *The Dark Night of the Soul* was his best-known work, he also wrote *The Spiritual Canticle* and *The Living Flame of Love*.

He was canonized in 1726. John of the Cross is a Doctor of the Church; his feast day is December 14. He is the patron saint of poets.

Sts. Thérèse (1873–1897) and Maurice

St. Thérèse was a young woman who lived only twenty-four years, but left behind a book that continues to inspire people to serve God in the small things in life—the "Little Way." Thérèse was born Marie Françoise Martin in Alençon, in the northern part of France, on January 2, 1873. She was the youngest of nine children. Her father was a watchmaker; her mother, Zélie, had a lace business (Alençon lace is highly regarded). Her parents had each hoped to enter the religious life, but instead, they married. Both are currently candidates for beatification. Thérèse's mother died when Thérèse was just five years old, and after her mother's death, Thérèse's sisters helped raise her.

She was apparently a happy child, keeping a number of pets, including doves and goldfish. She is said to have done savage imitations of neighbors and other people she and her family knew. She was also quite precocious. A photograph of her when she was older shows an attractive, dark-haired young woman with an almost impish look in her eyes.

Asked to Write

Two of Marie's sisters became Carmelite nuns, and Marie soon followed them to the convent—when she was just fifteen years old—taking the name Thérèse of the Child Jesus and spending her time cloistered in prayer and meditation. Although her life may have seemed fairly uneventful from the outside, her unique perspective became the seed of saintliness. She viewed every insult and slight as an opportunity to grow closer to God and to learn the way of love. She believed that each moment of suffering she faithfully endured could somehow ease the pain of others.

She had an opportunity to test this theory on a grander scale beginning on Good Friday, 1894, when she woke with a mouthful of blood. So began the final chapter of her life as she struggled with the physical torments of tuberculosis as well

Figure 7-4: Thérèse at 15, before becoming a Carmelite

as terrifying mental images. She was often tempted to despair but managed to continue to pray and seek to become love.

During this period, the abbess of the convent (who was also her sister Pauline) suggested to the frail young nun that she write about her life and her faith. Thérèse began that work in 1894 and completed it in 1897, when she was close to death. Thérèse of Lisieux took her least breath on September 30, 1897. Her final words were, "Oh I love him! . . . My God . . . I love you."

The twelfth century abbot Aelred of Rievaulx on friendship: "Let him choose from among them one whom he can admit in familiar fashion to the mysteries of friendship. And upon whom he can bestow his affections in abundance, laying bare his mind and heart even to their sinews and marrow, that is, even to the most secret thoughts and desires of the heart."

After her death, her life continued to bear fruit, both through her written words and the miracles ascribed to her. Her writings were published as *The Diary of a Soul*, which has become one of the most widely read spiritual autobiographies, translated into sixty languages. She once said, "After my death I will let fall a shower of roses. I will spend my heaven in doing good on earth."

Thérèse was canonized in 1925 by Pope Pius XI and was named a Doctor of the Church by Pope John Paul II in 1997, making her the third woman to be so named. Her feast day is October 1. She is a patron saint of France, foreign missions, and florists. In 1998, St. Patrick's Cathedral in New York City drew 6,000 people to a special mass celebrating St. Thérèse's elevation to Doctor of the Church.

A Glimpse of the Saint

The book *Maurice and Thérèse: The Story of a Love* by Patrick Ahern (Doubleday, 1998) offers a human glimpse of Thérèse. The book is a collection of twenty-one letters that she wrote to a struggling young missionary named Maurice Belliere. Through these letters, the two formed a deep and lasting bond. Early on in the letters, Thérèse wrote, "I feel as if our souls were made to understand one another." He responded that he felt exactly the same way.

She wrote her final, tender letters to Maurice from her deathbed. Although she was suffering from an agonizing illness, she knew that death would offer her an opportunity for a new kind of closeness. She wrote, "No more cloisters, no more grilles. My soul will be free to fly with you to the missions." Maurice never forgot Thérèse's promise to him. His gravestone is engraved with these words: "Spiritual Brother and Protégé of St. Thérèse."

Sts. Lioba and Boniface (Eighth Century)

Sts. Lioba and Boniface enjoyed a rich spiritual friendship. St. Lioba was an English nun who was a distant relative of St. Boniface. When she heard that St. Boniface was serving as a missionary in Germany, she was intrigued and she decided to begin a correspondence with him. Out of their correspondence grew a devoted friendship.

After twelve years of sending letters back and forth, Boniface asked if Lioba and some of her sister nuns might join him in Germany to help start monastic communities for women there. He knew that Lioba was an educated woman, schooled in the scriptures, the church fathers, and canon law. It was said that she was never seen without a book in hand.

The bonds so often present in the lives of the saints can serve as a model for those seeking to enter into authentic friendship with others. Through friendship, the saints were able to overcome the traditional barriers of sex, age, and rank. Friendship allowed these holy people to open their hearts and to experience the awakening of their souls.

By the time the women arrived, Boniface had become a bishop and was able to provide them with a monastery in Mainz. Lioba was successful in establishing the sister monasteries that Boniface had so hoped to see.

In 754 Boniface traveled to non-Christian Frisia as a missionary. As he left Lioba, he told her that it was his wish that she would be buried beside him so that "their bodies might wait for the resurrection and be raised together in glory to meet the Lord and be forever united in his love."

Boniface died as a martyr. Lioba often visited his grave, and when she died, more than twenty years later in 780, she was buried close to the bones of Boniface, in order to remain his companion, both in life and in death.

Chapter 8

Holy Animal Lovers

Some assume that saints were reclusive souls who just wanted to be left alone. But the lives of the saints offer an entirely different picture: not only do saints love other humans deeply, but many also experienced an almost surreal closeness with wild animals. This chapter will explore a small sampling of extraordinary encounters between holy people and animals such as otters, hyenas, horses, wolves and bears.

What Saints Know

Saints grow to love God, in all of humanity, and in all creatures. The following tales are ultimately love stories—in turns humorous and poignant, sublime and even surreal. All of these stories point to larger spiritual realities—suggesting that the purpose of life is to make God present in the world through living in harmony with God and all created beings.

This type of peaceful, love-inspired life is a mark of saintliness and points to the Garden of Eden, before sickness, sin, and death shattered the oneness of creation. The saints' interactions with animals also points to the life that is to come, where perfect love unites all redeemed creatures.

As Fyodor Dostoyevsky wrote in his book The Brothers Karamazov, "Love every leaf, every ray of God's light. Love the animals, love the plants, love everything. If you love everything, you will perceive the divine mystery in things."

Many of the following stories were kept alive through oral tradition, growing out of a symbolic world where not all stories were taken as literal truth. As the years progressed, many of these stories become spiritualized or mythologized, and one need not assume that every detail of the following accounts is straight historical fact. Instead, one just needs to be open to the possibility that these things *could* have occurred—that nothing is impossible in the lives of the saints—and that everything can become possible through love.

St. Cuthbert and the Otters

St. Cuthbert was born in 635 and eventually became a monk and served as prior of both Lindisfarne Priory and Melrose Abbey. He traveled to remote, rugged locations in order to preach. He also loved to keep long prayer vigils in wild places. Often he would stay with the monks at the Abbey of Coldingham, which was perched on a steep cliff overlooking the sea.

Late at night, after all of the monks had fallen asleep, he would sometimes sneak out of the monastery and head out to the sea, where he would wade into the water up to his neck, raise his arms to the sky, and pray with the rhythm of the waves. Although the monks realized that his bed was often empty, they were not entirely clear about what he did during his late-night adventures. One night, a monk decided to follow him discreetly, hoping that he would not be caught.

This is what he saw: Cuthbert waded deep into the sea, praying in his customary fashion. He prayed all through the night, and at the first light of dawn he returned to the shore and knelt for more prayer. When Cuthbert emerged from the sea he wasn't alone. He was followed by two otters, who panted on Cuthbert's feet to dry them, and snuggled against his body to try to warm him with their fur.

E-FACT

The eighth-century Lindisfarne Gospels were stored in Cuthbert's shrine for many years. They were lost at sea as the monks fled, fearing invasion. In a vision, they saw St. Cuthbert, who told them where to look. Three days later, they found the intact book, and to this day scientists believe that the stains on the book are from salt water.

The otters stayed with Cuthbert as he completed his prayer, kneeling before him in the sand. They did not depart until he offered them his blessing. The monk who had witnessed this remarkable sight was terrified. He could barely walk and stumbled several times on his way back to the monastery. There he watched Cuthbert pray the morning hours with the brother monks, and he knew he had to confess.

That morning, he fell on the ground before Cuthbert, weeping. St. Cuthbert said, "What is it, brother? What have you done?" The monk confessed to having followed him. St. Cuthbert offered his forgiveness on one condition—that he not share what he had seen until after his death. The monk agreed to this and kept the secret for all of Cuthbert's days. After the saint died in 687, the monk shared the story with anyone who would listen.

After St. Cuthbert's death, a shrine was created to house his bones on the Holy Island of Lindisfarne, in England. When, in 875, fear of a Danish invasion threatened the monastery, the monks packed up Cuthbert's relics. They carried the relics with them for seven years, until they were provided with a safe church to house them in. St. Cuthbert is commemorated on March 20.

St. Kevin

St. Kevin was born in Ireland in 489. His mother is said to have experienced no pain in childbirth. At his baptism he was given the name "Kevin," which means, "of gentle birth." His gentleness came through especially in relation to the animals that became his beloved companions during his solitary years in the wilderness of Glendalough.

E-XTRA

> One common element of saints' stories is that they are often said to enter the world through painless labors. The lives of the saints suggest a reversal of ancient curses, in particular, the curse from Genesis 3:16 in which God said, "I will greatly multiply your pain in childbearing; in pain you shall bring forth children."

One Lent, while St. Kevin was praying with his arms extended out of the open window of his hut, a blackbird lit on his hands and began to build a nest. According to the legend, St. Kevin stood patiently cupping his hands together as the blackbird build her nest and laid her eggs. He did not move or cease praying until all of the baby birds had hatched and flown from the nest.

Another much-loved tale of St. Kevin involves his friendship with an otter. One cold winter night he trudged out into the icy waters of a lake to recite his prayers. Just after he victoriously recited his Psalter, the saint accidentally dropped it into the lake. He stood there a moment, feeling distressed and unsure of how to proceed. Just then an otter surfaced clutching the undamaged Psalter in his mouth. Later, when the monks at Kevin's monastery were starving, this same otter brought them salmon.

One day, when the otter appeared with his salmon, one of the monks had an evil thought—he imagined that the otter's pelt would make some lovely gloves. Fortunately for the otter (and not so fortunately for the monks) the otter was able to read the monk's mind and he never again returned. St. Kevin severely rebuked this monk for his cruel and greedy thought.

At another time, St. Kevin was praying in a hollowed-out tree trunk. He treasured his life of solitude and did not wish to be discovered in his hiding spot. But a farmer allowed his cattle to graze nearby, and one of the cows developed a particular fascination with St. Kevin, coming daily to lick his feet, which protruded from the bottom of the tree trunk.

To the astonishment of the farmer, this cow began to produce copious amounts of milk (some accounts say fifty times more than before). The farmer could not understand the change that had come over his cow, so one day he followed her, only to find her licking the saint's feet.

St. Kevin was not pleased by the interruption, especially not when the farmer realized how gaunt and sickly he looked. St. Kevin, who lived off of nettles and berries, had endangered his life by severe fasting. The farmer insisted that St. Kevin come with him to be nursed back to health. The cow very likely saved the saint's life by sharing his secret, but the miracle also brought the fame and crowds that St. Kevin had so hoped to avoid.

St. Kevin lived to be 120 years old, and died encircled by his beloved brother monks. His feast day is celebrated in Ireland on June 3 and in America on July 3.

St. Seraphim of Serov

St. Seraphim was born in 1759 in a small town in Russia. When he was nine years old he became deathly ill, but had a dream in which he saw the Virgin Mary who promised to heal him. The dream came just before a famous icon of her was carried through the town. Because of bad weather, the procession had to change course and the icon came just past Seraphim's childhood home. His mother laid him on the ground and they carried the icon over him. He recovered completely from his illness.

St. Seraphim entered a monastery as a novitiate when he was twenty years old. Before he left, his mother blessed him with a large copper cross, which he wore all his life. At one point while he was in the monastery, he again became seriously ill, and had a second vision of the Virgin Mary in which she appeared with St. John the Theologian. In this vision, she turned

Figure 8-1: St. Seraphim of Sarov

and said (about Seraphim) "He is of our kind." She then touched his side with her staff, and he was healed instantly.

He made his monastic vows when he was twenty-seven years old, taking the name "Seraphim." The word means "fiery" or "burning" in Hebrew—words that aptly expressed the character of St. Seraphim's luminous prayers.

In 1794 he moved out into the wilderness to live in a small log cabin, where he was able to devote himself to unceasing prayer, and the study of the scriptures and the lives of the saints. There he kept company with bears, wolves, foxes, and rabbits.

One time, an abbess and a nun from a nearby monastery visited him. To their horror, a bear walked out of the woods on his hind legs. St. Seraphim looked at the bear and said, "Misha, you have frightened my poor orphans. Please bring them something for consolation, as I have nothing to offer them." The bear left immediately.

A few hours later, while St. Seraphim, the abbess, and the nun were deeply engaged in conversation, the bear came stumbling into St. Seraphim's cell, carrying a small parcel wrapped in leaves. "Misha, what have you brought us?" St. Seraphim said.

The bear stood on his hind legs and handed him the leaves. Inside was a fresh honeycomb. Seraphim handed the bear a chunk of bread, and the bear lowered his great head as if to bow. He then gracelessly exited the cabin.

St. Seraphim loved both people and animals. Whenever a person came to see him, he would address him as "my joy." He also found great solace in his solitary life of prayer. One of his most famous sayings is, "Acquire inward peace and thousands around you will be saved."

St. Seraphim lived for many more years in the cabin, eating and sleeping very little. During the last years of his life, visitors began to flock to his cabin to glean wisdom from him. As he aged, however, he became unusually exhausted. On January 1, 1833, he made three visits to the spot he had chosen for burial. That evening, monks overheard him singing Pascha (Easter) hymns in his cell. He was found dead the following day, kneeling in prayer before his beloved icon of the Virgin Mary. He is commemorated on August 1 and January 15. His feast day is January 2.

St. Roch and the Dog

St. Roch was born in 1295 in Montpelier, France. According to one legend, he was born with a red cross on his chest. He was of noble blood, and his parents died when he was twenty. At that time, he gave his inheritance to the poor and went on a pilgrimage. During his pilgrimage, he encountered many people who had been stricken by the plague, and his heart broke for them.

He prayed with them, and was able to cure many of them by making the sign of the cross over them. Eventually, however, he contracted the plague himself. He did not wish to share his infection, so he resolved to quietly go into the woods and die.

While he was in the woods, however, a dog discovered him. This dog visited him many times, always bringing with him food from his master's

Figure 8-2: St. Roch and the dog

table, as well as gingerly licking the saint's wounds. One day, the dog returned with his master, who, upon seeing St. Roch in such a desperate state, carried him home and nursed him to health.

By the time that St. Roch had again become healthy, a civil war shook France. St. Roch decided to attempt to return to his home, and the dog followed him. But he was captured and wrongly imprisoned for spying. The loyal dog accompanied him to his prison cell. St. Roch devoted his last five years of life to caring for his fellow prisoners and praying from his cell. He never admitted that he was of royal blood, although his status would have likely freed him from the prison.

St. Roch died in 1327 of natural causes. He is commemorated on August 16 and is considered the patron saint of dogs and those who love them, as well as invalids and those suffering from knee injuries and pestilence. After St. Roch's death, numerous healings were connected to him. Many people believe that he is a healer of those who are suffering from infectious diseases. He was canonized 100 years after his death, around the year 1427.

St. Macarius and the Hyena

St. Macarius was born in Egypt in A.D. 300. From his youth up, he suffered from an extremely tender conscience. Once, when he was a child, he ate a fig that a friend had stolen, and he mourned this sin for the rest of his days. When he was thirty, he moved to the desert to live in solitude.

One day, a hyena knocked on the door of his cell with the top of her head. The "knock" sounded so human that St. Macarius expect to find one of his brother monks standing there. Instead, he found a hyena with its baby (or whelp) clutched in its jaw. The hyena held the whelp out to the saint, crying.

St. Macarius took the whelp in his hands and examined it, trying to understand what was wrong with the small creature. He turned it over and over and finally realized that the whelp was blind in both eyes. He groaned and spat into the whelp's face, making the sign of the cross over his eyes. Immediately the whelp could see and was able to suckle its mother and follow her to the river.

The next day, the hyena returned to the cell of St. Macarius and again tapped his door with her head. This time, she was covered with the wooly skin of a freshly killed sheep. When St. Macarius saw what the hyena had done, he was horrified. "Where have you been? And what have you done?" he said. "Since that skin comes from violence, I don't want it!"

St. Macarius strove to be compassionate toward all creatures, saying, "Christians should judge no one, neither an open harlot, nor sinners, nor dissolute people, but should look upon all with simplicity of soul and a pure eye. Purity of heart consists in seeing sinful and weak men and having compassion for them."

The hyena stretched out on the ground before him, bending her paws as if she was begging him to take it. St. Macarius considered the spectacle before him and softened slightly. "I told you already that I would not take that skin—unless you promise me that you will never again trouble the poor by stealing their sheep."

The hyena bobbed her head at him in a wordless agreement. St. Macarius insisted again that she promise that she would never again kill a living lamb, but that she would take her prey only from creatures that had died naturally. The hyena again nodded at St. Macarius, eyeing him steadily.

St. Macarius looked down at the hyena before him and said, "If you struggle to find food, you must always come to me and I will share a loaf of bread with you. From this hour, you must never hurt another creature." Prostrate before him, the hyena made her pledge.

From that day forward, she would occasionally visit St. Macarius's cell when food was scarce, and he was all too happy to share a loaf with her. And he, for his part, slept soundly on the sheepskin for the rest of his days. He lived to be ninety and is commemorated on January 19.

St. Columba and the Horse

St. Columba was born in Ireland on December 7, 521. He was of a royal line and his life was characterized by missionary zeal. He was also the founder of the monastery on the famed Holy Island of Iona in Scotland, which remains a popular pilgrimage sight to this day.

E-XTRA

According to one legend, St. Columba handwrote 300 books during his lifetime. Two of the books which he may have transcribed, *The Book of Durrow* and a Psalter called *The Cathach*, are still intact to this day. St. Columba is the patron saint of bookbinders.

One of the most beautiful legends of St. Columba involves his white horse. When he was very old and tired, he made his way to visit his brother monks, who were working in a field. He was so weak that he could not walk, but had to be carried in a cart. When he saw his brother monks he explained that during the recent Easter celebration he had felt a great longing in his soul to go and be with Jesus. He understood that he could go and be with his Lord if he wished, but he decided to linger a little longer on this earth, as he did not want to grieve his brother monks during the Easter season.

At these words, the monks were deeply grieved, because they knew that Columba did not have much more time on earth. He turned to the east and blessed

Figure 8-3: St. Columba and the White Horse

the island and islanders who dwelt there, as well as the monastery that he had founded and nurtured.

As his death drew near, St. Columba shared this secret with his companion, Diarmid—it was soon to be his day of rest, his own Sabbath. He was tired from the toil of this life, and his Lord had invited him to be with him. Columba understood that he would die around midnight, following the footsteps of his fathers in the faith. At this, Diarmid wept. Columba tried to comfort him as well as he could.

Columba then headed back to his monastery one last time, but he was so weary that he stopped to take a rest by the side of the road. As he was sitting beside the road, his white horse ran up to him and leaned his head against the holy man's chest, drenching his shirt with his tears, which poured into his lap.

Diarmid rose to push the horse away from his beloved friend, but Columba stopped him, saying, "Allow this lover of mine to shed his tears on my chest. For this horse, being an animal, understood instinctively that I was going to be with my Lord, yet you, as a man, could not foretell this."

Fyodor Dostoyevsky offered these instructions, through his character Fr. Zosima in The Brothers Karamazov: "Love the animals: God has given them the rudiments of thought and joy untroubled. Do not trouble it, don't harass them, don't deprive them of their happiness, don't work against God's intent. Man, do not pride yourself on superiority to the animals; they are without sin, and you, with your greatness, defile the earth by your appearance on it. . . ."

At this, St. Columba blessed the white horse that had faithfully served him for so many years, and the grieving horse continued on his way. St. Columba then returned to the monastery for his final Vespers (or evening prayer) service. Later that night, when the bell tolled for the midnight service, Columba returned to the monastery church but collapsed before the altar, surrendering his soul to God. St. Columba died in 597 when he was seventy-seven years old. He is commemorated on June 9.

St. Francis and the Wolf

St. Francis is the most famous animal-loving saint. He preached to birds, freed rabbits and fish from traps—commanding them to "never get trapped again"—and even inspired a lone grasshopper one cold winter night to come out with him and sing the midnight prayers. St. Francis's brother monks, who had skipped the Psalter and stayed put in their cozy warm beds, were both astonished and ashamed to see the fresh grasshopper tracks in the show the following morning.

One time, St. Francis even tamed a wolf. The wolf had been terrorizing the people of the nearby town of Gubbio, stealing their sheep and even attacking humans. The people of Gubbio had attempted to hunt the wolf, but the wolf was too fierce and cunning to be captured. The townspeople became so fearful that they refused to leave the confines of the city walls.

When Francis heard about the wolf, he decided to head out to the hills and see if he could forge a compromise between the wolf and the people of Gubbio. The townspeople begged him not to risk his life, but he insisted on speaking with the wolf directly. A few peasants and one friar bravely offered to accompany him, but the peasants lost their nerve along the way.

E-XTRA

The story of St. Francis and the wolf is featured in a beautiful children's book called *Brother Wolf of Gubbio: A Legend of Saint Francis*. This book was written and illustrated by Colony Elliot Santangelo, and published by Handprint Books in 2000.

When the wolf spotted St. Francis, it rushed toward him, baring its teeth and growling. St. Francis immediately made the sign of the cross over the wolf and commanded the wolf to never again harm the people of Gubbio. The wolf immediately dropped to the ground, as if in agreement. St. Francis then lifted his hand to the wolf, and the wolf pressed his paw to St. Francis's outstretched palm, sealing their agreement with a pledge.

The wolf then followed St. Francis back to Gubbio. There St. Francis explained to the townspeople that the wolf promised to never again steal their sheep or threaten their safety. But he asked if they would consider feeding the wolf so that it would no longer have to hunt. The people enthusiastically agreed to this arrangement, and St. Francis and the wolf again raised palm to paw in pledge.

For the next two years, the wolf begged his meals by going from door to door, not unlike his friend St. Francis. The people of Gubbio learned to love and care for him. They kept his belly full and the wolf never again caused any trouble. When the wolf finally died of old age, the townspeople grieved the loss, feeling as if they had lost some of St. Francis's unique grace, which had lingered with them through the presence of the wolf. St. Francis is the patron saint of animals and the environment. His feast day is celebrated on October 4.

Chapter 9

Literary Saints

Not only are the saints known through the stories about them, they can sometimes be encountered through their own words. Like many writers, the following saints sometimes struggled with their abilities—they weren't always sure how or when to use them, and they sometimes needed to be prodded to write. The words that finally came were often candid and transcendent, drawing the attention of fans and foes. This chapter will explore a few of the great literary saints, who struggled to become bold in prayer and bold with pen.

St. John Chrysostom (347–407)

St. John Chrysostom was born to Christian parents in 347 in Antioch, Syria. As a young man, he studied for a career in law, and his professor, Libanius, was in awe of his eloquence. He felt that John had tremendous potential. When St. John was baptized as a young man, he decided to devote his talents to the church instead of to a career in law.

He eventually became a monk, and later a priest. During his years of solitary prayer, he nearly ruined his health because of his strict ascetic disciplines. But those years were rich, fruitful years. Because of the long hours spent in prayer, he had many treasures to offer the world when he entered back into it.

During his years as a priest, his greatest strength was also his greatest liability. Short in stature—only five feet tall—he was nonetheless a powerful personality. His preaching drew large crowds, attracting much attention and many followers. But he also alienated some important people because of his desire to strip the church of excess and to challenge the local rulers to live more simply and charitably.

Figure 9-1: St. John Chrysostom

Loving the Poor

By the time he was forty-nine years old, he was elected to become Patriarch of Constantinople. During his reign, he raised the hackles of the Empress Eudoxia by openly chastising her in his sermons, as well as likening her to unflattering biblical figures like Jezebel. He was extremely critical of opulence and luxury, refusing all invitations to banquets and giving away many of the material treasures that accompanied his position.

In 401 A.D., he deposed six bishops and made more enemies. He was demoted and sent into exile, but an earthquake terrified those responsible for his banishment and he was recalled. St. John continued to be a lively speaker and writer, and refused to soften the tone of his sermons. Despite his many supporters, he was again exiled. After three years in Curusus in Armenia, he was sent to Pontus. The journey there was incredibly difficult—the weather was harsh and he traveled on foot. Although he often complained of exhaustion, he was forced to continue on, and he died on September 14, 407. His last words were, "Glory be to God for all things!"

St. John Chrysostom said: "Do you want to honor Christ's body? Then do not scorn him in his nakedness, nor honor him here in the church with silken garments while neglecting him outside where he is cold and naked. The rich man is not the one who is in possession of much, but the one who gives much."

Healing the Past

The bitter memory of St. John's death lingered in the hearts of many Christians. St. John's student, Proclus, who served as Patriarch of Constantinople, once preached a sermon about St. John. Those who heard the sermon were deeply moved. They begged the Patriarch to have the relics transferred back to Constantinople.

E-XTRA

Here's an excerpt from St. John's Easter Sermon, read in Orthodox churches to this day: "Let no one grieve at his poverty, for the universal kingdom has been revealed. Let no one mourn that he has fallen again and again, for forgiveness has risen from the grave. Let no one fear death, for the Death of our Savior has set us free."

The Emperor, Theodosius II (the son of St. John's archnemesis, the Empress Eudoxia), agreed to have the relics moved, but the men he sent were unable to lift St. John's body. When Theodosius received word that the transfer was unsuccessful, he suddenly realized his oversight—he had forgotten to apologize on behalf of his mother for all that St. John had suffered. He sent a formal apology to be read over the relics. Immediately afterward, his men were able to lift the relics.

When the relics arrived in Constantinople, the Patriarch opened the coffin and discovered that the body of St. John was incorrupt. The church swarmed with people, who stayed beside the body of St. John all through the day and night. When the Emperor approached the coffin, he tearfully asked for forgiveness. The following morning, St. John's body was carried to the Church of the Apostles, and all the people cried "Receive back thy throne, father!" At this, witnesses saw St. John open his mouth and say, "Peace be to all."

In Proclus's sermon he said, "O John! Thy life was filled with difficulties, but thy death was glorious . . . O graced one, having conquered the bounds of time and place! Love hath conquered space, unforgetting memory hath annihilated the limits, and place doth not hinder the miracles of the saint."

St. John is commemorated on September 14. He left behind an impressive collection of sermons and writings. His liturgy continues to be celebrated each Sunday in Eastern Orthodox churches (although it is not entirely clear how much of the service he was directly responsible for). The bulk of his sermons were not committed to paper, but many of his letters, exegetical works, and books, especially *On the Priesthood*, have become classics and are read to this day.

St. Augustine of Hippo (354–430)

St. Augustine was born Aurelius Augustinus in the North African town of Tagaste. His father, Patricius, was a pagan landowner, and his mother, Monica, was a Christian who fervently prayed for her son to become one, too. Augustine was an excellent student, and after finishing school he led the life of a young man with few worries and ample money. Later in life, he described his youth as a "desert of sin, pride, and sensuality." Although he studied law for a while, he eventually became a writer. He also took up a

Figure 9-2: St. Augustine of Hippo

mistress—the relationship lasted fifteen years, and he fathered a son named Adeodatus when he was eighteen years old.

Intellectually curious, Augustine was particularly intrigued by the mystery of evil. He began to be influenced by the Manichaeans, a cult that espoused dualism: a doctrine that holds that the universe is under the dominion of two opposing principles, one good and the other evil.

Augustine eventually left Africa for Rome to study and teach rhetoric. His mother, Monica, had not yet given up on her attempts to convert him. She planned to make the journey with him, but he tricked her, escaping with his mistress and son. He eventually ended up in Milan, where he was shocked to find his mother waiting for him.

He began to soften toward Christianity as he listened to the words of the local bishop, St. Ambrose. Ambrose baptized Augustine and his son in 387. Augustine was thirty-three years old. His relationship with his mistress came to a painful end—"she was torn from my side," he wrote. Most likely, however, it was Augustine's decision to have her return to North Africa.

A Religious Life

After baptism, Augustine lived a communal life of prayer for a few months with his mother, brother, and a few others. He and Monica then set out to return to North Africa. The two continually spoke about faith and the afterlife. Augustine said that "for one fleeting instant" the two of them seemed to touch the heaven they longed for. Monica told Augustine she was satisfied now, happy to see her son living a Christian life. Within days she became ill and died.

Augustine was devastated. He remembered how she had suffered for him, and he wrote to God: "This was the mother, now dead and hidden awhile from my sight, who had wept over me for many years so that I might live in your sight." Augustine returned to Tagaste alone.

Although he was not yet ordained, he founded what could loosely be called a monastery. His son died in 389. Within two years, he was ordained a priest. He began to preach, drawing crowds with his eloquent sermons. In 395 he was named coadjutor to the bishop of Hippo and became bishop himself the following year.

The Confessions and Other Writings

Augustine fascinates people because he experienced the full scope of life—a life of revelry marked by a fitful journey toward God, ultimately transformed by repentance. His writing is deeply human and full of his own struggles. One of his famed quotes speaks to the human condition: "Oh, God, make me chaste, but not yet."

Augustine touched on every area of life in his writings, from abortion to telling the truth to capital punishment (he was against it). He wrote more about marriage than any other early theologian—although he sometimes struggled to see the positive dimensions of sexuality. While he believed that marriage was essential for the human race, he cautioned that sex was an explosive force that could ruin society. His own experiences in this regard very likely tainted his thinking.

E-FACT

Augustine cautioned against an overly literal interpretation of Creation. He believed that God "made all things together, disposing them in an order based not on intervals of time but on causal connections." Some things were created in fully developed form and others were in "potential form," which developed over time.

During the period of 397 to 400, he wrote *Confessions*, in 416 wrote *On the Trinity*, and between 413 to 426 wrote *City of God*. He wrote more than ninety books, several hundred sermons, and hundreds of letters. He was a brilliant writer, responsible for permanently influencing Western Christian thought.

Augustine served as bishop of Hippo for thirty-five years, until his death at the age of seventy-five in 430, during the siege of Hippo. This man, who for so long had a restless soul, finally found peace. In his own words, "You have made us for Yourself, and our hearts are restless until they rest in You."

He is a Doctor of the Church. His feast day is August 28. He is the patron saint of theologians, printers, and England.

St. Jerome (c. 340–420)

Born in Aquilea, Dalmatia, Jerome was educated in Rome. He was interested in learning all things, but was especially attracted to classical poetry. One night in a dream he was told to devote himself to the Gospels. Upon awakening, Jerome decided to devote his life to studying God's words.

Like many of his contemporaries, Jerome decided to become a hermit. He retreated to the desert to live an austere life, although he did take his books with him. Instead of Latin he studied Hebrew, and he devoted himself to writing. He lived among other hermits, who managed to get under his skin. After four years, disillusioned by the experience, he came out of his hermitage, saying, "Better to live among wild beasts than among such Christians!"

Figure 9-3: Literary vocation

A Life's Work

Jerome was ordained in Antioch, which was, until the rise of Constantinople, the third most important city of the Roman Empire, after Rome and Alexandria. After more traveling and studying, he eventually took a post as secretary to Pope Damasus. The pontiff gave Jerome a special assignment: translating the scriptures from the Greek, which had been translated from the Hebrew, into Latin. Jerome elected not merely to translate the Greek into Latin, but to translate the original Hebrew into Latin. The job took him the rest of his life.

During those years he also wrote *Adversum Helvidium*, which denounced a book by Helvidius declaring that Mary had had several children besides Jesus. He conducted Bible studies with noble ladies as well, encouraging them to study the scriptures. One of them was St. Paula, who figured prominently in his future.

Jerome was a fiery priest. He made some enemies with his sermons, especially those detailing the virtues of celibacy, and those attacking the pagan lifestyle. Unfortunately, he couldn't resist citing some influential Romans by name in his sermons. Overall, Jerome was difficult to get along with; some say he was downright cantankerous.

E-XTRA

Although Jerome was a brilliant scholar, he was cautious about judging the less educated. He wrote, "He who is educated and eloquent must not measure his saintliness merely by his fluency. Of two imperfect things, holy rusticity is better than sinful eloquence."

When Pope Damasus died in 384, Jerome lost his protector. Rumors circulated that he had an improper relationship with Paula, and he knew it was time to leave Rome. He traveled to Antioch, where others of the Roman group of friends, including Paula, joined him. They traveled to Egypt and Palestine and eventually settled in Bethlehem.

Always the Scholar

Jerome remained principally a thinker and writer, continuing the Latin translations and writing essays. He even sparred with St. Augustine, who questioned Jerome's critical interpretation of the second chapter of St. Paul's Epistle to the Romans.

Jerome is best known for his translation of the Old Testament from Hebrew and his revision of the Latin version of the New Testament. His version, the Vulgate, was declared the official Latin text of the Bible for Catholics by the Council of Trent in the sixteenth century. From it almost all English Catholic translations were made until the last part of the twentieth century, when Pope John Paul II replaced it with the New Vulgate in 1979.

Jerome's prolific writings included over 100 letters, which are still read and interpreted by hagiographers. He died in Bethlehem on September 30, which is also his feast day. He is a Doctor of the Church and is the patron saint of librarians and students.

St. Romanos the Melodist (490–556)

St. Romanos was born in Syria in the fifth century. He was a convert from Judaism and was baptized as a young boy. He eventually became an altar boy, and later became a singer and reader in the church in Constantinople. He was always the first to arrive at church and the last to leave. His voice, however, was mediocre. He loved to sing with the choir, but the choir didn't always love to sing with him, and they only occasionally invited him to join in.

Still, he was loved for his purity of heart and devotion, and the bishop of Constantinople was so impressed with him that he made him one of the official singers in a prominent Constantinople church. Unfortunately, this decision sparked envy in the other singers, who resented Romanos's seemingly unwarranted promotion.

On Christmas Eve the services drew massive crowds, including the Emperor and his court. The Patriarch was also present, and the choir was under great pressure to perform well. Each year, a singer was asked to improvise a solo hymn. When it came time for a singer to step forward, the jealous singers pushed Romanos forward, saying, "If you are so good, sing a hymn as we do."

Romanos panicked. He could not speak, let alone sing. He trembled as the crowds looked on. Finally, with tears in his eyes, he crouched behind the other singers.

After the service, he sat in the empty church. Incense lingered in the air, and the vigil lamps sparkled before the icons. He felt like a complete failure. He gazed at an icon of the Virgin Mary, asking her if she might help him find appropriate words to glorify her son.

That night, he dreamt that the Virgin Mary held a scroll out to him and directed him to swallow it. As Romanos swallowed the scroll, sweetness filled his body. He was overcome with joy and awe.

The next morning, during the Christmas service, a singer was again expected to step forward to sing an improvised hymn. This time, Romanos was ready. He sang the words from the night before, stunning the crowds and impressing the Patriarch, who came up afterward to ask who had taught him the hymn.

An excerpt from St. Romanos's Christmas hymn: "Today the Virgin gives birth to him who is above all being, and the earth offers a cave to the unapproachable One. Angels with Shepherds give glory, and magi journey with a star, for to us there has been born a little Child, God before the ages."

Romanos shared his experience with the Patriarch. The other singers, who had once derided him, prostrated themselves before him and begged for forgiveness. St. Romanos continued to compose hymns for the rest of his life. Over 1,000 poetic hymns are attributed to him. He is commemorated on October 1.

St. Thomas Aquinas (1225–1274)

Thomas is considered by many to be the greatest of the Catholic theologians, as well as one of the most brilliant minds in the Western world. Church doctrine that he wrote is still heeded today, and his prayers and hymns continue to be popular.

Thomas was born in a castle near Aquino, in southern Italy, the youngest of four sons. Thomas's father was the son of the count of Aquino and also a relative of the king of France. Thomas was well educated: he was sent to a nearby monastery when he was just five years old. Later he attended

Figure 9-4: Thomas Aquinas

the University of Naples. After a few years of study, he told his family that he wanted to become a Dominican friar. They were appalled.

Although he successfully entered the order, his family kidnapped him and held him in their castle for a year. The lockup, however, was unsuccessful. When his parents realized the depth of Thomas's determination to become a Dominican, they released him.

The Student

Thomas rejoined the Dominican order and was sent to Germany for further studies. He was a quiet student, never contributing much to the class, although his razor-sharp mind absorbed everything. His classmates called him "the dumb ox," for his perceived simplemindedness and his very real plumpness.

Thomas earned a doctorate at the University of Paris and taught there. This was quite a learning center at the time—Ignatius of Loyola and Francis Xavier studied there, among other renowned figures in the arts, politics, and religion. Thomas began writing works on philosophy and commentaries on scripture. Little by little, admiration for him grew until he was recognized as a genius.

In 1266 Thomas began his masterpiece, *Summa Theologica*, which continues to serve as the basis for Catholic theology. At the time, it was the most comprehensive work of Catholic faith ever written. In the past, theologians addressed specific dogmatic problems within a narrow framework. Thomas took a broader view, struggling to reconcile Christian doctrine with reason, as well as integrating the thoughts of the Greek philosophers. Although he believed that fundamental Christian doctrines are impossible to explain by reason, they are not necessarily contrary to reason and they can be discovered by natural reason.

Thomas allowed for differing viewpoints in theological discussions. His views were often considered controversial, especially when he adapted the philosophy of Aristotle, a pagan, to Christian theology.

E-FACT

Although few people recognized Thomas's special gifts when he was young, his teacher, St. Albert the Great, saw Thomas's potential. St. Albert predicted that "the lowing of this 'dumb ox' would eventually be heard all over the world."

Vatican II, which was convened by Pope John XXIII in 1962 and concluded by Pope Paul VI in 1965, brought church leaders to Rome to discuss and update theology and policy. Up until that council Thomism—which is what it had become known as—had dominated the education of candidates for the priesthood in Roman Catholic seminaries. But it was a "package" approach to Thomas's work: the questions were offered with the answers. That style of learning and teaching contradicted Thomas's very spirit. Post–Vatican II theologians sought to restore Thomas's work as that holy man had created it: open to dialogue and not insular.

Gentle Genius

Despite his massive work output—and he wrote many other commentaries throughout his life—Thomas was a humble and holy man and is said to have experienced visions and ecstasies. He is known never to have lost his temper, even when engaged in lively debate, and was never heard to make a harmful remark about anyone.

In one often-repeated story about Thomas, he was attending a state dinner given by King Louis IX. He was so lost in thought that he suddenly brought his sizable fist down on the table and blurted out, "And that settles the Manichaeans!" A comment he once made, about gardens, is poignant and revealing: "No possession is joyous without a companion. Notwithstanding the beasts and the plants, one can be lonely there."

So Much Straw

Thomas was not to complete the *Summa*. He suddenly stopped work in 1273, when he was living in a Dominican house in Naples. One day during mass he experienced something that caused him to permanently put down his writing implements. He said, "I cannot go on. . . . All that I have written seems to me like so much straw compared to what I have seen and what has been revealed to me."

He never explained what he saw that day, and for centuries hagiographers have puzzled over his words. Just three months after this life-changing incident, Thomas fell ill on his way to the Council of Lyon. After receiving his last confession and taking communion he said, "I am receiving thee, Prince of my soul's redemption: all my studies, my vigils, have been for love of thee." He died two days later, on March 7, 1274, at the age of forty-nine. He is interred in Toulouse, France, in the Cathedral of Saint-Sernin.

E-XTRA

In contrast to many of the saints who sought to grow spiritually through ascetic efforts, consistently depriving their bodies of food and sleep, Thomas offered these words about self-care: "Sorrow can be alleviated by good sleep, a bath and a glass of wine."

Thomas Aquinas was canonized in 1323 and declared a Doctor of the Church in 1567. His feast day is March 7. He is the patron saint of Catholic universities, chastity, pencil makers, and students.

Hildegard of Bingen (1098–1179)

Hildegard was the tenth child born of noble German parents in the province of Rheinhessen. During that time, it was not unusual for a family to offer up a child as a "tithe." A sickly child, at the age of eight she was given to the care of her aunt, Blessed Jutta Von Spanheim, to live with her in her cottage next to a Benedictine monastery. This abandonment devastated Hildegard.

Jutta raised Hildegard, and when the girl reached eighteen, she became a Benedictine nun. By this time Jutta had attracted a like-minded group of women around her. When Jutta died, Hildegard, at the age of thirty-eight, became prioress of the community.

Around 1147 she and her sister nuns moved their community to Rupertsberg, near Bingen, and founded a convent. She went on to found another convent some time later.

As a child Hildegard had visions, and she finally told her confessor about them when she was in her early forties. She felt a deep desire to write down all that she had seen and experienced, but she was afraid. When she shared some of her visions with a monk named Godfrey, he asked his abbot what Hildegard should do. This abbot ordered Hildegard to make a record of her visions. When Pope Blessed Eugenius III heard of her visions, he encouraged her to publish whatever she wished. After years of concealing her most private experiences, she began to embrace them and share them with the world.

E-FACT

Hildegard demonstrated unique gifts as a child. At the age of four, she was able to "see" and describe a calf growing inside of a cow in vivid detail. But Hildegard did not know what to think of her visions. When she asked her nurse if she saw similar things her nurse said no. Hildegard was terrified.

When Hildegard finally started writing, she couldn't stop. She wrote plays and songs, poetry and commentaries on the Gospels, as well as natural history and medical books.

Between 1141 and 1151 she penned her masterwork, *Scivias* (Know the Way), in which the mystical nun presented a look at human beings and the cosmos as radiating from God's love, which she said were "rays of His splendor, just as the rays of the sun proceed from the sun itself."

When Hildegard was eighty she became embroiled in a controversy. She and her sister nuns had chosen to bury a man who had been excommunicated by the local archbishop in their cemetery. When Hildegard was told that the body must be removed, she refused, saying that the young man had confessed, received communion, and been anointed before he died. In order to leave the body undisturbed, Hildegard personally removed all signs of his burial.

Hildegard died on September 17, 1179, when she was eighty-one years old. Although three attempts have been made to canonize her, she was never formally canonized. Yet her feast day of September 17 is celebrated by the Benedictines and Anglicans, and on the eight-hundredth anniversary of her death, in 1979, Pope John Paul II described her as "an outstanding saint . . . a light to her people and her time who shines more brightly today."

Chapter 10

Missionary Saints

Since the earliest days of Christianity, those who embraced the Gospel have sought to share it with others. During different times in history, this work has encompassed a variety of tasks: creating alphabets, writing theology, building churches, and finding concrete ways to minister to those in need so the message would not just be heard, but also seen. This chapter profiles missionary saints, compelled by love to carry their message to the ends of the earth.

Sts. Cyril (Died 869) and Methodius (Died 885)

These two brothers were born in Thessalonica. The brothers—Methodius was a monk and Cyril was a priest—were sent to Moravia in 863, in response to a request from a local ruler for Christian missionaries.

Cyril and Methodius were culturally sensitive, seeking to convey the Gospel in the local language. Their approach was labor intensive. Not only did they work to learn the local tongue—they were helped in this work by previous trips to the Slavic world—but they also created the Slavonic alphabet so that they could begin the rigorous task of translating the Gospels.

Although the brothers were extremely successful in their missionary endeavors, their approach was not without its detractors. The German bishops firmly believed that the official language of the Church should be Latin. They had already sent missionaries to Moravia who had been largely unsuccessful.

When Cyril and Methodius traveled to Rome to present their case before the pope, he offered them his complete support. Years later, however, after Cyril had died and Methodius had become an archbishop, tensions arose again and Methodius was forced to spend two years in prison. He was eventually released and vindicated.

Robert Ellsberg on saints: "For the sake of loving God, the saints did not forswear the love of other people, places, or things that made them happy. Quite the contrary. They believed that love is key. But behind each door it opens, there is another that leads to something wider."

To this day, the Slavonic language is used in many Eastern Orthodox churches. The ideals of Cyril and Methodius live on in the Orthodox Church. When Russian missionaries brought Christianity to Alaska, for example, they worked to translate many of the church hymns into the various languages of the native Eskimos, believing that people needed to worship in their own language. The brothers are commemorated on February 14.

Augustine of Canterbury (Died 604)

Pope Gregory the Great asked Augustine to re-establish Christianity in the Southern part of England after pagan Anglo-Saxons of Denmark and Germany had overwhelmed the local Christian population.

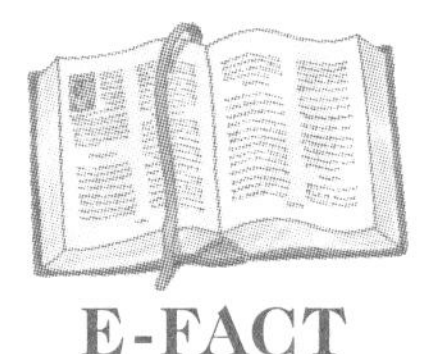

E-FACT

Canterbury remains the religious capital of England. None of the cathedral that stands today is from Augustine's time, however. The last of several Saxon buildings on the site was destroyed by fire in 1067. Most of the current structure was then designed and completely finished.

He and forty of his monks were received by King Ethelbert and Queen Bertha of Kent. Augustine built a church and monastery at Canterbury, on land given to him by the king, but ran into opposition as he sought to make converts. The king, however, was converted, and his change of heart inspired others to do likewise.

Augustine was the first Archbishop of Canterbury. To this day, the Archbishop of Canterbury remains the head of the Church of England, or the Anglican Church nationally. The church that Augustine constructed was the first cathedral ever built in England, and Canterbury remains the religious capital of the country. St. Augustine's feast day is May 27.

St. Anthony of Padua (1195–1231)

Anthony was born in Lisbon, Portugal, and first entered religious life in Coimbra, in northern Italy. There he met a group of visiting Franciscans en route to Morocco, and they impressed him with their missionary zeal. Tragically, the missionaries were martyred in Africa. Their remains were brought through Anthony's part of Italy on the way back to final interment at the monastery.

Anthony was moved to enter the Franciscan order and was later posted in Morocco. He became ill, however, and was forced to return home. Back in Italy he took a number of small assignments and was considered a typical

Figure 10-1: St. Anthony of Padua

young brother—until the day he was asked to preach at an important religious event.

Anthony stunned the audience with his eloquence. His fame spread and soon he received a letter from Francis authorizing Anthony to preach and to teach theology to the Franciscan friars. Anthony preached all over Italy and into France. He was a dynamic evangelist, convincing both to the clergy and the laity. He was called "Friend of the Poor" because he so often encouraged his listeners to be generous with the poor. He was such a popular preacher that he often had to speak outdoors because of the large crowds he drew.

Anthony's dream of being a missionary to faraway places was never fulfilled, but he was able to convey the Christian message with power and grace. When he was dying at age thirty-six, he gazed upward. When a friar asked him what he was looking at, he replied, "I see my Lord." He is buried in Padua, not far from the Dolomite Alps.

E-QUESTION

What is St. Anthony's bread?

Alms or donations given for the intercession of this saint are known as St. Anthony's bread. Today many organizations exist that collect money for the needy in the name of St. Anthony, which is one type of St. Anthony's bread.

Anthony was canonized just one year after his death and was made a Doctor of the Church by Pope Pius XII in 1946. St. Anthony's feast day is June 13. He is the patron saint of Portugal, infertility, lost objects, the poor, and travelers. Anthony's role as "finder of lost objects" may be related to his own life. A novice (one who is in the probationary stage of being admitted to a religious order) carried off a book that Anthony needed. He prayed for its return and the novice, suddenly motivated by an unknown force, brought it back to him.

St. Ignatius of Loyola (1491–1556)

Ignatius was born in Spain in a castle at Azpeita, in the Basque province of Guipúzcoa, of a noble family. The youngest of thirteen children, he was christened Iñigo López de Loyola.

As a youth, Ignatius became a court page and then went into the military. At thirty he was seriously wounded when a cannonball shattered his leg during the siege of Pamplona. During a lengthy convalescence at the home of his brother and sister-in-law, he picked up a book on the lives of the saints and was struck by their heroism.

His own life, however, seemed to be standing still. Although his leg healed, it was never the same as before. It was slightly shorter than the other leg and had a raised bump.

Ignatius struggled with his handicap. In his third-person autobiography, he wrote: "Because he was determined to make a way for himself in the world, he could not tolerate such ugliness and thought it marred his appearance."

Figure 10-2: St. Ignatius of Loyola

Ignatius told the surgeons to remove the bump, a terribly painful operation performed at the time without anesthesia. Inspired by his reading about the saints, he decided that when he was healed he would become a soldier again, but this time he would fight for Christ.

The Beginning

By the time he turned thirty-one, Ignatius was feeling well enough to start his new life. He left his brother's castle for a pilgrimage to the Catalonian shrine of Our Lady of Montserrat. There he traded in his expensive-looking clothes for a beggar's, and laid his sword and dagger from military service at the shrine's altar of Our Lady.

Next, he walked to the nearby town of Manresa and began to beg for food. He allowed his hair to grow wild in atonement for the pride he had once taken in it. Unlike other saints in the beginning of their spiritual development, Ignatius received a number of mystical visions. In one, a ray of light emanated from the Eucharist on the altar while he prayed.

Frederick Buechner on compassion: "Compassion is the sometimes fatal capacity for feeling what it's like to live inside somebody else's skin. It is the knowledge that there can never really be any peace and joy for me until there is peace and joy finally for you too."

Ignatius wrote most of his *Spiritual Exercises* in Manresa. This was the guide to prayer for which he is most noted. It was not published until 1548. One of the book's themes involved discerning the will of God. A person struggling between two seemingly good options could read the *Exercises* and discover, through them, which path to choose.

Ignatius left Manresa in 1523, on his way to Africa. He begged for all that he needed en route. But it was not a successful missionary journey, and he was forced to return to Barcelona.

Now, the once-unenthusiastic student elected to fill another void in his life: education. Realizing how much he needed to know for the life he aspired to, Ignatius returned to school. He enrolled at the University of Paris and became friends with six men who would work with him for the rest of their lives: Blessed Peter Favre, St. Francis Xavier, Diego Lainez, Alfonso Salmerón, Nicholas Bobadilla, and Simón Rodríguez.

E-XTRA

Although Ignatius suffered much from his painful wound, he understood the value of laughter and gratitude, especially in the face of obstacles. "Out of gratitude and love for Him, we should desire to be reckoned fools," he wrote. "Laugh and grow strong."

The men listened to Ignatius's religious insights and plans for future missionary work. Not only were they willing to hear him out, but they also wanted to accompany him, with the exception of Francis Xavier, who was initially reluctant.

This small group formed the nucleus of the Jesuit order. Ignatius also began to attract followers based on his *Spiritual Exercises*. As his fame spread, he also attracted negative attention and was even sent to prison for a short time. Some of the concepts in the book were viewed as controversial. Ignatius was ultimately released because no heresy could be found in the book.

The Next Phase

Ignatius graduated from the university at forty-three with a Master of Arts degree. He and his six close friends relied on the *Exercises* as their guide. On August 15, 1534, the Feast of the Assumption, they went to the chapel of St. Denis in Montmartre, Paris, to make their vows of poverty and chastity. Their third vow—they saw themselves as missionaries—was to go to Jerusalem to convert the Muslims. If they failed in that venture, they planned to offer their services to the pope, who could direct them at his discretion.

The group reached Jerusalem, but Ignatius became ill and was forced to return to Spain to recover. He planned to meet the others in Venice. When they all met again, their number had grown to ten. Three more men had listened to Ignatius's message and wanted to accompany the others. They were ordained to the priesthood, although they were still not a formal religious order.

A threat of war in Jerusalem kept the missionaries from returning. The group decided to separate so that they could each take on different tasks: volunteering in hospitals and teaching the *Exercises* in various Italian cities. Months went by, and when conditions still did not look good for travel to Jerusalem, Ignatius called everyone back to meet in Rome.

The group agreed to stand by the decision made in Montmartre: to offer their services to the pope. But should they become a formal religious order, which would mean taking a vow of obedience to the Vatican, along with vows of poverty and chastity? The group prayed over the issue and then agreed that they would swear obedience. They unanimously elected Ignatius as the head of the order. On September 27, 1540, Pope Paul III signed a document establishing the Society of Jesus, who became known as the Jesuits. The pope immediately ordered some of the men to leave for missionary work in foreign countries.

Staying Home

Ignatius remained in Italy, putting together the constitution for the Jesuit order and handling the other responsibilities of a Superior General. He was patient and charitable, but he was also good at standing up to the men who flaunted their education.

In 1550, Ignatius was given funds to build the Roman College for the Jesuits, which became the model for all of his other schools of learning. This came against the backdrop of tremendous change in Europe. The ideals of the Reformation were beginning to gain power, and ships sailed from Spain and Portugal to explore the world. These new developments brought a sense of urgency to the work of the Jesuits.

Ignatius had been frequently ill, so when he became sick in July of 1556, no one was particularly alarmed. However, this turned out to be his last illness. By the time he died on July 31 at the age of sixty-five, he had watched the Jesuits grow from ten to more than 1,000 men located in various European countries, Brazil, and India. Four hundred years later, there are more than 22,000 members of the Society of Jesus, and his *Spiritual Exercises* has become a classic.

Ignatius's feast day is July 31. He was canonized in 1622. During the proceedings leading to his declaration as a saint, more than 200 miracles were attributed to him. "For the greater glory of God" was St. Ignatius's motto, both for himself and for the Jesuits. St. Ignatius Loyola is the patron saint of retreats and spiritual exercises.

St. Francis Xavier (1506–1552)

Francis was born on April 7 near Pamplona, Spain (where the famous running of the bulls takes place every year), in the Basque area. He studied at the University of Paris, and while there he met Ignatius of Loyola. He did not agree with all of Ignatius's ideas—Francis may have been a bit too fun-loving for the austerities of the missionary life, but he slowly warmed to Ignatius's ideals.

Eventually, he decided to join Ignatius as one of the first seven Jesuit priests. Francis took his vows at Montmartre in 1534. A few years later, after the pope formally approved the Society of Jesus, Francis and another priest were sent as the first Jesuit missionaries to the East Indies. Before leaving for the Orient, the pope appointed him "Apostolic Nuncio" to the Indies. For Francis, the journey would become an eleven-year odyssey from which he would never return.

Setting Sail

It took five months to get around the Cape of Good Hope, then, hugging the coast of Africa and making a few stops, the ship reached India and Goa, at the time a Portuguese colony. Onboard the ship Francis cared for the physical and spiritual needs of all.

Francis spent several months preaching at Goa. Christianity had originally been brought to Goa by the Portuguese, but the church there was struggling. Francis helped to restore the local church through his preaching, and he helped care for the local population through his acts of kindness. He sought to minister to the sick and to teach children.

Francis's reflections on the Japanese: "The Japanese are in all matters naturally curious, eager to learn as much as possible; and so they never cease to ply us with one question or another, and to inquire further about our answers. Especially they seek most eagerly to hear what is new about religion."

He also traveled widely in Southeast Asia and the South Pacific, visiting Malacca in Malaya, the small islands near New Guinea, and Morotai, close to the Philippines. Finally, after he heard about Japan, he decided to travel to that remote and isolated country. He was deeply impressed by the Japanese culture, and he stayed there for two years.

His experiences in Japan transformed his mindset and his methods of evangelization. He resolved to become aware of and sensitive to the cultures in each country he visited. He wanted to make his preaching relevant to the unique concerns of the different people he encountered.

While in Japan, he began to yearn to enter China, but he knew it would be extremely difficult, as the borders of China were closed to foreigners. Francis would not be deterred, however, although his desire was stronger than his body. On December 3, 1552, as his ship approached China, he fell ill and died. As he was dying, he said to his comrades, "Let us all meet again at God's judgement seat." He was forty-six years old.

Man of the People

Many consider Francis Xavier to be one of the greatest Christian missionaries since St. Paul. He traveled thousands of miles through underdeveloped, sometimes nearly impassable lands to preach and to minister to the sick and imprisoned, to teach children, and to alleviate suffering whenever he could. Here was a man who lived with the people in each land he visited, able to reach them only through an interpreter—and through the powerful example of his own life.

Some descendants of Francis Xavier's early converts are still paying tribute to the man who was known as "the Apostle of the Indies" and "the Apostle of Japan."

Francis Xavier is buried in the Church of the Good Jesus in Goa, India. His death was associated with an odd—some might say grotesque—act. His right arm was ordered to be severed from his body by the Jesuit Superior General. The arm was then returned to Rome, where it now reposes in the Church of the Gesu. Symbolically, Francis Xavier was the church's right arm in Asia, and he is responsible for hundreds of thousands of conversions in Asia.

He was canonized in 1622 by Pope Gregory XV and his feast day is December 3. He is the patron saint of Borneo, the East Indies, Japan, foreign missions, and tourists.

His Legacy

St. Francis Xavier is held in particularly high regard by the residents of Kagoshima, at the southern tip of Japan's main island. While he was in what is now Malaysia, Francis met a Japanese man named Yajiro, who spoke so glowingly of his home that the missionary was moved to see it for himself. He and two fellow Jesuits, along with Yajiro, who acted as translator, arrived at Kagoshima on August 15, 1549. Francis preached there and compiled a catechism.

In 1999 a memorial mass was celebrated in Kagoshima, with an envoy from the Vatican attending. The city also unveiled its third statue of St. Francis Xavier. Considering that today only 0.5 percent of that city's 1.8 million people are Catholic, that's quite a tribute.

E-XTRA

When Francis was preaching in Ceylon, now Sri Lanka, he struggled to convince a group of skeptics. He asked two men to bring him a man who had been buried the day before. Francis knelt by the body, prayed, and then ordered him to rise in God's name. The man stood up, alive, and the congregation was converted.

Bl. Junípero Serra (1713–1784)

Junípero Serra was a Spanish priest of the Franciscan order who founded eight of the twenty-one missions running the length of California. The first founded by Serra was in San Diego in 1769.

He was born and educated in Majorca, an island off the coast of Spain. He became a Franciscan in 1730 and was ordained a priest in 1738. For a time he taught philosophy in Majorca and then left for Mexico City to teach at San Fernando College. Then he traveled to Lower California (Baja, part of Mexico), where he was named superior of the Franciscan missions. Little by little his missionary work to introduce Christianity to the indigenous people took him deeper into the California that is now part of the United States.

The Other California Missions

The Spanish weren't the first visitors, but in 1769 the Spanish soldier and newly named governor of California, Captain Gaspar de Portolá, led an expedition that established forts first in San Diego and then in Monterey.

Portolá traveled with Junípero Serra, who was to Christianize the Native Americans. After he established the first mission in San Diego, there would be twenty more along the coast of California. The missions and the dates of their founding follow.

- **San Diego de Alcalá** (San Diego), 1769
- **San Carlos Borromeo de Carmelo** (Carmel), 1770
- **San Antonio de Padua** (near Jolon), 1771
- **San Gabriel Archangel** (San Gabriel), 1771
- **San Luis Obispo de Tolosa** (San Luis Obispo), 1772
- **San Francisco de Asís** (San Francisco, more commonly known as Mission Dolores), 1776
- **San Juan Capistrano** (San Juan Capistrano), 1776
- **Santa Clara de Asís** (Santa Clara), 1777
- **San José de Guadalupe** (Fremont), 1779
- **San Buenaventura** (Ventura), 1782
- **Santa Bárbara** (Santa Barbara), 1786
- **La Purísima Concepción** (near Lompoc), 1787
- **Santa Cruz** (Santa Cruz), 1791
- **Nuestra Señora de la Soledad** (near Soledad), 1791
- **San Juan Bautista** (San Juan Bautista), 1797
- **San Miguel Archangel** (San Miguel), 1797
- **San Fernando Rey de España** (San Fernando), 1797
- **San Luis Rey de Francia** (near Oceanside), 1798
- **Santa Inés** (Solvang), 1804
- **San Rafael Archangel** (San Rafael), 1817
- **San Francisco de Solano** (Sonoma), 1823

Junípero Serra died in 1784, and is known as "The Father of California." As he was dying, he whispered, "Now I shall rest." He was beatified in 1987. Concerns have been raised, however, about his treatment of Native Americans, and these concerns have stalled the canonization process, perhaps permanently. Because every aspect of a person's life comes under scrutiny as he approaches canonization, all allegations must be investigated before any conclusive decisions are made.

Cross-Culture Missionaries

Issues surrounding culture have a dramatic effect on the success or lack of success of a variety of missionary endeavors. In some cases, missionaries have brought an imperial or colonizing spirit to their work, imagining that they were bringing religion to uncivilized heathens who lacked culture, education, and will.

Other missionaries, however, have come to new countries with humility, seeking to bring the best of their faith while being open to learning from the native cultures. They have learned the local languages, learned the customs of the people, and sought to find a common ground to build upon.

In the most successful missionary endeavors, cultural awareness has permeated the heart of the work. The more personalized and culturally aware the approach, it seems, the better. When Eastern Orthodox missionaries worked in Alaska, they often came into conflict with the Russian fur traders who were also there, because the missionaries had a genuine love for the local people. As previously mentioned, in Moravia, the German missionaries who attempted to bring an all-Latin liturgy could not succeed in translating their faith to the masses, while Sts. Cyril and Methodius were able to experience widespread success because of their willingness to translate the Gospels and to create an alphabet that is still used to this day in religious contexts.

Often it is assumed that cultural awareness is a new idea that was never present in ages past. Missionaries brought a wide scope of cultural sensibilities with them to their work, and these sensibilities influenced the outcome. A willingness to listen to the locals and to shape an approach that is appropriate to each culture seems to have had a dramatic, positive effect.

Missionaries who bring love and awareness to their work have the capacity to be fruitful in a variety of contexts, and to be loved by the locals long after they have gone. Those who have attempted to impose an entire culture upon people, however, are often less successful in their endeavors.

Chapter 11

Healing Saints

Although many saints are known for their ability to cure physical and psychological disorders, this chapter will focus on saints (and those on the path to canonization) who are most well known for offering healing to others. Although medicine has changed dramatically since the earliest centuries of Christianity, saints throughout the ages have used prayer and whatever other methods were available to bring healing, hope, and comfort to those suffering from illnesses.

The Virgin Mary

There is no saint more famed for healing than the Virgin Mary. All over the world, Marian shrines mark locations where healings are believed to have occurred. Many of these shrines are listed in Chapter 17. The Virgin Mary is both a cosmic and a local figure. In apparitions, she most often appears wearing the local garb and speaking the local tongue.

The Virgin Mary sometimes brings healing to those who seek it, and sometimes (for whatever reason) does not. Likewise, she is known to have brought healing to some who never asked for it. In Zeitun, Egypt, a figure appeared on the dome of a church, and men working across the street were concerned that it was a nun who was about to take her own life. One of the men, a Muslim, pointed at the woman. His finger had been badly infected with gangrene and was going to require amputation. Instead, he was miraculously healed.

In the United States, a blind man reports that his vision was restored after he prayed before the weeping icon, "Our Lady of Cicero," located just west of Chicago. All over the world, people report cures associated with the Virgin Mary. Because cures can sometimes be subjective, the Eastern Orthodox and Roman Catholic Churches tend to be wary about accepting claims before they have been investigated.

E-FACT

Although in Lourdes, France, thousands of people believe that they have experienced healings or Marian apparitions, the Roman Catholic Church has not yet investigated every claim. Because of this, of the 5,000 reported cures, the church has only officially recognized sixty-six of them.

Many associate the Virgin Mary's healing abilities with her closeness to her son. They believe that it is her motherly compassion and intimacy with Christ that allows her to embrace the world. She is also associated with mercy, comfort, and hope, and is viewed by many as a "universal mother" caring for people all over the world, praying for them and bringing them healing.

Sts. Cosmas and Damian (Died c. 300)

Sts. Cosmas and Damian were twin brothers from the Middle East who were physicians. The two studied science in Syria and were widely known for their medical skills. They refused payment for their services—in fact, one of the brothers refused to speak to the other for a long time after he accepted an apple from a patient. According to one account, the brothers' most noteworthy success was the grafting of a leg from a recently deceased Ethiopian man onto a man whose leg had been destroyed by ulcers.

E-XTRA

The Eastern Orthodox Church venerates three pairs of brothers, all named Cosmas and Damian, all physicians. Some, however, believe there was only one pair of brothers. The widespread distribution of their relics may have fostered the belief in three pairs of brothers.

Little is known about the biography of these men, although it is widely believed that they were martyred during the Diocletian Persecution around 300. The brothers were not harmed by water, fire, or crosses, but were finally beheaded with swords. They died with their other brothers, Anthimus, Leontius, and Eurepius. Sts. Cosmas and Damian are commemorated by the Eastern Orthodox Church on three separate occasions because of the confusion (see sidebar) surrounding these brothers, July 1, October 17, and November 1. The Roman Catholic Church retains an optional memorial for them on September 26. They are the patron saints of physicians and surgeons.

St. Catherine of Siena (1347–1380)

Catherine was born in Siena, near Florence, the twenty-fourth of twenty-five children of a prosperous fabric dyer. When she was fifteen, her family hoped for a suitable marriage for her. Catherine shocked them by cutting her long golden hair and insisting there would be no ordinary marriage for her; she was to be wed to Christ.

Figure 11-1: St. Catherine of Siena

Her parents punished her severely. With Catherine's already considerable inner resources—she began having visions when she was six—she was able to create what she called a "secret cell." In her mind she retreated from the drudgery of life. Eventually her father softened in his approach. Perhaps he became convinced that Catherine was on the right track when he saw a dove hovering over her head as she prayed.

Catherine eventually elected not to join a formal religious order, and became a Dominican tertiary. She was overcome with doubt, demonic visions, and taunting voices, but she dispelled them with laughter. Jesus appeared to her after one of those episodes. "And where were you when all this was happening?" she asked. His reply: "I was in your heart." From then on Catherine received daily visitations from Jesus.

Catherine's words and actions have survived through some 400 letters; a collection of her mystical experiences, published as *The Dialogue*; and the work of her confessor, disciple, and later biographer, Blessed Raymond of Capua. She was illiterate, but was able to dictate her words.

Catherine of Siena, on the faults of others: "On thy lips let silence abide . . . If the vice really exists in a person, he will correct himself better, seeing himself so gently understood, and will say of his own accord the things which thou wouldst have said to him."

Catherine is responsible for several miracles, including one within her own family. Raymond, who claimed she cured him of the plague, tells the story of how Catherine's widowed mother, Lapa, was seriously ill. After her daughter's prayers to God came this message: It would be better for Lapa to die than to face the terrible trials that lay ahead. But Lapa did not want to die and refused a deathbed confession, so Catherine continued to pray for her recovery.

One day while her daughter was at church Lapa died. "Lord, my God," said Catherine, in tears, "are these the promises you made me? That none of my house should go to hell? . . . As long as there is life in my body I shall not move from here until my mother is restored." Lapa was then revived. She lived to be nearly ninety, but her long life was filled with sorrows.

A Public Role

After three years at home, Catherine went out into the world, ministering to the ill and caring for those shunned by society, such as prisoners and patients stricken by leprosy and the plague. She was always mindful of Christ's bidding to her: "The service you cannot do me you must render your neighbors."

In Siena, she began to attract disciples. They called her "Mama," although she was still in her twenties and almost all of her followers were many years older.

In 1374, Catherine believed that Christ commanded her to go to France. She complied and became a more public figure. She wrote to popes and magistrates, counseling them on their roles and how to perform their duties. It is a tribute to Catherine's intelligence and perseverance that her advice was so often heeded.

A Last Vision

Near the end of her life, Catherine was distressed when a second pope was elected because many people were unhappy with Pope Urban VI. Her last vision, which occurred several weeks before she died, expressed her angst. She felt that the weighty church had been placed on her back, and she dropped to the ground in terrible pain and in paralysis. Afterward, she said, "You, O Lord, call me, and I am coming to you; and I come not through my own merits but only through your mercy." Upon her death the marks of the stigmata appeared on her body.

Catherine was named a Doctor of the Church in 1970. Her feast day is April 29, the day of her death. She is the patron saint of nurses and nursing services, nursing homes, Italy, Siena, and fire prevention.

St. Vincent de Paul (1580–1660)

Vincent was born to a poor family in Gascony in southwestern France. His parents felt the priesthood was an educational and economic escape for their son. Vincent became a Franciscan, ordained at the age of nineteen.

He enjoyed being a priest. It opened doors to him, offering him entrée to some of the "better" addresses and homes. In his forties or fifties he was called to hear the confessions of a dying peasant. The man worked on the grounds of the estate of a wealthy family for whom Vincent served as family tutor and chaplain. Before slipping away, the greatly relieved laborer told Vincent that he would have died in the state of mortal sin had he not had the opportunity to confess. Vincent suddenly realized the power of his vocation and the good he could do. He decided to devote himself to the poor.

Setting the Standard

Vincent began to focus on doing good works, to the point that there did not seem to be anyone left out of his ministry: orphans, the physically ill, the poor, prisoners, and the mentally ill. Vincent even entered the area of war relief and, new for that time, care for the elderly. From donations he received he was even able to ransom Christian slaves in North Africa.

Figure 11-2: St. Vincent de Paul

He organized charities in a way no one had before, making sure that those who needed help received it. He learned how to use newspapers to solicit charitable contributions. With all that activity, Vincent still found time to write prolifically on spiritual topics.

Founding Orders

Monsieur Vincent, as he became known, also founded a religious society of secular priests known as the Vincentians, who are devoted to mission work. His fame continued among the noted and grew among the needy.

Vincent worked closely with St. Louise de Marillac. Vincent would have had a difficult time accomplishing as much as he did without her assistance. She assisted him in founding the Daughters of Charity, an "unenclosed" congregation of women—they did not live in a convent. About the work of the Daughters, Vincent said, "Their convent is the sickroom, their chapel the parish church, their cloister the streets of the city."

E-XTRA

By his own admission, St. Vincent was a very human saint, and was revered as a simple priest despite his many gifts. He is known to have once described himself as "by nature of a bilious temperament and very subject to anger."

Vincent lived to be eighty. Just a few days before he died, as he was settling into sleep, he said, "It is Brother Sleep. Soon the sister, Death, will come."

He was canonized by Pope Clement XII in 1737, and was named patron of all charitable societies by Pope Leo XIII in 1885. His feast day is September 27.

Bl. Damien of Molokai (1840–1889)

A Belgian, Bl. Damien of Molokai was born Joseph de Veuster of a farming family at Tremeloo. At the age of twenty he became a member of the Congregation of the Sacred Hearts of Jesus and Mary. Three years later he headed for Hawaii, then known as the Sandwich Islands, where he was ordained and took the name Damien.

The new priest's assignment was several areas on the island of Hawaii, the largest of the islands, and Molokai, considerably smaller than Hawaii and to its north. Oahu, where the capital of Honolulu is situated, is a bit larger than Molokai and lies to the west of that island.

In 1865, King Kamehameha V of Hawaii signed into law "An Act to Prevent the Spread of Leprosy." Hawaiian health authorities were anxious to control this disease. Yellow flags adorned homes, trees, or fences of anyone who was suspected of leprosy. All afflicted were taken from their homes and sent by boat to Molokai. They included representatives from every segment of the population: the elderly, children, criminals, single persons, babies, and married couples.

They were banished to Kalawao. The ocean ringed three sides of that protruding land, and 1,600-foot cliffs rose on the fourth, perfectly isolating the area for government officials' intentions. It was nature's prison. There was nothing resembling a civilized society, just a purgatory of sorts for diseased bodies who saw death as their only release.

Damien volunteered to serve at the leper colony. He arrived in 1873 and stayed sixteen years until his death. Besides serving his parish's spiritual needs, Fr. Damien also took on the roles of physician, law enforcement officer, and undertaker. He eventually created a society and community that the residents could take pride in.

First, he created a cemetery. Before his arrival those who died on the island were buried in shallow graves and left to be eaten by the creatures that roamed the island.

Damien built shelters and even a water supply system. He continually had to deal with the Hawaiian Board of Health, usually ending up frustrated at its bureaucracy. He also founded two orphanages for the colony.

Damien considered himself one of his flock and would not succumb to any fears of contact with the lepers. In 1884, he contracted leprosy. He continued working until just a month before his death.

Controversy

This seemingly saintly priest was not without controversy. Some who visited the colony considered him arrogant, crude, and even dirty. That's how he contracted leprosy, they claimed, by smoking from the same pipe as the lepers. If he hadn't been so careless, they said, he would have lived longer and would have been able to continue serving his people. Others refuted this theory with a more controversial idea—that he got leprosy from his relations with women on the island (a posthumous investigation later exonerated him of that charge).

After his death, a Reverend Dr. Charles McEwen Hyde, a Congregational minister in Honolulu, wrote to a Presbyterian colleague in Australia, making these charges against Damien, and more. His letter was printed in a local Presbyterian paper in Sydney.

Hyde's allegations brought a response from an interesting quarter. In 1905 the author Robert Louis Stevenson, who had met Damien four years earlier and had visited Molokai several weeks after Damien's death, wrote "An Open Letter to Rev. Dr. Hyde." Many pages long, it replied to Hyde's accusations. If Damien had imperfections, wrote Stevenson, he was ultimately only human and was "a saint and a hero all the more for that."

Road to Sainthood

In 1936 Fr. Damien's remains were moved from Hawaii to Louvain, Belgium, near Brussels, for an impressive burial ceremony that probably would have stunned this simple man.

Fr. Damien was declared Venerable by Pope Paul VI in 1977, and was beatified by Pope John Paul II in 1995. Since the beatification was so recent, there is no reason to believe Damien's path to sainthood will not continue.

St. Padre Pio (1887–1968)

Padre Pio da Pietrelcina was a Capuchin friar who for more than fifty years bore the *stigmata*—or the bleeding wounds—of Jesus. He was watched by the curious and the devoted, and forced to bear up under the burden of being called "a living saint."

Figure 11-3: St. Padre Pio

A humble priest, Padre Pio served most of his life in southern Italy. He was almost constantly in physical pain from his wounds, yet his greatest torment was the skepticism he endured within his own church. On the fiftieth anniversary of the day that he first received the stigmata, a friend wished him fifty more years. He jokingly replied, "What harm have I ever done *you*?"

Padre Pio died in 1968. Shortly before he died, he confessed to a fellow priest,

"I belong more to the other world than this one, pray to the Lord that I might die."

Miracles too numerous to count have been attributed to this priest. In confession he was reportedly able to read hearts. He was a mystic and had frequent conversations with Jesus, Mary, and the saints. He could also tell the future: in 1947 he told a young Polish priest, Karol Wojtyla, that he would one day become pope. Padre Pio died on September 23, 1968.

E-FACT

Some claimed that Padre Pio's stigmata might have been caused by too much concentration on Christ's Passion. To this, Padre Pio replied: "Go out into the fields and look very closely at a bull. Concentrate on him with all your might. Do this and see if horns grow on your head!"

In 1999 that priest, who became Pope John Paul II, beatified Padre Pio at the Vatican in front of a crowd of 200,000 people, with another 100,000 watching on huge television screens in an open area across the city.

The pope looked tiny atop the Vatican balcony, below which he hung a banner of Padre Pio's photograph that was at least a few stories high. He told those gathered: "By his life wholly given to prayer and to listening to his brothers and sisters, this humble Capuchin friar astonished the world."

The words of St. Padre Pio, on living faithfully: "God wants to wed the soul in faith and the soul which is to celebrate this heavenly marriage must walk in pure faith, which is the only suitable means for this loving union."

In order for Padre Pio to be canonized, proof of a miracle was required. This miracle occurred on June 20, 2000. A young boy named Matteo Pio Colella was suffering from meningitis. One evening, he was sent to the intensive care unit of the hospital in San Giovanni, which was founded by Padre Pio. In the morning, nine of his organs showed no signs of life. That evening, however, a prayer vigil was held for Matteo. While his mother and some of the monks from Padre Pio's monastery were praying, the child woke from his coma. He reported that he had seen an elderly man sporting a white beard and a long, brown habit. This man told him that he would soon be cured. Padre Pio was canonized on June 16, 2002.

St. John of San Francisco (1896–1966)

Michael Maximovitch was born into a noble family in the Ukraine. After attending military academy, he entered law school and then worked in law. During the Russian Revolution his family fled to Yugoslavia, where Michael studied at a theological school and was tonsured a monk, taking the name John.

From 1925 to 1927, he taught theology at a Serbian seminary. It was there that his students discovered his ascetic and loving nature. At night, he rarely slept, but was seen wandering the dormitories. If a blanket had fallen off of a student, he would cover the student and make the sign of the cross over him.

He became a deacon, then a priest. In 1934 he was elected as a bishop and asked to serve in Shanghai. He was not eager to take this position in the church, and he hoped a mistake had been made. A woman who ran into him on a streetcar in Belgrade reported that he told her that there seemed to be some confusion. He believed he had been called into town on behalf of another Hiermonk named John who was supposed to become a bishop. When he saw her the following day he reported that things were worse than he originally thought—it was him whom they planned to make a bishop of. Although he explained to the other bishops that he wasn't fit for the job because he had a speech impediment, they told him that Moses had similar problems, and elected him despite his concerns.

Travels

In Shanghai, he worked tirelessly to complete the cathedral and to create additional churches, as well as an orphanage and a hospital. His orphanage ultimately housed 3,500 children over the course of several years. When the Communists came to power, he was able to successfully evacuate all the children to other countries.

He visited the sick and shut-ins daily, taking communion to them. He also frequently visited the prisons and the asylums. In the mental institutions, he took communion to those who were severely ill. Not only did many of them welcome him with joy, but they also trusted him enough to accept communion from his hands.

Sometimes he went out into the streets searching for the sick and hungry. He would bring them home and house them in his orphanage. He also gave away his own clothing to anyone who seemed to be in greater need. Often he could not resist the temptation to give away his shoes as well and occasionally caused a minor scandal by serving in church barefooted.

E-FACT

St. John was admired both within and outside of the Orthodox world. In Paris, a Catholic priest told the young people in his church, "You demand proofs, you say now that there are neither miracles nor saints. Why should I give you theoretical proofs when today there walks in the streets of Paris a saint—Saint Jean Nus Pieds [St. John the Barefoot]."

There is at least one verifiable miracle associated with Bishop John, listed in the archives at the County Hospital. A lady named L.D. Sadkovskaya was thrown from a horse and had a fractured skull and a weak pulse. Doctors feared that she would not survive surgery, or that if she did, she would never again hear, see, or speak. Bishop John was brought to her room. After asking everyone to leave he prayed for about two hours for her. Afterward, he asked the chief doctor to examine her. He discovered that her pulse was strong and her condition had stabilized.

The doctors decided to perform the surgery, but only if Bishop John would agree to remain with them. The surgery was successful and the woman astonished the doctors by recovering her ability to hear, see, and speak.

Bishop John then served in Paris and Brussels. While there, he sought to increase Eastern Orthodox devotion to Western saints. Through his efforts, many of the Western saints shared by the Roman Catholics and Eastern Orthodox (those who lived before the two churches separated in 1054) were restored to the Orthodox Church calendar.

In 1962 Bishop John was appointed to serve in San Francisco. There he completed construction on the Cathedral and continued to serve those in need, continuing to visit the sick and care for the poor.

His Death

St. John died on a trip to Seattle, while he was with a wonder-working icon of the Virgin Mary. According to the report of one woman, he predicted this event, saying, "I will die soon, at the end of June . . . not in San Francisco, but in Seattle."

On the day of his death, July 2, 1966, he celebrated Divine Liturgy (the Eastern Orthodox service of Holy Communion) and then spent three hours praying at the altar. Shortly after he emerged from the altar, he died. He had no signs of illness, but people heard him fall. They placed him in a chair while he was still breathing, and he died peacefully, before an icon of the Virgin Mary that is said to be miraculous.

Frederick Buechner once wrote on the topic of healing, "The Holy Spirit has been called 'Lord, the giver of life,' and, drawing their power from that source, the saints are essentially life-givers. To be with them is to become more alive."

His body was taken back to San Francisco. Since his death, many have flocked to his tomb to pray beside it, and his life seems to continue in the hearts, dreams, and visions of the faithful.

Shortly after his death, one of his students reported that he had seen Archbishop John in a vision or dream. He was wearing his white Easter vestments and his face was luminous. St. John said one word as he censed his student with incense: "Happy."

Another person named M.A. Shakmatova had a dream in which a crowd of people carried Archbishop John into St. Tikhon's Church. St. John rose from the coffin and stood in the front of the church, in the Royal Doors, which separate the altar from the congregation. He anointed people and said, "Tell the people: although I have died I am alive!"

In 1993, his body was examined and found to be incorrupt. He was glorified as a saint on July 2, 1994. He is commemorated on that day.

Chapter 12

Desert Saints

This chapter will turn to a sampling of saints from the fourth century who sought to carve out a life of holiness for themselves in the most inhospitable of environments—the deserts of Arabia, Egypt, Syria, and Palestine. At first in small numbers, and then in increasingly larger ones, the desert fathers and mothers left the familiar behind in order to grow and be transformed. This chapter will explore some of the questions surrounding a "desert vocation," as well as offering a glimpse of the human lives behind these heroic decisions.

The Lure of the Desert

During the fourth century, many men and women who were seeking to grow spiritually took a new path—they set out to the desert, seeking a life of prayer and solitude. These "Desert Fathers and Mothers" astonished the local Christians—who by then were just beginning to gain acceptance with the wider population—with their new desire to dwell in regions that had been considered uninhabitable.

In the deserts of Arabia, Egypt, Syria, and Palestine, they struggled with ravages of hunger and thirst, scorpions and other wild beasts, and, of course, their own inner demons, which often manifested themselves in vivid and frightening forms. To these early pioneers of desert life, however, a life of prayer, fasting, and simple labor was exactly what they wanted, and there in the desert many of them found their way to a wholeness they could not have imagined.

Out in the barren heat of the desert, the monastics sought to achieve an inner balance that Robert Ellsberg refers to as "inner equilibrium." They no longer wanted to be ruled by their emotional lives. The isolation of the desert, and the fierce battles they found there, helped them to break free from greed, lust, anger, and pride. As Ellsberg wrote, "When all these passions were pruned away, the result was not an absence of feeling but apatheia—a balance and wholeness expressed in kindness, gentleness and compassion."

The desert also offered the opportunity for an increased sense of alertness. The desert fathers and mothers found that these barren places were fertile ground for those who wished to live in a more aware, prayerful state. This kind of awakening was particularly welcome against the shifting religious backdrop. In many parts of the Middle East, Christianity was just beginning to become acceptable. Instead of conforming to the status quo, the desert fathers and mothers sought a different, rockier path.

The desert offered the opportunity to become not just a better Christian; in the words of Desert Father Abba Joseph, the dry backdrop of the desert offered the opportunity to become "All flame."

To better understand what Abba Joseph was referring to, listen in on an exchange between a younger desert monk named Lot and the older, more experienced desert monk Abba Joseph: Abba Lot said to Abba Joseph: "Father . . . I keep my little rule, and my little fast, my prayer, meditation, and contemplative silence; and according as I am able to strive to cleanse my heart . . . what more should I do?" The elder stretched up his hands to heaven and his fingers became fire. He said, "Why not become all flame?"

St. Anthony of Egypt (251–356)

St. Anthony is the most famous and most well-known of the desert fathers. His simple, profound sayings have been passed down from one generation to the next and continue to have a profound impact on those of every age. He was the child of wealthy Egyptian parents who died when he was just eighteen years old. He was left to care for his sister and to manage their financial resources. But one day when he was in church, he heard the Gospel text in which Jesus tells the rich man to sell all that he has and to give it to the poor. Anthony felt as if the words were spoken directly to him. He knew that something had to change, but he did not quite know how.

He eventually headed out to the desert, where he spent his time in caves. He was able to fully devote himself to the work of prayer and manual labor, and to waging war upon all that was ugly in himself. He also had to contend with a host of external battles with the elements, but through his struggles, he grew and became wise, strong, and joyful.

Figure 12-1: St. Anthony of Egypt

As Anthony became older, he no longer needed the isolation he once sought. He welcomed pilgrims who came to him seeking advice, and he helped to establish a monastic community in the desert.

He lived to be 105 years old, and his biographer and friend, Athanasius, marveled at his soundness of health—remarkably, his teeth and vision are said to have remained intact for all of his days. Despite the harshness of the climate in which he lived—or perhaps because of it—he grew to be a powerful witness for a brave, unconventional life of solitude and prayer. His face so shone with joy that strangers could recognize him by his joyful face alone. He is commemorated on January 17.

E-FACT

St. Anthony's Monastery, located just two kilometers from the cave where St. Anthony lived, was founded in 356, just after the saint died. The monastery is a self-contained village, complete with gardens and a mill as well as a church dedicated to St. Anthony. To learn more, go to *www.stanthonymonastery.org.*

St. Paul the Hermit (c. 229–342)

St. Paul the Hermit was very likely the first to move out to the desert, although his move to the desert seems less intentional than those of his later followers. Paul was a wealthy young man from Thebes. When he was just sixteen years old, his parents died. That same year, when the Christians in Egypt came under persecution, Paul decided to take refuge in a cave in the wilderness.

While there, however, he discovered that the solitary life of prayer was an ideal fit for him. Even when it was safe to return home, he elected to remain in the desert. He remained in the desert many, many years. When the famed St. Anthony of Egypt heard that there was another desert father who had been living a similar life, he set out to meet the man. He wandered through the desert, calling for Paul. When the two finally met, they immediately embraced each other.

The two men had a joyous visit together. Paul had been in the wilderness so long that he wished to catch up on the comings and goings of the world. He asked Anthony if he had any news about persecutions, heresies, or progress in the city. While the two men chatted, a raven arrived with a loaf of bread for the two men to share. Paul took the bread casually from the bird and explained that he had been fed this way for nearly sixty years, although he noted that until now, the raven had brought him half a loaf of bread; because of St. Anthony's visit, the raven had the foresight to bring an entire loaf.

Paul had a pressing concern on his mind, however, which he wished to conceal from his new, dear friend. He sensed that he was going to die soon. He did not want Anthony to have to witness his death, so he sent Anthony home to get a cloak for him. Anthony did as he was told.

Although Anthony walked as quickly as he could, he did not get back to Paul in time to enjoy more conversation. Instead, as he traveled back, he saw St. Paul's soul ascending to heaven, flanked by angels.

Anthony fell on the ground, grieving the loss of this new and dear friend—who had taken him a lifetime to find—and had already departed this world. Anthony found Paul's body in the cave. His deceased friend had taken his last breath kneeling in prayer. According to legend, two lions were there guarding Paul's body. After Anthony discovered Paul, the two lions graciously dug a grave for Paul.

Anthony buried his friend and then took an old tunic to remember him by. Anthony cherished his one memento from their unforgettable meeting and chose to wear it on high holy days. St. Paul of Thebes is commemorated on January 5 or 15 in the East and January 10 in the West. (This story was first recorded by St. Jerome and is beautifully retold by Robert Ellsberg in his book *All Saints: Daily Reflections on Saints, Prophets, and Witnesses for Our Time*, from Crossroad Publishing Co.).

St. Mary of Egypt (Died c. 421)

St. Mary of Egypt is one of the most beloved saints of the Eastern Orthodox Church. When she was only twelve years old, she left her parents and moved to Alexandria, where she lived as a prostitute. Later in life, she recalled with horror that she did not live as a prostitute for money, but because of the passions. She was so driven by her desires that she would even refuse money for her services. She lived as a prostitute for seventeen years. She made her living by spinning flax and begging.

One year, when she saw the crowds preparing to go to Jerusalem to celebrate the feast of the Exaltation of the Cross, she decided to join them. Although she had no money, she boasted that her body would provide both

Figure 12-2: St. Mary of Egypt

"fare and food" for her. On the boat, she had many sexual exploits, seducing both the willing and the unwilling.

When she got to Jerusalem, however, something strange happened. At daybreak, she tried to enter a church to venerate the True Cross of Christ (read more about this feast and cross in Chapter 16). But something held her back—almost a physical force. No matter how hard she tried, she could not enter the church. To her astonishment, all those around her entered the church without any struggle. She suddenly realized that it was her own sinfulness that was holding her back. She asked the Virgin Mary to help her and asked for forgiveness. After praying, she was able to enter the church and kiss the True Cross. She then said to the Virgin Mary, "O Lady, Lady, do not forsake me!"

As she left the church, a stranger stopped her saying, "Sister, take these." She took the three coins, bought some loaves of bread, and set off for the desert, as the Virgin Mary had told her that in the desert she would find glorious rest.

Along the way, she stopped at a church, which was built into the banks of the River Jordan. She was baptized there and received communion. She then moved on to the desert, where she lived undetected by any other human being for forty-seven years.

One day a priest named Fr. Zosimas discovered Mary. He was confused and frightened by her naked, emaciated form, however, not sure if she was a demon or an angel. He turned away and prayed for courage, and then approached her again, only to have her flee. Her skin was brown and burnt from the sun and her hair was bleached white from it. He shouted to her, "Why do you run from an old man and a sinner? Slave of the True God, wait for me, whoever you are, in God's name I tell you for the love of God for whose sake you are living in the desert."

Although Mary had never met him or heard of him, she addressed him by name. "Father Zosimas," she said, "Forgive me." Fr. Zosimas was terrified—how did she know his name? But Mary, for her part, was embarrassed because she was completely naked. She asked the priest to loan her his cloak, which he did immediately. Both of them fell prostrate on the ground, each asking for the other's blessing.

Fr. Zosimas listened to Mary with awe. She seemed to know everything about him. Fr. Zosimas asked Mary to share her story with him, and although she was reluctant, it all came pouring out—the details of her former life as a prostitute, as well as her many hardships in the desert. Fr. Zosimas wept openly as she shared her story, but he asked her to continue on. He could see that she had achieved a level of holiness in the desert that was all the greater because of her former level of sin.

She asked Fr. Zosimas if he would return in one year on Holy Thursday with communion for her. He agreed to this. When he returned, one year later, she came walking across a body of water to meet him and he was terrified. He fell on his knees in awe before her, but she scolded him for kneeling like that. "What are you doing? You being a priest, carrying the holy mysteries?"

He got up off the ground, fumbling as he prepared the holy mysteries. After she took communion, she raised her arms and said, "Lord now let your servant depart in peace, according to your word, for my eyes have seen your salvation." She asked Fr. Zosimas to leave again, and not to return for a year.

When he returned a year later, however, he found her body on the ground. Her hands were crossed over her and she faced the east. Fr. Zosimas kissed her feet and washed them with his tears. He then wept for a long, long time.

She had left him a note in the sand beside her. In the note, she asked him to bury her in that exact spot, and explained that she had died just an hour after he brought her communion. She had signed the note with her name, which he had never heard before, "Mary, the sinner."

Fr. Zosimas understood that he had to bury her, but the task was formidable. The ground was hard and dry. He tried to dig into the dirt with a small piece of wood, but he quickly became sweaty and exhausted. Just then, a lion approached Mary's body and began to lick her feet.

Fr. Zosimas was terrified by the lion, but again he steeled himself by making the sign of the cross. As he did this he realized that perhaps the lion had been sent to help him. He asked the lion if he might dig the grave with his claws, and the lion complied.

Fr. Zosimas continued to pray and weep over the saint in the presence of the lion. He then buried her with the help of the lion. As he buried her, he alternated between grief and awe at the wonders that had been shown to him through this woman. He then returned to the monastery that he had come from to share what he had experienced. St. Mary of Egypt is commemorated on April 1 and the fifth Sunday of Lent in the Orthodox Church.

(This account is largely drawn from *The Great Canon, the Work of Saint Andrew of Crete*, Holy Trinity Monastery.)

St. Moses the Black (330–405)

St. Moses the Black, also called Moses the Ethiopian, was another desert saint who experienced remarkable transformation. An escaped slave, he was a leader of a group of robbers as well as a murderer.

One day he took refuge at a monastery from the local authorities. He was so moved, however, by the peaceful manner of the monks inside that he experienced a dramatic change of heart. He confessed his sins, repented, and asked if he could stay at the monastery.

E-XTRA

The monastery abbot, St. Isadore, took Moses to the roof to watch the sunrise. Isadore, sensing that Moses was discouraged, said, "Only slowly do the rays of the sun drive away the night and usher in a new day. And, thus, only slowly does one become the perfect contemplative."

His sins, however, continued to torment him. He was making a confession to St. Macarius one day when an angel appeared to him. The angel held up a tablet of his past sins and began to wipe them clean as he confessed them. Still, he had a difficult time adjusting to the disciplined life of the monastics.

Once, while he was staying at the monastery, four robbers attacked him. But he was of a powerful physique, and overpowered them. He tied them into a bundle and dragged them to the monastery chapel. He dropped them in front of the other monks, who were busy at prayer. He explained that now that he had them tied up, he was not quite sure what to do with them, and he did not think it would be Christian to hurt them. The stunned robbers repented and became monks themselves.

Moses eventually became the leader of a group of hermits who lived in the desert near Skete. He was also ordained as a priest. When Moses was seventy-five years old, he heard that robbers planned to attack his group. Instead of fleeing or taking up arms, Moses stayed to greet his attackers and was martyred along with seven of his brother monks. He is commemorated on August 28 and is viewed as the patron saint of African-Americans.

St. Simeon Stylites (c. 390–459)

Simeon was born on the Syrian border of Cilicia. As a thirteen-year-old herding sheep, he had a vision that he took to mean that his later life would be spent on pillars (stylites comes from the Greek *stylos*, "pillar"). He entered a monastery, but was asked to leave because of his excessive self-mortification, which included lengthy periods of fasting and self-flagellation.

St. Anthony the Great wrote, "The Fathers of Old went forth into the desert, and when they themselves were made whole, they became physicians and returning again, they made others whole."

Simeon became a hermit near Antioch; then he moved to the top of a mountain and his piety began to attract crowds. Going even farther to get away from them, he built a 10-foot-high pillar and lived on top of it. For the rest of his life he lived on successively higher pillars. The last was about 60 feet high and was his home for twenty years. None of the pillars measured more than 6 feet in diameter at the top.

Clad in animal skins and host to quite a number of vermin, he preached from those positions, made converts, and was considered a respected and holy man. Even emperors consulted him. Women, however, were not allowed near the pillar sitter's enclosure.

Simeon Stylites practiced other great austerities. He ate and slept very little. He was too tall to stretch out on the platform atop the pillar, but he would not accept any kind of seat. Once in a while he would stoop for rest; other times he would just let his body go slack.

He died this way, falling forward from a praying position. The date of his death has been passed on as either July 24 or September 2, and he was the first of what would become known as the "pillar ascetics." His feast day is January 5.

Chapter 13

American Saints

This chapter will explore the lives of some of the American saints. These saints helped to establish schools, convents, and orphanages on American soil, and some of them worked to combat issues that continue to be divisive in contemporary times, such as racism. The lives of these saints are an essential part of both the history of the Roman Catholic and Eastern Orthodox Churches as well as the history of the United States.

St. Elizabeth Ann Seton (1774–1821)

Mother Seton, as she is known, earns the first spot in this section because she is the first American-born saint. Pope Paul VI announced the canonization of this New Yorker in 1975.

She was a woman who lived through almost all that can be experienced in a lifetime: religious conversion, travel, marriage, motherhood, financial problems, discrimination, widowhood, betrayal, losing a child, founding a religious order, and taking vows. The recognition of her strong faith throughout what might be called a soap-opera life came in the form of eventual sainthood.

The Anglican Elizabeth

She was born Elizabeth Ann Bayley in New York City. Her father was a professor of anatomy at King's College, now Columbia University, and her maternal grandfather was the rector of St. Andrew's, the Anglican church on Staten Island.

Elizabeth was one of three girls. Her mother died when she was just three; her father eventually remarried, and soon there were six more siblings. Leading the life of a well-to-do young lady, Elizabeth learned to play the piano and speak French. At the appropriate age of nineteen she was married to William Magee Seton.

Figure 13-1: St. Elizabeth Ann Seton

The couple was happy, and in fairly short order had five children: Anna Maria, William, Richard Bayley, Catherine Josephine, and Rebecca. William Seton was a prosperous merchant, so the couple was not only happy but wealthy as well.

In addition to charity work, Elizabeth also explored her religion during those years, under the tutelage of an assistant to Trinity Church. She spread word of her new enthusiasm for her faith among family members and was overjoyed when her husband finally joined the church. "Willy's heart seemed to be nearer to me for being nearer to his God," she wrote.

Clouds on the Horizon

A mere six years after their marriage, the Setons' placid life suddenly began to fall apart. Willy's business, a family-owned company, failed, and by 1803 the firm was in bankruptcy.

Tuberculosis, a disease that had plagued the Seton family, now showed up in Willy, and the seriousness was perhaps exacerbated by his worry over the business. To try to halt the progress of the illness, the Setons sailed for Europe, taking their oldest child, Anna Maria, with them and leaving the other four with relatives. To finance the trip, Elizabeth sold the last of her silver, china, and whatever else she owned that would bring cash.

The desperate strategy did not work. The family landed in Leghorn, Italy, and went on to Pisa. Two days after Christmas 1803, William Seton died there.

E-XTRA

Because of the standard of comfort in her life, Elizabeth was able to involve herself in charity work in the city. Among other projects, she was one of the cofounders of the Society for the Relief of Poor Widows with Small Children.

Elizabeth buried her husband as quickly as Italian law mandated, but she was unable to return to America because of the bad winter weather and the fact that Anna Maria had caught scarlet fever. Her grief was overwhelming, but her enduring faith held fast. She wrote a friend, "If I could forget my God one moment at these times I should go mad—but he hushes all—Be still and know that I am God your Father." (Elizabeth Seton kept a journal for many years and engaged in exchanges of letters with many family members, friends, and colleagues who helped paint a rounded portrait of a deeply spiritual woman.)

She stayed in Leghorn for four months after her husband's death, befriended by two couples (the men were brothers). During that time she was introduced to Catholicism and became increasingly interested in that faith, to the point of studying the religion.

In 1804 she returned to New York, accompanied by the younger of the two brothers, Antonio Filicchi. Elizabeth was to remain in touch with that family for the rest of her life. They were instrumental in her conversion and there was much letter-writing between them.

Back at home and without her beloved Willy, Elizabeth was forced to set mourning aside and turn her attention to how she would earn a living. Apparently the Bayley family resources could not stretch beyond the Bayley family, because Elizabeth seemed to have received no financial help, or at least not enough, from her father. And with the Seton family business in bankruptcy, there was not likely to be much help from that quarter.

As she looked around New York to see what she could do, Elizabeth was stunned to find friends and even some family members taking a few steps back from her now that she was interested in becoming Catholic. She thought perhaps she could teach school, but those same friends did not want her influencing their children. Elizabeth was looked on with disdain in her Protestant circle, and indeed in all of the predominantly Protestant city.

She set about taking in boarders, a business that limped along for a while. One bright spot for her in that dark time was that she was baptized a Catholic in 1805.

An Answer

Finally the young widow was offered a position by a Catholic religious order in Baltimore, which asked her to found a girls' school. Other women joined Elizabeth, and by 1809, under her leadership, they founded a religious community, the Sisters of Charity of St. Joseph. They also established a school for poor children in a village named Emmitsburg, near the Pennsylvania border.

Initially the women lived in a farmhouse, along with Elizabeth's children. From then on, as the order grew, the girls lived in their mother's boarding schools, her two sons in a nearby Catholic school for boys. The new community, which now included eighteen nuns, was approved by Archbishop Carroll of Baltimore in 1812.

Elizabeth was named superior of the order. She modeled it on St. Vincent de Paul's Daughters of Charity, with a few variations in its bylaws allowing for differences between Americans and the French. She called it the Sisters of Charity of St. Joseph. The nuns would devote themselves to the education of the poor and to teaching in parochial schools. The nuns' habit was Elizabeth's black mourning dress with a shoulder cape and a black bonnet, which was later replaced by a white one.

From her groundwork grew the huge Catholic parochial school system in the United States. Mother Seton's work spread throughout North America, South America, and Italy, where she still had ties (principally the Filicchi family).

Another Loss

Elizabeth Seton was a strong woman, but when her daughter, Anna Maria, died at the age of sixteen, she experienced a totally different sorrow and test of her spiritual resources. Anna Maria was her oldest child, and the one most like her mother. An added bond between the two was the time they spent together traveling to Italy with Willy, as well as the following months in that country without him.

Her daughter's death was not unexpected: Elizabeth and Anina, as Anna Maria was known, spent much time together during her long illness, talking, praying, and strengthening their faith. On her deathbed Anina took vows as a Sister of Charity, and mother and daughter spoke of being reunited in eternity.

Still, Elizabeth was devastated by Anina's loss and sank into a deep depression. She wrote to a friend, "The separation from my angel has left so new and deep an impression on my mind, that if I was not obliged to live in these dear ones I should unconsciously die in her."

Serenity

The sharp anguish eventually eased. Elizabeth Seton continued in the huge task of administering and expanding her order, and continued looking after her children, who were never far from her, physically or in her thoughts. When the boys got older, she sent them to Leghorn to learn business from Antonio Filicchi. She died in Emmitsburg in 1821 of tuberculosis.

Mother Seton could have attained sainthood for her devotion in founding and running a religious order that became important in early American education and remains so to this day. But her canonization also reflects her deep spirituality. She was a woman who lived more than half of her life flourishing as a Protestant in New York. When it became apparent that she was about to convert to Catholicism, she suffered discrimination in that city and was not free of it until she moved to Maryland. Despite prejudice, despite her financial problems, not to mention the death of her husband and two children—she lost her youngest daughter, Rebecca ("Bec"), in 1816 when the girl was fourteen—her faith remained strong.

The move toward canonization began in 1907. In 1959 Mother Seton was given the title "Venerable." In 1963 she was beatified, and she was canonized in 1975. Her feast day is January 4.

St. John Nepomucene Neumann (1811–1860)

Two American saints are firsts: John Neumann was the first male American saint, and Frances Xavier Cabrini was the first naturalized American citizen to be canonized. St. Rose Philippine Duchesne, like Neumann and Cabrini, was another saint who was an immigrant to this country.

John was born in Bohemia and educated in Prague. He wanted to become a priest, but, curiously, when he applied he was told that there were enough clerics at the moment in that region.

The archbishop of Thebes reported John Neumann as "a little inferior for the importance of such a distinguished city, not in learning nor in zeal nor in piety, but because of the littleness of his person [John Neumann was five foot two] and his neglect of fashion. . . . The populous City of Philadelphia surely merits a bishop of another type."

He was not discouraged because he actually longed to be a missionary in the United States, He sailed to New York, arriving with literally his last dollar in his pocket. Ordained there, he was transferred to Buffalo, which fit his concept of "frontier priest" more than Manhattan did. He covered a

Figure 13-2: St. John Neumann

sizable geographic area outside that upstate city, because he was younger and stronger than the other priest assigned there. He walked constantly to baptize, officiate at weddings, give the Eucharist, and comfort the dying.

He did not stay in the Buffalo area long but traveled to other regions as a missionary. When he was thirty-one he joined the Redemptorist Order. The first Redemptorist professed in this country, John Neumann served in parishes in Baltimore and Pittsburgh, until he was eventually consecrated bishop of the sprawling city of Philadelphia at age forty-five.

John most emphatically did not want that post. He pleaded with his superiors in Europe to intercede for him with Pope Pius X, to keep the pope from choosing him. It didn't work. He went to Philadelphia, overseeing that city's rapid development, fueled by the growing number of immigrants. He built churches and schools—more new schools than any bishop in the country—and produced a German/English catechism for the newcomers.

A few years after his death, reports of favors and cures obtained through his intercession began and they continue to this day. A man noted for his piety and humility, John Neumann is said to have lived in a tiny room and to have owned only one habit. He is buried in Philadelphia. He was canonized as in 1977, and his feast day is January 5.

St. Frances Xavier Cabrini (1850–1917)

The woman was a whirlwind, accomplishing an astonishing amount in her lifetime. She was born Maria Francesca Cabrini in Lombardy, Italy, the youngest of thirteen children. Orphaned at eighteen, she wanted to become a nun but, in delicate health, was refused entry to two religious communities.

Figure 13-3: St. Frances Cabrini

Help was to come from another quarter, however; a local prelate asked if she'd like to take over a poorly run orphanage. She was delighted by this possibility. After completing that assignment, she and seven followers moved into an abandoned friary and founded the Institute of the Missionary Sisters of the Sacred Heart, specializing in educating girls. Soon there were branches in other Italian cities.

In 1899, the archbishop of New York asked Frances and five of her sisters to come to New York to work. It turned out to be a peculiar offer. When the nuns arrived, the archbishop took back his invitation and suggested they return to Italy.

The women stayed. Frances went on to establish numerous schools, orphanages, hospitals, and convents, not only throughout the United States but in Central and South America, England, and France. She even returned to Italy six times to organize more convents there. In this country, Frances was especially helpful in assisting Italian immigrants.

When faced with a seemingly insurmountable problem, she would ask, "Who is doing this? Are we—or our Lord?"

E-XTRA

At the time of her death in Chicago, she had established more than fifty schools, orphanages, hospitals, convents, and various other charitable centers including St. Cabrini Home, which in still in operation in New York's Mid-Hudson Valley.

She was canonized in 1946. Her feast day is November 13, and she is the patron saint of hospital administrators, emigrants, and immigrants.

Saints for Their Times

Away from their immediate sphere of influence, neither Bishop Neumann nor Mother Cabrini is very well known in this country. Their work took place at a time when the United States was receiving a great number of immigrants from Europe. Both Bishop Neumann and Mother Cabrini were instrumental in organizing those waves of newcomers and providing services for them that are, in many cases, still in existence today. The time was right for their unique energy and talents.

St. Katharine Drexel (1858–1955)

Katharine Drexel died in 1955. It is easy to recognize, and even identify with, such a contemporary person, even if she wears a nun's habit that has long since been updated by her order. She lived so recently that several of the sisters remember Katharine Drexel and speak of her with affection.

The Heiress

Katharine Drexel's name may be a giveaway to some that she was a member of the wealthy Philadelphia banking family. Indeed, her father was a partner of J.P. Morgan in a firm that later became the major Wall Street financial house Drexel Burnham Lambert.

Katharine's mother died just five weeks after her birth. Her Catholic father, Francis, of Austrian descent, eventually remarried, and her stepmother, Emma, had a good deal of influence on the young girl. The Drexels were a religious family, and Katharine and her two sisters, Elizabeth and Louise, were brought up learning to give to the needy. Three days a week Emma would open the doors of their townhouse at Rittenhouse Square to cheerfully hand out food, clothing, and cash to those who needed assistance.

Katharine led the life of a young woman of means. She had a governess and tutors. At fifteen she traveled to Europe with her family for the first time and took in the typical tourist sites. (She pronounced Westminster Abbey "gloomy.") Back at home, Katharine made her social debut. But even while her days were filled with fittings and parties, she still made time for charity.

After her stepmother died in 1883, Katharine's father took his daughters to Europe again. This time the young woman visited the home of her namesake, St. Catherine of Siena, and her growing desire to enter a religious order was reinforced.

Returning to Philadelphia, Katharine talked to her priest, a longtime family friend, who urged her to wait awhile and see if the determination was still as strong in a year or two. During that interval Katharine and her father and sisters traveled to the Northwest, exposing her to a part of the country along the way that would play a prominent role in her future.

In 1885 Francis Drexel died. He had established a trust for his three daughters of $15 million, the largest estate ever recorded in Philadelphia up to that time. Fortune hunters were tripping over themselves to get to the girls' front door. Elizabeth and Louise both eventually married, but all three girls used their money to help others.

Katharine's Choice

There were plenty who needed help. The years of Katharine's life, like the lives of John Neumann and Frances Xavier Cabrini, spanned a time of monumental growth in this country. With immigrants pouring in from both coasts, there was a movement toward settling the middle of the country.

Katharine took the road less traveled in her work for charity: She elected to concentrate on Native Americans and African-Americans. These two sectors of the population received almost no attention from government or society at the time. The Native Americans had been here for centuries, and African-Americans were not considered "recent" immigrants.

The rail trip Katharine had taken with her father across America had, at least from a distance, acquainted her with the part of the country that needed her help. Katharine had also spoken with two missionaries, one from Dakota and the other from the Indian Bureau in Washington, D.C. She started small, endowing schools on Native American reservations around the nation with part of her inheritance.

On another trip to Europe with her sister, Elizabeth, she met with Pope Leo XIII. When she pleaded with him to send priests for the Native Americans, he responded, "Why not become a missionary yourself?"

So she did. In 1888 the young heiress entered the convent of the Sisters of Mary in Pittsburgh, Pennsylvania, to begin training for the sisterhood. She ultimately intended to found a new order, but first she had to become an "established" nun.

At the age of thirty-seven, Katharine took her final vows. By that time, with everyone now knowing about her eventual plans, she had found twelve women who wanted to work with her.

Her congregation was known as the Sisters of the Blessed Sacrament for Indians and Colored People, later to be just the Sisters of the Blessed Sacrament, or SBS. Soon even more like-minded women were joining the order.

Difficult Times

The ministry had its rough moments. Walking the streets of Harlem and other big-city neighborhoods in the 1950s, the sisters often passed by white people who called them "nigger sisters." When the nuns would tell Katharine about the remarks, she would say, "Did you pray for them?"

E-FACT

> In 1922 in Beaumont, Texas, the Ku Klux Klan said they would tar and feather the white pastor at one of Mother Drexel's schools—and bomb his church as well. The nuns prayed. In two days a tornado hit Beaumont and destroyed the Klan's headquarters. Two Klansmen died in the storm. The Klan never bothered the nuns again.

Katharine Drexel was still allowed to administer her trust fund, which brought her about $300,000 a year. Besides funding her own projects, she readily donated money to the causes of others—a million dollars, for instance, went to the Bureau of Catholic Indian Missions. In the 1920s she contributed $750,000 toward the founding of Xavier University in New Orleans, the first Catholic college established for African-Americans. The archbishop there had asked her to help provide a training college for African-American teachers. She had her lawyer handle the details of the purchase because she felt certain the owner wouldn't sell to her.

On her own, Katharine Drexel was responsible for building nearly 100 schools in cities and suburbs, and a dozen schools for Native Americans.

Special Acclaim

They seem remarkable even these days, but imagine how extraordinary Katharine Drexel's accomplishments were in her time. In noting all that she gave, Augustus Tolton (1854–1897), who lived at the time of Katharine Drexel and was, in those early years of her work, the first African-American priest to be acclaimed by black Catholics, wrote: "In the whole history of the Church in America we cannot find one person that has sworn to give her treasure for the sole benefit of the Colored and Indians. As I stand alone as the first Negro priest of America, so you, Mother Katharine, stand alone as the first one to make such a sacrifice for the cause of a downtrodden race."

By the terms of Francis Drexel's will, when one of his daughters died her part of the Drexel trust would be divided between the other two. Katharine eventually inherited Elizabeth's share and, when Louise died in 1945, the entire income from the trust.

She lived to be nearly 100 years old. In poor health for the last twenty years of her life, she stayed close to her order's motherhouse and spent most of her time in a wheelchair. But she continued her commitment to civil rights, including funding the NAACP in some of its projects.

By the time of her death she had spent just about all of her inheritance. Katharine Drexel is buried at the motherhouse of the Sisters of the Blessed Sacrament in Bensalem, Pennsylvania. She was beatified by Pope John Paul II in 1988, and canonized on October 1, 2000. Her feast day is March 3.

More than 3,000 Americans, including members of the Sisters of the Blessed Sacrament and faculty, alumni, and students from Xavier University in Louisiana, attended the jubilee mass canonizing Katharine. The Xavier University Concert Choir sang at the liturgy. Also seated near the altar was a man who had regained his ability to hear in 1974 and attributed this to Mother Drexel's intercessions.

St. Herman of Alaska (1758-1837)

Fr. Herman was a lay monk and missionary, from a merchant class family that lived near Moscow. In 1773 he was sent as part of a missionary team of monks to Alaska which was then "Russian America." His team traveled east for a year, finally arriving in Alaska in 1774. For a time, Fr. Herman was in charge of the mission based in Kodiac as well as the school.

Love for the Natives

The monks continually came into conflict with the Russian-American Company, because they protested the harsh way that the company treated the natives. The monks refused to remain silent about the injustices they witnessed and became the targets of the hostitlity of Alexander Baranov, the company leader. Baranov even went so far as to tell the monks that they could not have contact with the Christian communities they served.

When the monks attempted to protect the natives by placing them under imperial protection, Baranov only increased his threats, causing the monks to cease serving the Orthodox faithful for a time.

Fr. Herman moved to Spruce Island in 1808. There, he lived in a small hut, tending a garden full of potatoes, garlic, and turnips. He was often overheard singing, chanting, and praying from his hut. Beneath his tattered habit, he ltive—he slept on some deerskin over a bench and used two bricks for a pillow. He kept company with a family of wild minks. Although he loved living as a hermit, he left his hut often so that he could tend to those in need.

E-FACT

People sometimes asked Fr. Herman how he could tolerate his isolated existence. He replied, "I am not alone. God is here, just as He is everywhere. The holy angels are here. . . ."

One time after an earthquake, a tidal wave threatened the island. Fr. Herman placed an icon of the Virgin Mary in the sand and prayed there. He then told the natives not to be afraid, the water would not rise above the icon. Just as he promised, the water stopped at the icon and the locals were spared.

Love for the Children

Later, in 1817, when a plague swept through Kodiac and several other islands, many people became sick and died. Fr. Herman stayed with the sick, praying for them and tending to their needs. The plague left many orphans, and Fr. Herman brought them back to Spruce Island with him, where he created an orphanage and school for their care.

Fr. Herman gathered the children together who had lost parents and brought them back to his home, where he created an orphanage and school to care for them.

When he was around eighty years old, on December 13, 1837 Fr. Herman knew that he was close to death. He asked one of his spiritual children to read from the Acts of the Apostles and light some candles. His cell became fragrant with a sweet floral scent, and his face shone.

The canonization of Fr. Herman was completed on August 9, 1970. He was the first Eastern Orthodox saint to be canonized in America. He is commemorated on September 24.

St. Innocent of Alaska (1797–1879)

St. Innocent (John) was born on August 26, 1797 in Russia. His father was a church server, and died when John was only six years old. John attended seminary, married and was ordained a priest in 1821.

Two years later, when he was twenty-five years old, he volunteered to take his family to the rugged Alaskan island of Unalaska. He traveled 2,200 miles over the course of a year with his mother, his wife, infant son Innocent, and brother Stefan. They finally arrived at Unalaska—a volcanic, windswept island—on July 29, 1824.

There, he and his family dug an underground hut for the family to live in, similar to the ones the natives inhabited. Fr. John also created a school for the locals were he integrated his growing knowledge of the local culture and customs into his lessons about Christianity. He also began work on a church and a pine home with wood from Sitka and trained members of his parish in carpentry so that they could assist him. Over the years, he built furniture for his home, as well as clocks and musical instruments for friends and family.

For the next ten years, he traveled by kayak, dogsled, reindeer, and ship to serve more than a thousand Russians and native Alaskans spread over ten different settlements. Out of his devotion for the local people, he translated many hymns and services into their native tongues, as well as creating an alphabet and translating portions of the Bible. He also wrote the first book in Aleutian: *An Indication of the Pathway into the Kingdom of Heaven.*

In 1838, when Fr. John was visiting St. Petersburg and Moscow to consult with church authorities about his work in Alaska, he received word that his wife had died. He wanted to return to his children immediately, but was persuaded to become a monk by Church authorities. As a monk, he took the name Innocent.

In 1940 he became a bishop and continued his missionary work. He continued to devote himself to the local people, traveling between the islands and working on translations of the services and scriptures into the local Yakut language. On November 19, 1867 he was appointed the Metropolitan of Moscow. He continued to care for the Church in Russia and America. He suggested that the Russian Church in America be based in San Francisco instead of Sitka, and he expressed his desire that the services would be translated into English, that the clergy would speak English, and that Americans would be encouraged to become priests. His prayerful desire and tireless efforts helped seed what is now known as The Orthdox Church in America.

He died on March 31, 1879. He was canonized on October 6, 1977. He is commemorated on October 6 and March 31.

To read more about Eastern Orthodox saints in America, try *Portraits of American Saints*, compiled and edited by George A. Gray and Jan Bear (from Diocese Council and Department of Missions Diocese of the West Orthodox Church in America, Los Angeles, California, 1994). This unique, readable book offers vivid profiles of contemporary American Eastern Orthodox saints and provided valuable source material for this chapter.

Chapter 14

The Horrible Fates of Early Martyrs

The word "martyr" comes from the Greek word *martyria*, meaning "witness." The person who offers up her life eloquently expresses her faith, sometimes creating a chain reaction—witnesses may come to faith, and those who already believe may be inspired to live more boldly toward death. This chapter offers a glimpse into the lives—and deaths—of some the earliest Christian martyrs. These early martyrs suffered in ways that may seem unimaginable today, and they suffered courageously for a faith that was obscure and relatively unknown in their own time.

A "Good" Death

For centuries, Christians have desired a peaceful and painless death, with ample opportunity to tie up loose ends and heal relationships. The Catholic writer Flannery O'Conner believed that her long battle with lupus preceding death was a sign of God's mercy—she wished that everyone would have years to prepare, as she did. But martyrdom can come suddenly, and the death of a martyr is rarely tidy, almost never painless.

The early martyrs did not have a long history of saints' stories to draw upon, nor did they have firm footing in an established church. Their faith ran deep, however, and they refused to deny their faith when called upon to do so—and then were slain for it.

The author David Nichol wrote: "It is the martyrs who show us how to die. We call upon them and upon the ancestors to take us into their company. What they teach us, above all, is to go into death wholeheartedly, to embrace the experience with one's whole heart and in joy."

In many cases, few biographical details of the early martyrs survive. But some of these names might ring a bell with saint-watchers, who remember hearing and reading about the dramatic deaths of St. Agnes, St. Perpetua, St. Felicitas, St. Polycarp, and a number of other men and women who are still remembered in the twenty-first century. Their memories are cherished not only for how they died, but because their deaths brought life to others. As the early Christian theologian Tertullian wrote, "The blood of the martyrs is the seed of the church."

The Making of a Martyr

Practitioners of the new Christian faith faced their greatest opposition between the years 33 and 313. In 313 the Emperor Constantine converted and legalized Christianity, and life became less risky for Christians. Before that Christians suffered massive persecution. Those that converted from Judaism inevitably experienced tension as they sought to carve out a distinctive life of faith.

There were thousands of Christian martyrs during the persecution. In some cases, death was inevitable, because Christianity refuted the legitimacy of the Roman Empire's deities—including the emperor, who considered himself divine. Civil law forbade the practice of the Christian faith or even assembling for the propagation of that belief. The treatment of the Christians, ranging from merely dismissive to outrageous cruelty, depended on the whim of the emperor.

Christians often met in secret. Many were caught, forced to admit their belief, and then executed. But not all confessed their faith. This type of compromise raised many issues. Were those who said whatever authorities wanted to hear—and therefore did not die—still true Christians? Or did they have to begin all over again in the faith with a fresh baptism—assuming the first did not take—and hope for more courage the next time around?

Few are called to martyrdom in the ultimate sense. None are supposed to seek it. All Christians, however, are called to follow in the footsteps of Christ, and for some, this difficult journey culminates in martyrdom. Others are called to die in smaller ways every day of their lives, to surrender to love and to offer their lives for others in daily concrete ways. Both callings are rooted in Christ, who did not desire death but willingly surrendered to it for the sake of the world. His pain was real, as was the pain of the martyrs. And yet he, like so many after him, must have been sustained by a sense of ultimate hope and larger purpose, realizing that death is the door to life.

Not unlike the pagans, Christians brought food and other items to the graves of their loved ones or friends. For Christians, the idea was to be joyous, as indeed the Christian faith was in the first few centuries. The Roman Catholic Church returned to the joy surrounding death in the years after Vatican II. Funerals were no longer conducted with the celebrant in black vestments and the service accompanied by dirge-like music—the "Dies Irae," for example, a hymn that starts: "Day of wrath, O day of mourning." Today, most Christian funerals emphasize the movement into God's light. Present-day funerals also tend to celebrate the life of the deceased. White, not black, is the operative color used in these services. In these churches, the clergy wears white vestments to symbolize the hope of the Resurrection, although those who attend the funeral are still likely to wear black.

Interestingly, civil authorities did not interfere with early Christian graves, having a respect for death that apparently crossed religious lines. In time shrines and basilicas were built over some of those martyrs' tombs. These houses of worship remain today.

The following stories do contain some legendary aspects, but the stories remain largely true. It is inevitable that certain fantastic elements have entered in, as these stories have been told and retold for nearly two thousand years. Still, the stories retain a heartbreaking, genuine quality that continues to challenge and inspire.

The Holy Innocents (First Century)

Not everyone who dies for the faith *chooses* to die. Although martyrs are most often characterized by a willingness to surrender to death, there are many who died for the faith who never experienced a moment of "decision." They were taken to death without consent, dying as victims. Many of them are nonetheless honored as martyrs of the Church.

This is especially the case in heartbreaking situations when those who die are children. The first martyrs for Christ were indeed children, as recorded in the book of Matthew. They died not because of anything they said or did, but simply because of the rage of King Herod, who heard that a child had been born who was to be "King of the Jews." (Matthew 2:2) When Herod could not destroy this newborn king, he spent his rage on all of the other children under two in and around Bethlehem.

E-XTRA

> The earliest Christians believed that King Herod's horrific massacre of children had been foretold in Jeremiah 31:15 (New International Version): "A voice is heard in Ramah, mourning and great weeping, Rachel weeping for her children and refusing to be comforted, because her children are no more."

The wise men, upon hearing of the birth of Christ, saw the rising of his star and started asking about this newborn child who was to be King. When Herod heard of this, he asked the wise men to find the child and then report back about his location. But the wise men, having been warned in a dream not to return to Herod, disobeyed him and provoked his jealous rage.

E-QUESTION

Exactly how many children did Herod order to be killed?
There are disputes about the number of children who died under Herod's rage. While the Byzantine liturgy listed 14,000 Holy Innocents, a list of early Syrian origin mentions 64,000. Others believe that these numbers are unrealistically large and that fewer than twenty children may have died.

Herod was reportedly so brutal by nature—he may have even killed his own son in this massacre—that Augustus said, "I'd rather be Herod's pig than Herod's son." (Macrobius, *The Saturnalia*) Herod assumed that his massive act of violence would end the threat to his throne. But like any ruthless leader, he created devastation without actually accomplishing his goal. Joseph had already been warned in a dream that he was to depart with the child to Egypt, and Jesus remained safe.

Many children died in his stead; this event is referred to as "The Massacre of the Innocents." These children died without choice or knowledge of the person they were dying for. The agony of their parents must have been extreme.

These "Holy Innocents" have been remembered by the church since at least 485. They are commemorated on different days in a variety of churches. The Roman Catholic Church commemorates this feast on December 27, the Lutherans and Anglicans on December 28, and the Eastern Orthodox Church on December 29.

St. Stephen (Died c. 34)

St. Stephen is one of the earliest martyrs of the Church. Although many of the details of his life have not been recorded, a few facts have survived the test of time, especially through the account offered in the Acts of the Apostles.

St. Stephen was one of the first seven deacons in the early Christian Church. He was a convert from Judaism, and he enjoyed lively debates with

Figure 14-1: St. Stephen

other Jews about Christianity. His robust manner eventually caused him to get into trouble.

Stephen was accused of blasphemy and brought before the high priest. He responded to the charges brought before him by turning them against his accusers, saying that they had always persecuted their prophets and turned away from the law, and now they had killed Jesus. (Acts 7:51–52)

Stephen's words infuriated his accusers. But he continued to speak, describing a vision of Christ. "Behold, I see the heavens opened, and the Son of man standing at the right hand of God." (Acts 7:56) These words caused his accusers to run him out of the city and pelt him with stones until he died.

Like Christ, he died praying for forgiveness for those who took his life. As he was dying he said, "Lord Jesus, receive my spirit." In the centuries to follow, many more martyrs followed his example—dying horrible deaths with words of forgiveness and peace on their lips.

E-FACT

In Greek, the name Stephen is translated as *Stephanos*, which means "crown" in Greek. His crown was the victory of dying bravely for Christ. To this day, in Eastern Orthodox weddings, couples are crowned with "Stephana" flowers, reminiscent of the honor of dying for love.

St. Polycarp (c. 60–155)

This saint had more than a devout faith for which he was willing to die. He was a literate man who influenced the church of his time. His is the oldest account of Christian martyrdom outside of the New Testament.

Polycarp was a disciple of John the Baptist and served for many years as bishop of Smyrna. When he was young, he kissed the chains of St. Ignatius of Antioch as he traveled to Rome for martyrdom. It is unlikely that Polycarp suspected that he would eventually share the fate of Ignatius, although Ignatius did help prepare him for that possibility. In a letter to Polycarp, Ignatius wrote, "A Christian does not control his own life but gives his whole time to God."

He was arrested when he was eighty-six years old and ordered to repeat "Caesar is Lord" and curse Christ. Polycarp refused, saying, "Eighty and six years I have served him and he never did me any wrong. How can I blaspheme my King who saved me?"

His sentence: death by burning. "Come, do what you will," the elderly bishop told his accusers, adding, "Leave me as I am, the one who gives me strength to endure the fire will also give me strength to stay quite still on the pyre, even without the precaution of your nails."

The flames blazed around this holy man, like a wind-filled sail, but they did not touch him. Finally, an executioner stabbed him to death. An account of his martyrdom claimed there was such a quantity of blood "that the fire was quenched and the whole crowd marveled." St. Polycarp's feast day is February 23.

St. Barnabas (Died c. 61)

A missionary, Barnabas is especially important because he preached the gospel to the gentiles. In one Greek town, he and St. Paul so impressed the locals that the two men struggled to prevent the Greeks from offering them sacrifices. They were believed to be the Greek gods Zeus and Hermes.

Barnabas was originally a Jewish Cypriot named Joseph. He was renamed Barnabas by the apostles after he sold his land and donated the proceeds to the young church. His name means "son of encouragement," sometimes translated as "son of consolation."

None of the authentic writings of Barnabas survive. The "Letter of Barnabas," by an anonymous Christian of the late first or early second century, expounds on the superiority of Christianity over Judaism. At one time, some scholars believed that Barnabas also wrote a New Testament letter to the Hebrews. Later historians believe that neither work can be traced back to Barnabas. Both are too extreme in their statements about Judaism. These documents do not seem consistent with the life and tone of

Barnabas, although he and St. Paul did struggle to answer many questions relevant to non-Jews who converted to Christianity—most notably the question of whether converts must be circumcised even if they are not of Jewish lineage.

Although Barnabas was not officially one of the apostles, St. Luke included him as an apostle because of the calling he received from the Holy Spirit. His willingness to vouch for and share in St. Paul's ministry also placed him in a position of influence in the early church. Barnabas appears to have been stoned to death in Cyprus around the year 61. His feast day is June 11.

Sts. Perpetua and Felicitas (Died 203)

Perpetua was a wealthy woman of Carthage, in North Africa, the mother of a newborn baby son known as Vivia or Vibia. Perpetua is usually linked with St. Felicitas (or Felicity), her pregnant young servant. The two suffered the same fate.

E-XTRA

The moving story of these two women, St. Perpetua and St. Felicitas, who were both mothers and martyrs, was so loved in North Africa that it caused St. Augustine to complain that this story was read more commonly than the Gospels.

What makes Perpetua's martyrdom so touching is that she recorded her thoughts as a young woman facing death, and these accounts survive. She describes her fear and hunger, as well as her painfully swollen breasts when she was separated from her newborn.

At age twenty-two, Perpetua was arrested with Felicitas and several friends for a transgression related to the banned practice of Christianity. They were all held in a private home, where they were baptized by friends, and then moved to a prison.

At her trial, Perpetua was conflicted over her responsibilities. She had an aged father who pleaded for her life, and of course she had her baby boy. (Her husband is not mentioned in the narrative of her life.) When confronted with the threat of death, she said simply, "I am a Christian."

Although she was willing to leave everything (including her child) behind for her faith, she never speaks of motherhood in a negative way. In fact, in her account, the baby is brought to Perpetua in prison and she nurses him. She notes, "Straightaway I became well, and was lightened of my labor and care for the child; suddenly the prison was made a palace for me, so that I would sooner be there than anywhere else." All could not be made right with her father, however. A non-Christian, he could not understand her dedication to this religion or grasp her joy in foreseeing eternity. She says to him, "What happens at this tribunal will be what God wants, for our power comes not from us but from God."

When she placed her son in the care of a person who would be able to tend to him after she was gone, she was greatly relieved. But her relief was short-lived. The news that she and Felicitas would die fighting beasts in the amphitheater certainly must have staggered her.

Just as Thomas More calmly awaited his execution in the Tower of London, and remained calm even as he climbed the scaffold, Perpetua was equally serene and accepting. Her last words: "Thus far have I written this, till the day before the games; but the deed of the games themselves let him write who will."

An eyewitness completed Perpetua's story: Felicitas was eight months pregnant when she was arrested. After a night spent in prayer, her labor began and she rejoiced that she was able to hand her daughter over to a Christian friend so that the babe would be spared the terrors of the amphitheater.

On the day before their execution, Perpetua, Felicitas, and their fellow prisoners and friends celebrated a "love feast" in the prison. This night was marked by sorrow and joy—they were going to their death, but they found peace and happiness in those last hours despite the horror awaiting them.

The next day the prisoners entered the arena. Again Perpetua was asked to deny her faith. Again she refused, saying, "For this cause came we willingly unto this, that our liberty might not be obscured. For this cause have we devoted our lives." They were tossed about by a wild cow, but the two women survived.

An executioner was called to put them to death by the sword, but apparently he was new at the job and was not able to strike a perfect final blow.

Perpetua guided his hand. The eyewitness added, in closing the account of this saint, that just before the swordsman took aim, Perpetua and Felicitas, formerly mistress and slave, exchanged a kiss. This gesture symbolized the reality that they were now—and always would be—sisters in Christ. They are commemorated on March 7.

St. Cyprian (c. 200–258)

A learned man, Cyprian was a lawyer and teacher before he converted to Christianity. He became a great scholar of the Bible and is considered a major figure in early Christian literature.

Cyprian was named bishop of Carthage, and at one point he had to flee persecution. He continued to rule his see by letter. That didn't set too well with his flock, who were quite critical of his flight. When he did return, many of "the faithful" were no longer true to the Church. A priest who stayed when Cyprian left was now in schism, which is a formal breach of unity among people of the same faith. Between coping with that priest and deciding how the lapsed could be welcomed back into the church and standing firm on the primacy of the pope, Cyprian had his hands full.

More was to come. When he was fifty-two years old, Carthage was stricken with a plague that was to last two years. Cyprian and his Christians were blamed.

At that time he wrote "On the Mortality" to comfort those in his diocese. Cyprian ran into still more trouble when he ran afoul of Pope Stephen I. The saint refused to recognize the baptism of heretics, which Stephen had declared valid.

Finally, compounding those difficult times, an official decree went out forbidding clerics from the practice of Christianity and requiring them to participate in the official state religion. When he refused, Cyprian was arrested and exiled to a village some distance from Carthage. In a year, a new edict came down, this one calling for death for bishops, priests, and deacons. Because Cyprian continued in his refusal to recognize pagan gods, he was beheaded on September 14. His feast day is September 16, two days after his martyrdom.

St. Alban (Third Century)

St. Alban lived in Britain during the time of the Roman occupation. He may have been a soldier—he is believed to have been a man of some consequence in his society. Although Alban was not a Christian, he willingly shared his home with a Christian priest who feared for his life under the persecution.

Alban watched his guest with curiosity. He was so impressed with the priest that he suddenly longed to learn about the Christian faith and to be baptized. His guest willingly taught him all that he knew. But Alban's time with this priest was short-lived. The priest was to die at the hands of the Romans.

Alban, although new to the faith, asked the priest to allow him to trade clothes with him so that he could die in his stead. When the persecutors came to his home, he was there waiting for them, dressed in the priest's clerical garb.

He was led to trial. When the judge discovered Alban's trickery he was enraged and threatened Alban with death. But Alban was unafraid. He confessed that he was a Christian and was beheaded. The story does not end there, however. The judge was so inspired by Alban's courage and resolve that he decided that he also wanted to be baptized. St. Alban is commemorated on June 20.

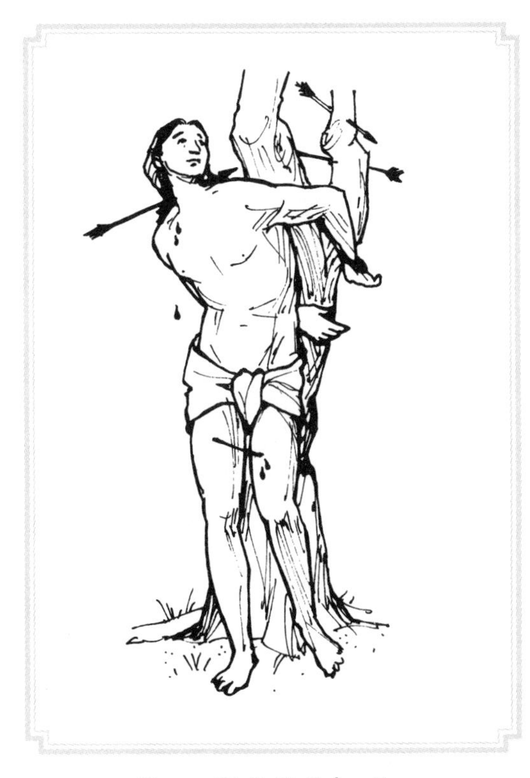

Figure 14-2: St. Sebastian

St. Sebastian (Died c. 288)

St. Sebastian is vividly depicted in art as the young man standing at a pillar whose hands are tied behind him, looking upward toward heaven. He has been shot with nearly a dozen arrows.

Sebastian may have been born in Gaul (France), and was a soldier in the Roman army. Although he was a covert Christian, he made numerous converts, including some government officials. Sebastian is also said to have cured his wife, Zoe, of her deafness.

Sebastian's Christianity was finally brought to the attention of Emperor Diocletian, who was persecuting the followers of the new faith. He ordered archers to execute Sebastian. The arrows hit him and he was left for dead, but he didn't die. A Christian woman found him and nursed him back to health, only to have Sebastian once again denounce the emperor for his cruelty to Christians. He was again sentenced to die, and this time his executioner took no chances, beating him to death.

Sebastian was indeed a real person, and is buried on the Appian Way. However, some of the details of his story could be pious fiction. His feast day is January 20, and he is invoked for protection against plague.

St. Dorothy (Died 303)

Yet another victim of Diocletian's scourge was Dorothy, who refused to make sacrifices to the gods. She was tortured and was to be executed. On the way to the place where she was to die, she met a young man, a lawyer named Theophilus. Teasing her, he asked her to send him fruits from "the garden" that she had claimed she would soon enter. She knelt for her execution, prayed, and an angel appeared with a basket of three roses and three apples. Dorothy had them sent to Theophilus, saying she would see him later in the garden. The lawyer converted to Christianity, and soon he, too, was martyred. Her feast day, formerly February 6, is no longer observed.

Chapter 15

Holy People of the Holocaust

Although many speak of the horrors of the Holocaust, few speak of the holy people who laid down their lives for others in the camps. The following accounts detail the lives of a small sampling of those who bore witness to this statement from the Talmud: "Whoever saves a single life saves the world entire." Whether they were forging baptism documents to save lives or bringing comfort to those dying in the camps, these saints sought to do all that they could during this time of pain.

Relevant Saints

"Indifference is the great poison of our age," wrote St. Maximilian Kolbe, martyr of Auschwitz. In the face of great human suffering it can be tempting to become numb and to turn away. The following holy people chose instead to go to the heart of the suffering and to remain present with those who needed them most—eyes and hearts open wide until their last breath.

These saints remained anchored in concrete acts of kindness despite the violence and despair around them. By sheltering Jews, caring for neglected children, and sharing their meager food and water rations, they managed to live for a larger purpose and to bring meaning out of meaninglessness.

These saints are particularly relevant for contemporary times: most of them went through a period of atheism early on in life, and later on, all of them engaged huge questions—such as: How does one keep faith in the face of despair and how does one continue to believe in a loving God despite evidence to the contrary?

In the face of seemingly unanswerable questions, these people managed to grasp hope as the nightmare of the Holocaust progressed. Mother Maria Skobtsova remained hopeful even while watching smoke rise from the chimneys of the crematoriums. "But it is only here, immediately above the chimneys, that the billows of smoke are oppressive," she said. "When they rise higher, they turn into light clouds before being dispersed into limitless space. In the same way, our souls, once they have torn themselves away from this sinful earth, move by means of an effortless unearthly flight into eternity, where there is life full of joy."

St. Maximilian Kolbe

Raymond Kolbe was born on January 8, 1894 in Poland. He was such a mischievous child that one day his exasperated mother said, "What will become of you?" Raymond was deeply troubled and took the question to the Virgin Mary. In prayer he asked, "What will become of me?" The Virgin Mary then appeared before him with two crowns, one red and the other white. The white symbolized purity and the red martyrdom. She asked Raymond if he would like to choose a crown. He asked for both and from that moment his life was infused with a new sense of purpose.

His belief in his ultimate destiny may have strengthened him as he struggled with health issues. As a child, he was often sick, hospitalized multiple times for tuberculosis. As he aged, he continued to suffer from tubercular attacks, crippling headaches, and abscesses all over his body.

A Franciscan Life

When he was sixteen he joined the Franciscans, taking the name Maximilian. In 1918 he was ordained as a priest. He eventually created a friary in Poland called the "City of the Immaculate," which eventually swelled to contain 650 friars. Likewise, he helped to found the "Knights of Mary Immaculate," which published journals related to Marian devotion. One of his journals was distributed to more than 800,000 people. In the 1930s he traveled to Asia to create Marian communities in Japan and India.

He was back in Poland when the Nazis invaded in 1939. Fr. Kolbe sent most of the other friars home. He then opened the friary doors to shelter 3,000 people, among them 2,000 Jews. In May of 1941, he was arrested and taken to Auschwitz.

E-XTRA

This is a prayer related to St. Maximilian Kolbe: "O Lord Jesus Christ, who said, 'Greater love than this no man has that a man lay down his life for his friends.' Through the intercession of St. Maximilian Kolbe whose life illustrated such love, we beseech you to grant us our petitions . . . [add specific petitions here]."

At the camp, he suffered three months of heavy labor and abusive beatings. Even as his health deteriorated, he barely slept at night. Fellow prisoners remember him going from bed to bed, saying, "I am a Catholic priest, how can I help you?" Others crawled across the ground to his bedside to make their confessions and to receive consolation.

The Red Crown

There was a custom at Auschwitz that when one prisoner escaped, ten would be killed in retaliation. When one of Fr. Kolbe's bunkmates disappeared in July of 1941, he and the others were lined up. Ten of these men were selected for the starvation bunker. When one of the men, Francis Gajowniczek, was called, he began to weep, saying, "My poor wife and children, I will never see them again."

Fr. Kolbe asked the guard if he could take this man's place. When asked who he was, Fr. Kolbe said, "I am a Catholic priest from Poland; I would like to take this man's place because he has a wife and children." Fr. Kolbe then was taken to the underground death bunker with nine others. The men had nothing to eat or drink but their own urine. But something unusual happened in the death bunker: agonized wails transformed into prayers and songs, as Fr. Kolbe helped his bunkmates prepare for death.

By August 14, only Fr. Kolbe and three others remained alive. They were killed with shots of carbolic acid. Fr. Kolbe was the last to die. He lifted his arm to the executioner, and died with a prayer on his lips.

Moments after he died, his expression was calm and radiant, his eyes open and head drooping against the back wall. This was the death he had always hoped for. As he had once said, "I would like to use myself completely up in the service of the Immaculate, and to disappear without leaving a trace, as the winds carry my ashes to the far corners of the world."

Bruno Borgowiec, a man charged with tending to the men in the starvation bunker said, "At every inspection, when almost all the others were now lying on the floor, Fr. Kolbe was seen kneeling or standing in the centre as he looked cheerfully in the face of the SS men. . . ."

Fr. Kolbe was canonized in 1982 in Rome by Pope John Paul II, who had often prayed at the site of his death. The man Fr. Kolbe had saved, Francis Gajowniczek, was present at the ceremony. "For a long time I felt remorse when I thought of Maximilian," he said. "By allowing myself to be saved, I had signed his death warrant. But now I understand that a man like him could not have done otherwise. Perhaps he thought as a priest his place was beside the condemned men to help them keep hope. In fact, he was with them to the last."

St. Edith Stein

Edith Stein was born in 1891, in Breslau, Germany. She was born on Yom Kippur, the Jewish Day of Atonement. When Edith was only two years old, her father died suddenly and her mother was left to raise eight children. Through all of the difficulties her mother faced, she remained a devout Jew. Although Edith admired her mother's convictions, she did not share them. By the time she was thirteen, she had become an atheist because she felt that there were too few authentic believers.

Conversion

In college, however, Edith's atheism began to collapse. She was a brilliant student, one of the first women to be admitted to study at the University of Göttingen. There she studied under Edmund Husserl, the founder of phenomenology. By the age of twenty-three she had completed her dissertation on empathy.

E-FACT

St. Edith said of the Holocaust, "I realized that it was his Cross that was now being laid upon the Jewish people, that the few who understood this had the responsibility for carrying it in the name of all, and that I myself would do this, if only he would show me how."

The study of philosophy and the conversion of many of her friends to Christianity caused her to begin to seriously consider its claims. She began to read the Bible and other spiritual writings. At twenty-nine, she picked up a copy of the autobiography of St. Teresa of Ávila. She read through the night and by the morning, she said, "This is the truth." She rushed out to purchase a Catholic missal and catechism.

She was baptized the following January. Although she wanted to enter the Carmelite order immediately, her advisors asked her to wait because her conversion had already devastated her mother. Edith continued to accompany her mother to synagogue, feeling more deeply connected with her Jewish heritage than she had before.

Edith taught for a short time in Münster, but as the Nazi movement gained momentum, she lost her teaching position. She also foresaw the horrors ahead and attempted to gain an audience with Pope Pius XI—to request that he issue a papal encyclical against the Nazis—but her request went unanswered.

E-XTRA

A prayer said to St. Edith Stein: "Saint Edith Stein, holy martyr, philosopher of the truth, defender of the human person against the evils of this age, enlighten our minds, illumine our hearts, fill our lives with the passion of your love for the Cross. Amen."

Sr. Edith entered the Carmelite convent in Cologne. She took the name "Sister Teresa Benedicta a Cruce" (meaning Blessed by the Cross). Her mother, who was not present at the ceremony, accused Edith of abandoning her people during their time of persecution.

A Death of Solidarity

As the war on the Jews was declared on November 8, 1938, Edith feared that her presence at the nunnery endangered her sister nuns. She was smuggled into Holland. Although she did not fear death—and in fact wanted to offer her life as a sacrifice for her own people—she did not wish for anyone else to be unnecessarily harmed.

In 1940 the Nazis occupied Holland and Edith and her sister Rosa (who had also converted) were forced to wear the yellow star. On July 26, 1942, the Catholic bishops of Holland issued a statement denouncing the persecution of the Jews. This provoked a harsh retaliation from the Nazis, who immediately rounded up all Catholic Jews. On August 2 the Gestapo arrived at the convent. Edith reassured her sister, saying, "Come Rosa, we're going for our people."

E-FACT

A fellow prisoner said of St. Edith that it was almost painful to see her: "She carried so much pain that it hurt to see her smile . . . Every time I think of her sitting in the barracks, the same picture comes to mind: a Pieta without the Christ."

Edith died in the gas chamber at Auschwitz on August 9, 1942. Forty-three years later, on this same day, a little girl was born in America and named after St. Edith. Teresa Benedicta nearly died when she was two years old from an accidental Tylenol overdose. Her family and friends asked for the intercessions of St. Edith, and the little girl miraculously survived, to the astonishment of her doctors. St. Edith was canonized on October 11, 1998, by Pope John Paul II.

Mother Maria Skobtsova

Figure 15-1: Mother Maria Skobtsova

Mother Maria Skobtsova is perhaps the most unconventional saint to grace these pages—a brilliant, chain-smoking, twice-divorced, left-leaning nun with an enormous heart. Like Mother Teresa of Calcutta, Mother Maria went out into the streets of Paris, seeking the destitute and bringing them home to care for them.

Elizaveta Pilenko (nicknamed Liza), was born in Latvia in 1891. Her wealthy parents were devoutly Orthodox and taught her about the faith from childhood. She took to Christianity naturally—by the time she was seven, she asked her mother if she was old enough to become a nun. But when she was a teenager, her father died and her faith crumbled. "If there is no justice," she said, "Then there is no God."

Orthodox theologian Metropolitan Anthony Bloom's first impression of Mother Maria: "On the table there was a glass of beer and behind the glass was sitting a Russian nun in full monastic robes. I looked at her and decided that I would never go near that woman." (Later on he was more favorably impressed with her and enthusiastically supported her canonization.)

Like many of the martyrs in this book, she felt the desire to sacrifice her own life for others from a young age. As a teenager in St. Petersburg, she was drawn to intellectuals and revolutionaries but disillusioned by their lack of action—they did not seem to understand the reality of dying for a cause; instead, they dwelt in the more abstract realm of ideas.

Two Marriages

In 1910, when she was eighteen years old, she married Dimitri Kuzmin-Karaviev, who was an alcoholic. This marriage only lasted three years. During these years she gave birth to her first child, Gaiana, published her first book of poetry, *Scythian Shards,* and began to feel the desire to study theology. She was accepted at the then all-male theological academy of the Alexander Nevsky Monastery in St. Petersburg.

Mother Maria said: "At this moment God is visiting his world. And the world can receive that visit, open its heart—"Ready, ready is my heart"—and then in an instant our fallen lives will unite with the depths of eternity." —from the essay Insight in Wartime.

As World War I was beginning, she moved back to her family's country home in the south of Russia. She began to feel convinced that Christ really did exist.

In 1918, after the Bolshevik Revolution, she was elected deputy mayor of Anapa. When the White Army took control of Anapa, the mayor departed and she became mayor. She was accused of being a Bolshevik, and put on trial. The judge in the trial, Daniel Skobtsova, saved her life and she and he were married shortly afterward.

When she was pregnant with her second child, she, Daniel, Gaiana, and her mother fled the country. In Georgia, she gave birth to her son, Yuri, and in Yugoslavia she gave birth to her second daughter, Anastasia. The family arrived in Paris in 1923.

The Death of a Child

In 1926 the entire family developed influenza. Everyone got better except for Anastasia, who grew thinner each day. She was finally diagnosed with meningitis, and for almost two months her mother sat by her bedside, unable to cure her daughter, watching her deteriorate.

Anastasia died on March 7, and Liza's second marriage collapsed shortly after that. Her son Yuri went to live with his father. A few years after Anastasia's burial, a more permanent spot opened up in another section of the cemetery. As Liza followed her daughter's coffin, she re-experienced many of the earlier emotions from her daughter's death. She also felt the stirrings of a new vocation. "I became aware of a new and special, broad and all-embracing motherhood," she wrote.

E-XTRA

Tensions often arose between Mother Maria and the two nuns who assisted her. She was often late to services or missed them entirely because of the demands of hospitality. She also rushed out of services to answer the doorbell, refusing to neglect those in need. Her two sister nuns eventually left to form a more traditional convent.

In 1935 her other daughter, Gaiana, died suddenly. These two deaths dramatically altered the course of her life. She longed to care for those who struggled most intensely—drug addicts, recent immigrants, and those who were mentally ill.

Her bishop encouraged her to become a nun, but she was only willing to live a consecrated life if she could continue to be engaged with the people she cared for. Her husband eventually granted her an ecclesiastical divorce and she became a nun.

A "Bohemian" Convent

With the support of her bishop, she obtained a home to share with those who needed a place to get back on their feet. Her home also became a place of theological discussion and debate. To make room for more guests, she slept in the basement beside the boiler on an iron bedstead. Two years later, she rented a larger home at Rue de Lourmel. She could now serve meals to one hundred instead of just twenty-five. Over the years she rented several other properties so that she could care for more people.

During World War II, many Jews came to stay with Mother Maria and the priest who had been sent to assist her, Fr. Dimitry Klepinin. Mother Maria was also able to gain entrance to a stadium where many Jews were being held. For three days, she sought to bring comfort, to care for children, and to distribute food. With the help of garbage men, she was also able to smuggle four children to safety in trash bins.

E-FACT

The story of Mother Maria's rescue of these children from the stadium has been vividly retold for children in the book *Silent as a Stone: Mother Maria of Paris and the Trash Can Rescue*, by Jim Forest and illustrated by Dasha Pancheshnaya, published by St. Vladimir's Seminary Press.

Mother Maria was arrested on February 10, 1943. After some time in transitional camps, she spent her final days at a camp in Ravensbrück, Germany. There she was a source of inspiration for many, leading theological discussions and remaining cheerful even as her health failed and she needed to be held up by other prisoners for roll calls.

On March 30, 1945, Holy Saturday, her life ended in the gas chambers. Before she died, she asked a fellow prisoner to memorize this message for her loved ones. "My state at present is such that I completely accept suffering in the knowledge that this is how things ought to be for me, and if I am to die, I see this as a blessing from on high."

Fr. Dimitry Klepinin and Yuri

Fr. Dimitry was closely associated with Mother Maria, as he was sent to serve at her chapel in 1939, when he was thirty-five years old. He was a modest man and source of strength for Mother Maria and her son Yuri during those difficult years.

Fr. Dimitry was born in 1904 in Piatigorsk, Russia, to a devout Orthodox family. His father was an architect. After the family moved to Odessa, his mother Sophia established an Orthodox school and worked among the poor in Odessa. She was imprisoned in 1919 by a group called the Cheka, which would later become the KGB. She was, however, released after a short time.

Spiritual Cornerstones

In an article published online at *www.incommunion.org*, his daughter Helene Arjakovsy-Klepinin described two spiritual cornerstones in Fr. Dimitry's life: just after his mother was arrested, Dimitry went into a church to pray. He stood still with his hands behind his back and was scolded by a nun for standing this way. He vowed to never set foot in a church again.

Figure 15-2: Fr. Dimitry Klepinin

Ironically, the death of his mother in 1923 brought him back to the faith. He described his experience at her grave in a letter to a friend, "For the first time in my life I understood the meaning of suffering, when I realized that everything I hoped for in life had evaporated. . . I recalled the words of the Lord, 'Come unto Me, all ye that labor and are heavy laden and I will give you rest,' I went to my mother's grave with a heavy load of worldly sorrows, everything seeming so muddled up and forlorn, and suddenly 'I found the light yoke' of Christ."

In 1929, Dimitry graduated from the St. Serguis Theological Institute in Paris. Later, he was involved with the Russian Student Movement. He married Tamara Feodorovna Baimakova in 1937 and was ordained later that same year. Two years later he was called to serve at the parish of the Protection of the Mother of God, the shelter established by Mother Maria.

E-FACT

Within the Eastern Orthodox Church, married men are allowed to be ordained as priests, although they may not marry (or remarry) after they have been ordained. Within the Roman Catholic Church, married men have been barred from ordination since the Middle Ages.

Forging Documents

By 1942, Jews began to come to him, seeking baptism. He spent hours teaching them about the faith. Later, he was asked to issue false baptismal certificates. Although he never baptized anyone who did not show a genuine desire to be baptized, he willingly created the false baptismal certificates, saying, "In all times the Church has been a refuge for those who fall victim to barbarism."

On February 8, 1943, Nazi security police found a letter in Yuri's pocket that contained another request for Fr. Dimitry to create a false baptismal certificate. Fr. Dimitry was required to come for questioning before the Gestapo.

About Pascha (Easter) in occupied Paris: "Outside there were restrictions, fear, war. In the church, illuminated by the light of candles, our priest, dressed in white, seemed to be carried by the wings of the wind, proclaiming with a radiant face: 'Christ is risen!' Our reply, 'He is risen indeed!' tore apart the darkness." (from Helene Arjakovsky-Klepinin's article at www.incommunion.com).

The following morning, Fr. Dimitry served liturgy in a small chapel dedicated to St. Philip (a martyr-bishop who had been killed for protesting the crimes of Ivan the Terrible). He then walked to the Gestapo offices where he was interrogated. He immediately admitted everything, surprising the

German officer, Hoffman, who had assumed he would have to work to get the details out of Fr. Dimitry. In a *Young Life* article published in 1970, Sophie Koulomzin offered this account of Fr. Dimitry's interrogation:

> Hoffman said curtly, "And if we release you, will you promise never again to aid Jews?"
>
> Fr. Dimitry answered, "I can say no such thing. I am a Christian, and must act as I must."
>
> Hoffman stared at him in disbelief for a moment, and then struck Fr. Dimitry across his face. "Jew Lover!" he screamed. "How dare you talk of those pigs as being a Christian duty!"
>
> The frail Fr. Dimitry recovered his balance. Staying calm, he raised the cross from his cassock and faced Hoffman with it.
>
> "Do you know this Jew?" he said quietly.
>
> The blow he received knocked him to the floor.

After six more hours of interrogation, the soldiers came to the house to arrest Mother Maria. They told her, "Your priest has sentenced himself." Fr. Dimitry then said goodbye to his wife and two children, one four years old and the other six months old. He asked his wife to look after an elderly woman who lived nearby. Only later did the family come to understand why his visits to this lady were so lengthy: he used to chop wood for her, build her a fire, and bring her food and cook it for her.

Life in the Camp

Fr. Dimitry, Yuri, and their coworker Ilya Fondaminsky were transferred to a camp called Compiegne. There Fr. Dimitry helped prepare Yuri for the priesthood. Tamara was able to send Fr. Dimitry his vestments and service books, and working together with other prisoners, they created a small chapel, complete with hand-painted icons, an altar table, a hand-carved cross, and a chalice. Eucharist was celebrated daily and the Orthodox and Roman Catholics held alternate services there. Ilya Fondaminsky, a Jew, was finally baptized in their chapel. Afterward he wrote to a friend that he was "Ready for anything, whether life or death."

In January of 1944, Fr. Dimitry and Yuri were sent to a camp at Dora where they both became ill. Yuri developed furunculosis—his skin was covered in boils. His illness caused him to be sentenced to death. Fr. Dimitry died four days later, from pneumonia.

Just before his death, an old friend brought him his monthly note card on which he could write a short message to his loved ones. He just stared at the card, and then looked up at his friend. There were no more words. He died later that evening.

E-XTRA

After being liberated in 1945, fellow prisoner Pianov wrote of Fr. Dimitry, "I can say that that year with Fr. Dimitry was a godsend. From my experience with him, I learned to understand what enormous spiritual, psychological and moral support one man can give others as a friend, companion and confessor."

Glorification

Mother Maria, Fr. Dimitry, Yuri, and their companion and coworker Ilya Fondaminsky were canonized on May 1 and 2, 2004, at the Cathedral of St. Alexander Nevsky in Paris. They are commemorated on July 20.

They were the first modern Eastern Orthodox saints to be canonized in Western Europe. According to witness Nancy Forrest (to read her full account, visit *www.incommunion.com*) the services surrounding the canonization were beautiful and unusual. A very old white-haired woman was there at the church, seated in a place of honor—she was a survivor of the camps who had been with Mother Maria in her final days.

Many members of Fr. Dimitry's family were also present, including his daughter Helene Arjakovsky-Klepinin and her children. According to Nancy Forrest, Helene's daughter Tanya said that she and her mother felt as if "they had been taken out of themselves," the services were so beautiful; they had to pinch themselves to make sure they were really awake.

The most significant moment in the services occurred when the icons of the newly canonized saints were brought out into the church. The icons featured five saints: Fr. Alexis d'Ugine Medvedkov and the martyrs, Mother Maria, Yuri, Fr. Dimitry, and Ilya Fondaminsky.

E-FACT

Fr. Serge Hackel, Mother Maria's biographer, was present at the glorification as well, wearing tattered, handmade vestments. They were originally crafted by Mother Maria for Fr. Dimitry, and were discovered when a German film crew came to Paris to create a movie about Mother Maria.

Archbishop Gabriel, from Flanders, who had originally petitioned for the canonization of these saints, described them in a letter: "Faced with the trials of our times, they bring us a message of comfort and hope of absolute faithfulness to the Gospels of Christ: humility, gentleness, self-denial, concern for the weak and the oppressed, service to one's neighbor, a spirit of sacrifice and love, because, 'There is no greater love than to give one's life for one's Friend.'"

To learn more about Mother Maria and Fr. Dimitry, read Sergei Hackel's *Pearl of Great Price: The Life of Mother Maria Skobtsova 1891-1945* published in 1981 by St. Vladimir's Seminary Press. This book provided many valuable details for this chapter.

Chapter 16

A Bone to Build a Dream On

Everyone wants a piece of the saints—quite literally. Strange as it may seem to modern sensibilities, Christians have long treasured the bodies of the saints, believing that their relics held life-giving properties. Likewise, it has been common practice to dig up the bodies of the saints after some time to examine them for corruption, because of the traditional understanding that the bodies of God's holy ones often remain intact, sometimes even emitting a sweet fragrance. This chapter will explore the historical and theological roots of relic-lore.

The Unlikely Love of Relics

While it may seem strange that the Christians have traditionally treasured relics, this perspective was rooted in a different way of seeing the world. In the minds of the early Christians, the bodies of the saints were transformed into "temples of the Holy Spirit." (1 Corinthians 6:19) This transformation did not end when a saint entered eternal life, as the bodies of the saints were never viewed as "dead matter." Instead, these bodies have been long thought of as "asleep," awaiting the Resurrection.

For centuries, Christianity has contained both literal and figurative dimensions. It has been previously mentioned that Tertullian wrote, "the blood of the martyrs is the seed of the church." There are multiple ways to understand this. By laying down their lives for God, the early martyrs expressed their faith in a way that was so eloquent, courageous, and compelling that they could not help but plant seeds through this act. Those who saw Christians die this way often experienced a change of heart as a result.

E-XTRA

St. Augustine once said of the bodies of saints, "The bodies of saints will therefore rise again free from every defect, from every deformity, as well as from every corruption, encumbrance, or hindrance. In this respect, their freedom of action will be as complete as their happiness."

Historically, churches were built on the sites of holy relics, and relics have been contained in the altars of churches. When an Orthodox church is consecrated, relics from the body or clothing of a saint or a holy object she used are sealed into the altar as a way of sanctifying the space, and assuring the faithful of the continued presence of the holy ones. When possible, relics from the saint for which the church was named will be included, thus providing a concrete link to that person.

Biblical Roots

The scriptures (both the Old and New Testaments) do support some of the traditional beliefs surrounding relics. In the Old Testament (2 Kings 13:20–21), a dead man was once resurrected after touching the bones of the prophet Elisha. In the New Testament (Mark 5:25–29), a woman was healed after she touched the hem of Christ's robe. Likewise St. Paul's handkerchief healed in Acts 19:11–12.

On relics, from 2 Kings 13:20–21 (New International Version): "Elisha died and was buried . . . Once while some Israelites were burying a man, suddenly they saw a band of raiders, so they threw the man's body into Elisha's tomb. When the body touched Elisha's bones, the man came to life and stood up on his feet."

In all of these stories, the physical and spiritual are intertwined, so that the holiness of a person is not confined to his soul, but radiates throughout his body. This intermingling of the physical and spiritual does not end at death but continues even after the soul has continued on.

Relics and Pilgrimages

Historically, Christians traveled many miles to pray before the relics of a saint. It was believed (and still is, within many pockets of Christendom) that by praying before the relics of a saint one might experience healings or other spiritual blessings, in the same way that an encounter with a living saint can be transformative. This belief was connected to the idea that those who die in Christ do not die, but continue to live. The bodies of the saints, therefore, remained as a link to the holy person who now dwelt with God in heaven.

The belief in the holiness of relics was confirmed at the Seventh Ecumenical Council in Nicaea, Asia Minor, 787. At this council it was decreed that "Our Lord Jesus Christ granted to us the relics of Saints as a salvation-bearing source which pours forth varied benefits to the infirm. Consequently, those who presume to abandon the relics of the Martyrs: if they be hierarchs, let them be deposed; if however, monastics or laymen, let them merely be excommunicated."

Handling Death

Although in contemporary times one might be tempted to scoff at this view of relics, many contemporary practices surrounding death and burial would be scandalous to those of an earlier time. The way in which Western culture has institutionalized death might seem heartless to the earliest Christians, who saw their care for the dead as an extension of their care for the living. Imagine if Jesus had died in this age—there would have been no Joseph of Arimethea to tenderly care for Christ's body and no myrrh-bearing women to discover the resurrected Christ—instead, there would have been a fancy funeral parlor and undertaker who would have been hired to handle the whole business quietly and out of sight.

Joseph of Arimethea (First Century)

Joseph of Arimethea, who was fairly well-to-do and a clandestine follower of Jesus, was present at the Crucifixion and persuaded Pontius Pilate to let him have Jesus's body. He wrapped it in the finest linens and herbs and laid it inside a tomb that was carved from rock on the side of a hill. Joseph either paid for this tomb for Jesus or placed him in his own family's resting place, a brand new tomb, located in Jerusalem. It was said of Joseph that he was "waiting for the kingdom of God."

E-FACT

Patrick Henry Reardon, in *Christ in the Saints* (Conciliar Press, 2004), wrote that when Michelangelo painted his final Pieta, he drew Joseph in his own likeness. "That tomb, originally planned for Joseph, has been unoccupied these many centuries, a symbol of the hope we have for our own graves," Reardon wrote.

Little else is known about St. Joseph. He is supposed to have gone to Gaul (France) as a missionary. He is also said to have inherited the chalice used at the Last Supper. His feast day is commemorated on March 17. He is the patron saint of funeral directors and undertakers.

The Myrrh-Bearing Women

The Myrrh-bearing women were a small band of women, all closely associated with Jesus, who went to his tomb to anoint his body with myrrh and other spices. Only a few names are known: Salome, Joanna, Mary Magdalene, and "the other Mary."

These women went very early in the morning, hoping to continue their loving care for Jesus. They rose to anoint him with their spices. Instead of finding Jesus, however, they found an empty tomb. A man standing near the tomb—who could have been an angel or a gardener—announced to them that the tomb was empty because Jesus had already risen. These women were able to be the first to experience the Resurrection because of their willingness to care for Christ's body with their own hands.

Traditions Surrounding Corruption

In the famed Russian novel by Feodor Dostoyevsky, *The Brothers Karamazov,* there is a scene that might be particularly puzzling to those unfamiliar with the ancient traditions surrounding relics. Soon after the beloved spiritual father, Elder Zosima, dies, those from the village flock to his body, bringing sick children, as if they had been waiting for him to die so that they could experience a miracle. And yet the body, to the surprise of all who knew Elder Zosima, soon begins to stink. Immediately questions are raised about his holiness, and those who loved him most were devastated.

St. Ephraim the Syrian, on holy martyrs, "Even after their death they act as if alive, healing the sick, expelling demons and by the power of the Lord rejecting every evil influence of demons. This is because the miraculous grace of the Holy Spirit is always present in the holy relics."

Even in the book, however, one of the monks points out that saintliness is not always accompanied by incorruption. Although many of the saints' bodies did not decompose, there is no official church dogma related to this issue. While a lack of bodily corruption could be viewed as support for a person's saintliness, bodily corruption does not mean that a person was *not* holy.

As strange as this scene from *The Brothers Karamazov* may be, it does offer a glimpse into a more ancient Christian understanding. The belief that a lack of bodily decay points to saintliness may be partially based upon the idea that saints, by living lives of holiness, were able to anticipate the Resurrection in their own bodies, where the body and soul are reunited and continue to live with God. Because of this, their bodies often remained fresh and without decay, even in death—which is, for the saints, just more life.

A Sweet Aroma?

In Thessaloníki, Greece, the body of St. Demitrius, the Myrrh-Gusher, has continued to emit the bitter-sweet aroma of myrrh for many centuries. To this day, one can visit the church where his body is kept, lean over his casket, and smell this unforgettable aroma.

According to legend, St. Demitrius not only lays prone in his tomb, but he also walks through the town on a regular basis doing anonymous good works. This saint has apparently been so busy that he has worn out his shoes multiple times, so that they have had to be continually replaced.

E-QUESTION

Does the Bible speak of these types of aromas?
In 2 Corinthians 2:15–16, "For we are the aroma of Christ to God among those who are being saved and among those who are perishing, to one a fragrance from death to death, to the other a fragrance from life to life."

The sweet aroma that comes from his tomb is not a completely unknown phenomenon. Many of the bodies of the saints through the centuries have emitted a sweet scent, both during life and after their deaths. When St. Francis experienced the stigmata, his wounds occasionally gave off a sweet scent. Likewise, after St. Teresa of Ávila had been buried, her grave is said to have given off a sweet scent. During her lifetime, when she sinned, she used to say that she felt like she "smelled bad."

Classically, this type of unusual manifestation of God's grace has been taken as a sign by those who already believe and has not necessarily been viewed as compelling for those who do not believe—these "signs" do not always translate well into secular society, and perhaps they were never supposed to.

Although there is no firm theology surrounding the sweet aroma that comes from many bodies of the saints, this phenomenon points to a few theological beliefs. One, which dates all the way back to the Garden of Eden, is that sickness and death are a result of the Fall. The resulting corruption and stench was believed to be an earthly, not heavenly, phenomenon. Because the saints were able to make heavenly realities present through their lives, it was believed that even in death they made the Kingdom of God present on this earth. Likewise, because their lives were pure and represented a reversal of all that went wrong in Eden, it was believed that even their deaths represented a reversal of the ancient curse of sickness and death that came through Eden.

Often, in the lives of the saints, earthly realities are overturned. Unlike those on earth who sought earthly wealth and honor, the saints often gave up riches and fame to follow Christ. Although many of them experienced devastating illnesses while they lived on this earth, in death, their bodies often (but certainly not always) were able to emit a sweet-smelling aroma suggestive of the life to come.

Relics on the Black Market

One of the more tragic realities associated with relics is that although much good has come through them, abuses have occurred. The Church has officially forbidden the buying and selling of relics, but this has not stopped people from stealing little tidbits of relics. While the holiness of relics is supposed to suggest the goodness of God present in the bodies of saints, there are stories associated with relics that are a bit bizarre.

After St. Teresa of Ávila died, her body was cut up and distributed to those who admired her. Her confessor retained her left pinkie for himself. This finger, oddly enough, eventually ended up in the possession of the head of state in Spain, Generalissimo Francisco Franco. He placed Teresa's pinkie on his bedside table and kept it there until his death in 1975.

St. Jerome, in a letter to Riparius on relics: "We do not worship, we do not adore, for fear that we should bow down to the creature rather than to the Creator, but we venerate the relics of the martyrs in order to better adore him whose martyrs they are."

The Coveted Head of St. John the Baptist

In the Eastern Orthodox Church, the first, second, and third "findings" of the head of St. John the Baptist are commemorated. These commemorations are related to the quirky history surrounding St. John's head, which has been "lost" and rediscovered multiple times.

The head was first "found" by a nobleman named Innocent who built a cell for himself on the Mount of Olives. One day while digging into the earth to build a foundation for the church he hoped to build, he found the head of St. John the Baptist. Just before his death, he hid the head to protect it.

E-FACT

Within the Eastern Orthodox Church, on feast days devoted to St. John the Baptist, a pious custom dictates that one is not supposed to use round plates, because of the way that St. John was gruesomely beheaded. Because his head was placed on a platter, it is considered especially inappropriate to eat large, round objects—such as cabbages—on round plates on those days.

Later, two monks who visited the Mount of Olives rediscovered the head of St. John the Baptist. It was then passed between some Christian families, finally falling into the hands of a heretic named Eustace, who tucked it into a cave. Fortunately, a monastery was built on this site, and the abbot of the monastery, led by a vision, recovered the head once more in 452. Presently, no one is quite sure where St. John's head resides.

Vanishing Relics?

There are two significant figures in Christianity who have left behind no bodily relics. These two figures are Christ and the Virgin Mary. Both of them, however, reportedly left behind relics that are associated with things they touched or wore.

E-XTRA

The mother of the famed Emperor Constantine, Helena, found the Cross of Christ when she was in Jerusalem in the year 325. St. Helena ordered that a church be built on that spot and the Church of the Holy Sepulchre (or tomb) remains to this day.

The lack of relics associated with both Jesus and his mother have often been taken as support for the belief that both of them ascended into heaven, instead of remaining in the tomb to await the Resurrection. The relic most commonly associated with Christ is small slivers of wood from the "true cross." Although it really cannot be determined how many of these slivers—which have been embedded in icons and crosses all over the world—are authentic, it is believed that some of them are.

Figure 16-1: St. John the Baptist

The most famous relic associated with the Virgin Mary is her "belt," which was housed at the Blachernae Palace Church in a suburb of Constantinople. This church—perhaps because of its association with the relic—was also believed to be the site of a famous tenth-century apparition of the Virgin Mary in which she spread her protective veil over the congregation, astonishing those who witnessed it and giving rise to the celebrated feast of "Pokrov," a commemoration of the protection of the Virgin Mary.

Relics have had a rich and valuable place in the spirituality of Christians for centuries. The value of relics is not in their "shock value," and they are not "magical items." Relics remain as concrete links to the saints who have gone before, as well as to the spiritual realities they represent. They speak to the mystery of the Incarnation—through which physical matter was redeemed. Relics also speak to the hope of the Resurrection, to the way in which Christ's death transformed the way that Christians understood—and encountered—the deaths of their loved ones and their own death.

Chapter 17

Shrines and Saintly Stops

A pilgrimage is a journey to a place that has been hallowed by prayer and the footsteps of the holy ones who once walked there. Pilgrimages were extremely popular in the Middle Ages, and have again come into the public consciousness because of the widespread phenomenon of apparitions of the Virgin Mary. This chapter will explore a sampling of saintly stops around the world—offering a glimpse of spiritual destinations that feed the soul, heart, and mind.

The History of Pilgrimages

People have been making pilgrimages since at least the third century. Those who embarked on pilgrimages came from every rank of society—the poorest of the poor to monarchs and rulers. Likewise, the motivations of pilgrims varied—some came seeking healing, others for penance, still others out of mere curiosity.

E-XTRA

The prolific British author A.C. Benson, son of a late nineteenth-century Archbishop of Canterbury, Edward White Benson, likened life to a pilgrimage. He wrote, "As I make my slow pilgrimage through this world, a certain sense of beautiful mystery seems to gather and grow."

Pilgrimages were especially common during the Middle Ages, when the journeys to popular locations such as Jerusalem, Rome, and Santiago de Compostela in Spain (where the Apostle James is believed to have been buried) were arduous. The difficulty of the journey did not decrease the appeal of the pilgrimage. If anything, the hard road functioned as a catharsis. As pilgrims struggled toward holy places, they prayed with groans, offering their sufferings up to God and believing that with each step they took, they were a few steps closer to holiness and transformation.

Shrines, Cathedrals, and Basilicas Defined

A shrine is a building or complex that is a pilgrimage destination; the main focus is a cult figure, such as a saint. Lourdes, France, has a famed shrine dedicated to the Virgin Mary. There one can bathe in springs that are believed to be miraculous. One can seek spiritual, emotional, or physical healing, and many believe that they find what they seek.

A shrine can also be located in a church, marked by a relic, icon, or statue that the faithful visit for purposes of veneration.

A cathedral is a church where a bishop, archbishop, or cardinal presides. A cathedral serves as the seat of that particular diocese or archdiocese. It is usually, but not always, the most prominent religious edifice of that faith in a particular geographic area.

A basilica is a church with historical significance and one that continues to play a role in the religious life of a region. Basilicas generally have rich liturgical lives, celebrating more historical feast days than other churches and with more solemnity. Basilicas are expected to be models of liturgical celebration as well as places of pilgrimage.

"Major" basilicas are principal papal churches found only in Rome. They are of special historic note. Among them are St. Peter's, St. Mary Major, St. John Lateran, and St. Paul's Outside the Walls.

"Minor" basilicas carry special recognition from the Holy See. In this country they include the Sacred Heart Basilica on the campus of the University of Notre Dame in Indiana, the Cathedral of St. Augustine in St. Augustine, Florida, and the Mission Dolores in San Francisco (one of the chain of missions originally established by Bl. Junípero Serra). Confusing though it may seem, a church does not have to have "Basilica" in its name to be considered a minor basilica.

Figure 17-1: The National Shrine of the Immaculate Conception

Shrines in the United States

Although there are shrines and holy places all over the world, the next few pages will offer a small sampling of a few best-loved sites, both in the United States and abroad. Many of these places have rich historical and cultural traditions associated with them, and some are reported to be sites of apparitions of the Virgin Mary. If a person were to make a pilgrimage, he could expect to come away changed in ways that cannot be imagined or anticipated beforehand.

Washington, D.C.

The Roman Catholic patron saint of America is Mary. The National Shrine of the Immaculate Conception in Washington is a fascinating complex. The basilica there is the largest Roman Catholic church in the Western Hemisphere. It is Romanesque and Byzantine in style and is highlighted by a blue-domed roof.

The bell tower is reminiscent of St. Mark's in Venice, and holds a fifty-bell carillon. Regularly scheduled carillon concerts increase in number during the summer tourism months. The shrine also houses the largest collection of contemporary Christian art in the United States, most in honor of Mary. Some fifty-plus chapels are part of the complex, each of them also featuring an aspect of Mary or her life. This basilica offers the opportunity to come to know Mary better by learning about the different phases of her life. There is also a garden dedicated to Mary, offering a quiet place for prayer, retreat, and reflection.

Baltimore, Maryland

A well-worn path leads to the St. Jude Shrine, which honors the patron saint of lost causes and desperate situations. Located in the heart of Baltimore, the shrine has been open since 1917. Besides areas for prayer and gratitude, it features a Millennium Room in the visitors' center that offers a unique mix of history of the shrine and futuristic interactivity, including a virtual Wall of Honor, which memorializes friends and family, and celebrates birthdays, anniversaries, and other milestones.

Emmitsburg, Maryland

In the northwestern part of this state, just below the Pennsylvania border, is the National Shrine of St. Elizabeth Ann Seton. It was built in 1965, a full decade before Mother Seton's canonization.

This basilica holds the relics of St. Elizabeth Ann Seton. The grounds feature the Stone House where she lived with her companions in 1809 and the White House where they resided after 1810. It was here that she founded the first parochial school in the country.

There is also a museum dedicated to her life and work, and an information center. The nearby cemetery marks the place where Mother Seton was originally buried after her death in 1821.

A handful of miles from the Seton shrine is the Grotto of Lourdes, at the foot of the Catoctin Mountains. This is a shrine to Mary, a simple mountain sanctuary that was much loved by Mother Seton, who called it "wild and picturesque." This shrine offers ample opportunity for meditation on this woman's exceptional life. Stone and bronze Stations of the Cross lead the way along original pathways to the Grotto and the Corpus Christi Chapel.

St. Augustine, Florida

This town of 20,000 along Florida's northeast coast, just off Interstate 95, is the oldest permanent European settlement in the United States, dating from 1565. St. Augustine is commonly called America's oldest city, and was also home to the first Catholic Mass in the United States.

The mass was held in 1565 at the waterfront Mission of Nombre de Dios. The mission is topped by a huge cross, rising 200 feet and viewable from several miles around. The mission also includes a shrine to "Our Lady of la Leche" or "Our Lady of the Milk" dating back to 1615. This particular name for Mary is related to piety associated with the Virgin Mary's role as a nursing mother. There is also a charming, very small ivy-shrouded chapel, built in 1918.

Cicero, Illinois

At St. George's Antiochian Orthodox Church, an icon of the Virgin Mary holding her infant son began to weep on April 24, 1994. Since that date, tens of thousands of people have come to the church to pray before the icon. Some report healing as a result. Others believe that the weeping icon is a call to prayer, particularly for the troubled Middle East.

"I am a Palestinian. Most in our Church are from the Middle East. This is a very troubled part of the world. I believe the icon is giving us a wake-up call—telling us to pray for the world. The world is not doing very well." –Fr. Nicholas Dahdal, priest at St. George's.

Although the icon is not currently weeping, one can still glimpse four tear-streaks, two from the Virgin Mary's eyes and two from the eyes of her son. Many continue to come to the church to pray before the icon. In 1997, there was a fire in the church that destroyed much of the interior. The icon, however, remained virtually unharmed.

Darien, Illinois

The National Shrine of St. Thérèse is situated in this town west of Chicago. Contemporary in design, it features a chapel and museum dedicated to the "Little Flower," as well as special programs honoring Thérèse of Lisieux.

Libertyville, Illinois

The St. Maximilian Kolbe Shrine is situated in the Marytown friary, home of the Conventual Franciscan Friars of St. Bonaventure Province. The shrine honors the Polish saint who died in a Nazi prison camp in World War II. The unique community of Marytown is also the center of the Militia of the Immaculata Marian consecration movement, which was founded by that saint in 1917 (to learn more about St. Maximilian Kolbe and other Holocaust saints, see Chapter 15).

Golden, Colorado

The Mother Cabrini Shrine can be found just beyond the foothills of Golden, a western suburb of Denver. At this location, St. Frances Xavier Cabrini created a summer refuge for orphans. Mother Cabrini arranged large white stones in the shape of a heart, surrounded by a smaller stone cross and a crown of thorns. Nearly 800 steps lead to a 22-foot-high statue of the Sacred Heart. The steps are adorned by the Stations of the Cross, the Mysteries of the Rosary, and the Ten Commandments. It was here that Mother Cabrini discovered a spring of water on a barren hilltop, and the water still flows.

The shrine is administered by the Missionary Sisters of the Sacred Heart of Jesus, founded by Mother Cabrini, the first naturalized American citizen to be canonized.

Shrines in Canada

If you have an opportunity to travel to Canada, there are several significant Canadian shrines worth seeing. The following shrines testify to Canada's rich spiritual heritage and are architecturally significant as well.

Montreal, Quebec

St. Joseph's Oratory is a magnificent basilica and shrine dedicated to the patron saint of Canada. It is situated on the north slope of Mount Royal and, at 860 feet above sea level, is the highest point in Montreal. It is said to have the second-largest dome in the world, after St. Peter's Basilica in Rome. Founded as a tiny chapel in 1904 by Br. André, a member of the Holy Cross Order of Roman Catholic brothers, by 1922 it had grown into a 5,000-seat basilica.

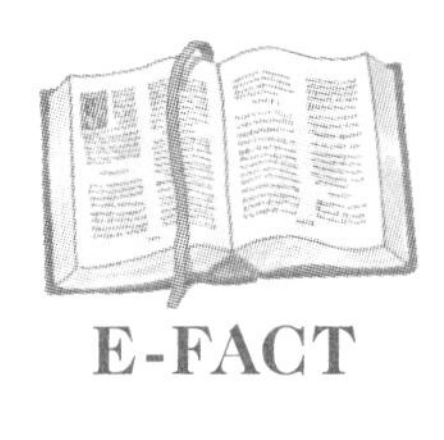

E-FACT

The carillon found at St. Joseph's was initially designed for Paris's Eiffel Tower but was found unsuitable for that landmark. It came to the oratory on loan in 1955 and is now a permanent fixture. Carillon concerts are held during the week and on weekends.

Quebec City

The famed Basilica of St. Anne de Beaupré is in the village of Beaupré, about 25 miles northeast of Quebec City, although it is usually included in "What to See in Quebec City" listings. Now quite large, the shrine began as a small monument of thanksgiving. In the 1650s, shipwrecked sailors rescued from the waters of the Gulf of St. Lawrence showed their gratitude to St. Anne, mother of the Virgin Mary, by founding a chapel in her name.

This chapel attracted the faithful in such large numbers that within a few years the little wooden structure had to be replaced by a larger fieldstone church. By 1876 the shrine had become the size of a basilica. Destroyed by fire in 1922, it was rebuilt the following year in a neo-Roman style.

Today the basilica can accommodate more than 3,000 and has over one million visitors a year. Some leave behind crutches, canes, and folding

Figure 17-2: Basilica of St. Anne de Beaupré

wheelchairs as a testament to their faith and the intercession of St. Anne. The fountain in front of the basilica is believed to have healing powers. The shrine is particularly crowded the week before St. Anne's feast day (July 26), as pilgrims make a nine-day novena ending in a candlelight procession on the eve of the feast.

Shrines in Mexico

The history of Mexico involves stories of conflict between the Spanish invaders and the local Aztec people. When missionaries came from Spain to bring the Roman Catholic faith to the local people, they struggled to establish credibility. Some historians believe that Mexico would not have become a Roman Catholic country if not for the intervention of the Virgin Mary at Guadalupe. The following shrine commemorates this extraordinary encounter.

E-QUESTION

Why do sailors pray to St. Anne?

There is an ancient tradition associated with seeking the intercessions of St. Anne for those who are lost at sea or storm-tossed. The famed Reformer Martin Luther asked for Anne's prayers when he was at sea during a violent storm, and when the storm became calm, he became a monk out of gratitude.

Our Lady of Guadalupe is one of the major shrines in the world and is an important attraction in Mexico City. This is where the Virgin Mary is believed to have appeared to Juan Diego, a young Indian boy, in December 1531. It was there that she requested that a shrine be built in her honor.

Figure 17-3: Our Lady of Guadalupe

The Virgin Mary's visit came during a time of violence and devastation. Just ten years prior to her visit, the Spaniards had brutally attacked the Aztecs. Although Spanish missionaries labored to bring the Gospel to the Aztecs, their efforts had been largely unsuccessful because of the tensions between the Spaniards and the Aztecs.

The Virgin Mary appeared as an Aztec to an Aztec, bringing a message of peace and reconciliation. Her visit was taken as a sign of a new era in which the Spaniards and the indigenous Mexicans could live peacefully side by side.

Juan Diego told his bishop about the apparition, but the older man was skeptical. A few days later, the youth returned to the site of the apparition and the lady once again appeared. He relayed the bishop's request for proof of her visitation, whereupon Mary instructed Juan to gather roses from the frozen, stony ground and take them to him. To his surprise Juan saw a great many Castilian roses and gathered them up in his cloak. When he stood in front of the bishop and opened his cloak, the roses tumbled out. The bishop fell down on the ground before the cloak (or tilma), which bore an image of the Virgin just as she appeared to Juan Diego. The famed Tilma of Guadalupe hangs above the main altar of the shrine today.

Juan Diego is buried at the site. The shrine, in the north of Mexico City, is always crowded, but particularly so on December 12, the feast of Our Lady of Guadalupe.

Shrines in Europe

Europe has a particularly rich spiritual history and many European countries continue to draw thousands of pilgrims to this day. Most of the popular shrines commemorate contemporary apparitions of the Virgin Mary.

Pilgrims have come to these shrines from all over the world, hoping for healing or spiritual refreshment, or simply to satisfy their own curiosity.

Ireland

Our Lady of Knock has become a major shrine in the west of Ireland, near Connemara, in County Mayo. In 1859, in the small village of Knock, the Blessed Virgin appeared to fifteen villagers near the local parish church. It was a "silent" apparition: Mary did not speak. The spot has since become a center of Irish Catholicism, and Knock has become so popular that it now has an airport to welcome visitors.

Also in Ireland is a famed natural monument to St. Patrick—Croagh Patrick is a mountain 2,500 feet high a few miles inland from Clew Bay on the west coast in County Mayo. The statue of St. Patrick guards the ascent to the mountain, the most sacred in Ireland.

E-XTRA

Croagh Patrick has been a pilgrimage site since the fifth century, when Patrick spent the forty days of Lent on its peak, praying and fasting. Today, every year on the last Sunday in July, as many as 60,000 people climb the mountain, some in bare feet, many ailing, seeking healing and spiritual growth.

Although the first part of the climb is not that difficult, the second leg can be exhausting, as movement slows and becomes labored. Be prepared: it takes five hours to climb Croagh Patrick, going up and then back down again. At the summit, however, is a magnificent view of the west and a small chapel, which, besides offering an opportunity for prayer, is a welcome refuge on a drizzly or chilly day.

Lourdes, France

This town of 18,000 in southwestern France on the edge of the Pyrenees is the site of one of the most famous shrines in Christendom. Between February and July 1858, the Virgin Mary appeared eighteen times to a young shepherdess, Bernadette Soubirous, who at the time of the first apparition was collecting firewood along the river Gave. One month after that vision, some 20,000 people followed Bernadette to the river, but she was the only one who saw Mary.

E-FACT

In one of the apparitions, Bernadette was instructed to drink and bathe from a spring that wasn't there. It started flowing the next day. This spring evolved into the miracle baths at Lourdes. There have been more than 5,000 cures reported from these waters, but the Church officially recognizes only sixty-six.

In March, just a month after the apparitions began, Bernadette was asked to have a chapel built to honor the Virgin Mary, who told the girl, "I am the Immaculate Conception." Today the complex at Lourdes attracts several million pilgrims and tourists annually.

Fatima, Portugal

Located in a small town about 100 miles north of Lisbon, this is the second most popular shrine in Europe after Lourdes. Fatima is the site where the Virgin is said to have appeared on May 13, 1917, to three shepherd children: Lucia dos Santos and her two cousins, Francesco and Jacinta Marto.

The three claimed to have seen a woman standing on a cloud in an evergreen tree. Her message directed the faithful to pray for peace (at that time the Great War was being waged in Europe). She asked the children to return on the thirteenth of each month until October.

Word of the vision spread. On October 13 there were an estimated 70,000 people in the field awaiting the apparition. Mary was visible only to the children, but many claimed to witness the "miracle of the sun." A golden ball of light twirled in the heavens and then plunged toward the earth before rising back to the sky. Those who witnessed this fell on the ground in terror, believing that the world was coming to an end.

At Fatima, the Virgin Mary is said to have correctly predicted the rise and fall of Communism, as well as World War II. The visions began during World War I, and she told the children that although the current war would end, a worse war would follow.

The apparitions at Fatima are said to be closely associated with "secrets," which were not to be revealed until specific times. The third secret was supposed to be revealed in 1960, but when Pope John XXIII opened the message containing the secret he read it and quickly resealed it. Every pope since then has read the message, but the contents remained a mystery.

This has led the faithful to believe that the message included information about an apocalyptic event and, especially at the turn of the millennium, many called for the disclosure of the secret. The third secret was finally revealed at Fatima in May of 2000 when Pope John Paul II presided at the beatification ceremony of Francesco and Jacinta (Sr. Lucy was still alive at the time). The third secret, he said, involved the shooting of a bishop dressed in white, which the pope interpreted as the assassination attempt on his own life in 1981 in Rome.

Like Lourdes, the apparitions that occurred at Fatima are viewed as "accredited" by the Roman Catholic Church, but the faithful are not required to believe in the apparitions or the healings associated with them. The last of the three "seers," Sr. Lucy dos Santos, died on February 13, 2005. She was ninety-seven years old. The case for her canonization has not yet been opened, as the Church generally waits five years after a death to begin the process.

Rome, Italy

St. Peter's Basilica is a magnificent structure, originally constructed as a church to house the tomb of St. Peter, by Emperor Constantine in the fourth century. The original building was repeatedly damaged by fire and then rebuilt. Then in the sixteenth century Pope Julius II asked the noted architect Bramante to draw up plans for a new basilica.

After John Paul II survived the assassination attempt at St. Peter's Square, he visited the shrine at Fatima and deposited bullet fragments into the crown of a statue of the Virgin Mary. He credited her with his survival. The assassination attempt occurred on May 13, 1981, the anniversary of the first apparition at Fatima.

The dome was designed by Michelangelo, who also painted the ceiling. The canopy over the altar is from the later architect and master, Gian Lorenzo Bernini, who, in the seventeenth century, also designed the ellipse outside that is St. Peter's Square. The basilica contains the tombs of many popes. All of the buildings in the religious complex are part of Vatican City, an independent state within the city of Rome.

Figure 17-4: St. Peter's Basilica

Outside the Vatican there are other "must-see" churches in Rome: the basilicas of St. Mary Major and St. John Lateran, and St. Paul's Outside the Walls, where St. Paul of Tarsus is buried.

Czestochowa, Poland

Our Lady of Czestochowa (pronounced chesh-ta-HO-va), or the Jasna Gora shrine, is named for the abbey of the Pauline Brothers where it is situated. It is also known as the Shrine of the Black Madonna. The Black Madonna is not, as some think, of African origin. The icon, probably brought from Byzantium, has never been cleaned or polished.

Czestochowa is an industrial city of about 250,000 in south-central Poland. The Madonna's role in nearby Jasna Gora (Hill of Light) came about in the fourteenth century when Prince Ladislaus Opolszyk was transporting the icon, which historians say is a ninth-century Greek or Greek-Italian work, from the Ukraine to Opala. At Czestochowa he stayed overnight at the Jasna Gora abbey, storing the portrait. In the morning the wagon holding it would not move. Ladislaus took that as a sign it was meant to stay in Czestochowa, and he built a chapel there to display it and a monastery for monks to care for it.

E-XTRA

The icon in Czestochowa is slightly damaged: the Virgin Mary's cheek contains scars, created by bandits. When they attempted to steal the icon, it became so heavy that they could not carry it. In a fit of rage, they slashed the Virgin's cheeks and threw the icon into a ravine.

Our Lady of Czestochowa was declared the Queen of Poland in 1656. It is the nation's principal shrine, which was much loved by Pope John Paul II. On major feast days, as many as 500,000 people make the pilgrimage to Jasna Gora to venerate the icon, and this tradition remained strong even during the Communist and German occupations when religious pilgrimages were extremely risky.

Medjugorje, Herzegovina

On June 24, 1981, in the Croatian mountain village of Medjugorje (med-JOO-gaw-ree), the Virgin Mary appeared to six children—and continues to do so. The apparitions have occurred at both the original site and in the village church of St. James. Identifying herself as the Blessed Virgin Mary, Queen of Peace, she has asked for reconciliation and prayer. She has also said, "I have come to tell the world that God exists." Many who have visited Medjugorje have experienced healing and spiritual growth.

Ever cautious, the Roman Catholic Church has no formal position on these apparitions, although Pope John Paul II has visited the site, and some bishops have spoken favorably of it. Medjugorje has become so popular that it currently competes with Fatima and Lourdes as a pilgrimage site, despite the ravages of war surrounding it. According to a *Wall Street Journal* article from November 9, 1992, "The war has enhanced Medjugorje's fame as an oasis of peace and mystery."

Chapter 18

How the Veneration of Saints Grew

How did martyrs get to be saints, anyway? Did someone write down a Christian's name when he or she was slain, adding a note about that individual's bravery as a martyr, and then pass it along to other Christians? Actually, that is something like what actually happened. One did not have to be a martyr, however, to become a saint. This chapter will explore the lives of a few of the earliest saints.

Virgins and Ascetics

Around the fourth century there arose two divergent "lifestyles" for women. Certain Christian women elected to stay unmarried and chaste, considering themselves brides of Christ (e.g., St. Agnes and St. Lucy). Choosing to remain virgins caused problems for many women, especially if they were not in Christian families. Even Christian parents often gave their daughters a difficult time about the decision, especially if a proper marriage was needed to improve the family fortunes.

E-FACT

Not everybody who admitted to being a Christian during this time was killed for his faith. Men and women who had the good fortune to live through their ordeals or court trials were called confessors. They might have suffered a good deal in prison and may even have endured exile, but they survived. After their death they were accorded the same honor that went to martyrs.

These women usually entered a religious order. For many of them, remaining a virgin and becoming religious was a declaration of independence—the only way out of leading a life traditionally imposed on them. While their motives were almost certainly piety and a desire to commit their lives to God, no doubt there were women who just did not want to marry or who did not want to marry the man chosen for them.

In religious life, too, a woman could learn, sometimes rising to the position of superior in her convent. The convent was not always a cloistered life of prayer: some women taught, some wrote, and some did works of charity outside the convent walls.

Christian men, especially monks, chose the path of the ascetic. A monk, or even a man affiliated with no religious order, would walk off into the desert or woods, existing on food he could pick from the vegitation. He spent his time in prayer and contemplation—and sometimes self-flagellation and other extreme mortifications. All of this was done to become closer to God. The hermitlike, celibate existence was difficult and, when taken to an extreme, was similar to a slow martyrdom.

Ascetics sometimes viewed this way of life as a temporary measure to atone for a sin or crime or to plead a favor with God. For example, Joachim, father of Mary, went into the desert and fasted and prayed for forty days (see Chapter 2). Usually this was a choice for a longer period, sometimes even the remainder of a man's life.

Saint Who?

Until about the fifth century, saints were honored only in the place they came from, which was usually a village. They were recognized as saints by acclamation in that community; in those days the infant church had no requirements as to who should or should not be canonized. "Polycarp—the man was a saint!" someone would say with gusto. Others would agree: "No doubt about it!" The town would note his name and from then on pay him the veneration due one so worthy. This would include praying for his intercession in one matter or another, celebrating the day he died, and, of course, passing on his story orally and in writing.

Records were kept of those who died as martyrs, as well as prominent religious figures and holy men and women. Their names were read during church services.

E-XTRA

All martyrs, known and unknown, were honored in an umbrella celebration called Feast of All Martyrs, which was instituted in the fifth century. It later evolved into the present All Saints' Day.

This system worked well in small towns. Naturally, no one outside those hamlets knew about those particular saints. People were specially appointed to keep track of listings of the names of martyrs and other Christians of note who died in large cities such as Rome. In times of intensive persecution, however, so many were killed that only the more famous names were recorded.

News traveled more slowly in the early centuries than it does now, but people were just as curious then about what went on around them as we are today. Towns and cities began exchanging lists of martyrs and other holy people, especially those famous for, say, how they died or their acclaim as preachers. They would sometimes trade relics of the person as well, which is how a relic of an Italian saint could end up in a church in another country. If a town had the name of a special martyr and a relic of him or her, the residents considered themselves twice blessed and twice as protected by that saint.

Getting Organized

The towns and cities that kept a record of native holy people, whom they could venerate and around whom they could hold festivals, were fortunate. But as Christianity spread, new nations that adopted the religion found themselves in a quandary when it came to saints. Obviously they had no Christian history, so they requested lists—usually from Rome, the largest city—with the names of many saints. From that base they added their own saints as they acquired them. Lending out lists and getting new lists from other countries is how some saints became universally known.

During the Middle Ages, the system became more organized. Lists of saints who had broad appeal were sent from the Holy See in Rome to every nation or community. For example, there was a consensus in Rome that the gospel writers should be known and venerated by Christians everywhere, so they were placed on what would become a universal list. As new Christian nations developed their own holy people, they would send those names to Rome for inclusion in the growing master list.

Going Overboard

Veneration of the saints was admirable, but sometimes it went to excess. Cults developed around certain saints; the faithful became obsessed with relics, sometimes dividing them up into smaller and smaller parts and selling them.

These were not cults as we know the term today; rather, they were supporters of a particular holy person, interested in advancing his or her cause toward sainthood or venerating the saint. Unfortunately, some Christians became obsessed with miracles and superstitions surrounding their favorite saint, which made the Church feel there might be too much emphasis on saints at the expense of worshiping God.

Thus a practice was established of having the regional bishop decide, after reading the would-be saint's biography and account of miracles attributed to him or her, whether that person should be approved as a saint, with a feast day assigned in that region.

This was a start, but papal approval of favorite saints carried more prestige than the acknowledgment of a mere bishop. Involving Rome also allowed decisions to be made on unbiased knowledge of the life of a candidate for sainthood. Thus in 993 Ulric of Augsburg, a bishop, was declared a saint in the first papal canonization.

Back to Reason, and Sensible Veneration

The canonization process was refined over the centuries until, in 1284, papal approval was the only legitimate path to official recognition of sainthood for Roman Catholics. By then lists of saints' names had been compiled, and the days when huge numbers of martyrs were being regularly added to the lists were over.

Relics, too, gave way to more practical symbols. After all, there were only so many bits of bone and hanks of hair to go around, and the church frowned on selling them! Also, the burial sites of saints belonging to the earliest age of the church were uncertain, and saints who were, for example, burned to death sometimes left no relics.

The new symbols that cropped up could be more easily seen by the faithful, or even bought by them. They could be mass-produced as well—or at least as mass-produced as those early centuries would allow. They could be sizable and expensive works of art, or they could be small reminders of a holy person—a drawing, or perhaps a medal or a ring.

Paintings depict saints in a form unique to that person's life, or perhaps death. St. Cecilia, for example, a patron of musicians, is painted playing an organ. St. Peter, the first pope, holds keys, symbols of "the keys of the kingdom." St. Nicholas is portrayed with three golden balls or bags of gold, symbolizing his gift to the three young sisters without a dowry. And of course there is St. Sebastian with those punishing arrows.

The Rise of Patron Saints

The practice of appointing saints as patrons of specific occupations, or to intercede for those suffering from particular illnesses, or for other special causes came about as local people believed that a particular saint had performed miracles for them or interceded for them for a special favor, which was usually related to an incident in that holy person's life.

E-FACT

As missionaries traveled the globe to spread the word of Christianity, they named sites where they landed, and eventually preached, after saints. In America, a whole state was named after one: Maryland, for Mary, the mother of Jesus. A huge number of towns and cities in this country are also named after saints.

The naming of patron saints is an ongoing, continuing practice; patrons are named for practically every aspect of life. This is an informal process, not at all like canonization. Churches, children, and cities are named for saints, as a way of invoking their presence as well as offering young people a holy example to live toward.

Chapter 19

Disappearing Saints

Over the years, superstitious and legendary elements have been incorporated into some of the saints' lives. It also seems that some of the saints who have been loved for centuries may not actually have existed. This chapter will explore the "back stories" related to some of the saints who no longer occupy a prominent place in the Roman Catholic Church calendar, whether because their stories were disproved or because it was decided that there wasn't enough evidence to support them.

What Is Hagiography?

Hagiography is the genre that the more ancient saints' stories generally fall into. This genre should not be thought of as a straight, historical relating of facts. Hagiographers (or the writers of this type of literature) sought to express spiritual ideals, to edify their listeners, and to entertain.

The ancient stories of the saints often contain fanciful elements that were built around a kernel of truth. This was not a major concern for hagiographers, who did not have the strict, literal compulsion to "get the facts right" that is present in contemporary academia. Instead, the hagiographers sought to be good storytellers. They often relied on shaky sources like oral tradition, and many stories had already been exaggerated and distorted before they were captured on paper. Hagiographers were also generally not overly concerned with citing their sources, and plagiarism was generally acceptable. Because so many stories were copied and mingled with others, it can sometimes be difficult to identify the real saint behind the multitude of stories.

Because of the unique genre of hagiography, contemporary religious scholars and historians puzzle over the ancient narratives. What is one to make, for example, of the three separate accounts of two brothers named Sts. Cosmas and Damian who were all physicians and pharmacists? Could it be possible that three such pairs of brothers existed, all in the same general location and with similar life stories? Or is this multiplication of accounts the result of hagiographers?

The Bollandists

Because of the many challenges associated with hagiography, a Catholic group called the Bollandists formed in Belgium in the eighteenth century. This group is charged with the weighty task of separating fact from fiction, of puzzling over the ancient manuscripts and determining historical accuracy and authenticity.

They have been commissioned with the work of revising the Roman Martyrology, checking for accuracy and correcting chronological problems. They have also sought to identify the saints who may not actually have existed. The work of the Bollandists is incredibly challenging, because it is far easier to prove that a person existed than it is to show that she never lived.

In many instances, details of demoted saints' lives, beyond name and perhaps date and place of death, are legend rather than fact. They have not been declared fictional characters; it is still thought that there is a kernel of truth to their existence. Nor is the Church tossing them out, but just relegating them to what you might call another list—sort of a B-list. The Church wants to be fair to the public in presenting saints who have a well-documented life.

The men and women who follow still show up on some calendars of saints' feast days (the difference between those calendars and a liturgical calendar is explained in Appendix C) and are patron saints of specific causes.

St. Barbara

Her birth and death dates are unknown, but it is said that she lived in the Middle Ages. According to legend, Barbara was martyred by her pagan father because of her faith. Before her death she was held prisoner in a tower where, during one of her father's absences, she had three windows built to explain the Trinity. When her father returned, he took her before a judge, who had her tortured. Still not satisfied, her father took her to a mountaintop and killed her. He was destroyed by fire as he came down the mountain.

Figure 19-1: St. Barbara

Her feast day of December 4 is still listed in some reference works, and she is the patron saint of architects and builders. However, the Church says her existence is doubtful.

St. Catherine of Alexandria

Catherine was said to have lived in the early fourth century, the daughter of an aristocratic family in the Egyptian city of Alexandria. She studied philosophy, rather unusual for a young lady at the time, and became convinced of the truth of Christianity. At eighteen, determined to convert the emperor, she allowed him to have her tested by fifty of the top minds of his court. They could not dispute anything she argued, and so they converted. Then they were burned to death.

The emperor was so impressed with Catherine he asked her to be his consort. She declined and was imprisoned. While incarcerated, Catherine converted the emperor's wife. Then the torture began. The legend goes that everyone who came in contact with her—her jailer, the imperial guards—was killed.

Catherine was next. She was subjected to four wheels, each studded with sharp nails. Two wheels turned in one direction and two in the other, two of them coming down on her body from the top and the other two mauling her from below. She was to be mangled to death. To this day, a wheel with spikes projecting from the rim is known as a Catherine wheel.

E-FACT

St. Catherine was one of the most beloved saints of the Middle Ages, and was considered "one of the fourteen most helpful saints in heaven." Preachers loved to incorporate her story into their sermons, and she was the subject of much poetry, despite some of the fantastical elements of her story.

The wheel, however, could not claim her. An angel struck the contraption before it hurt Catherine. There is no happy ending here, however, unless you consider her moving on to glory: she was finally beheaded. St. Catherine of Alexandria is the patron saint of librarians, lawyers, maidens/virgins, and craftsmen. Her feast day, November 29, was dropped from the liturgical calendar in 1969.

St. Christopher

The most famous disappearing saint is Christopher. In 1969, four years after the end of Vatican Council II, Christopher was demoted. What has been handed down of his life, the Church says, appears to be primarily legend.

Figure 19-2: St. Christopher

How many drivers in days of old (pre-1969) carried St. Christopher medals or statues of him on the dashboard of their car so that the patron saint of travelers would protect them? How many still do, despite his having been downgraded? These drivers must think, "Well, it can't hurt."

The patron saint of travelers has also appeared on medals in the wallets of tourists and business travelers, and small statues tucked in their luggage. A going-away gift to a relative or friend was often a St. Christopher medal. Here was a saint who sold a lot of product in religious stores.

Christopher became a Christian and set out to convert others. Unfortunately for him, as you have read throughout this book, those early few centuries of Christianity were particularly difficult for the newly converted, and Christopher was martyred by the Roman emperor Decius. He was burned at a stake, but the flames did not touch him. Beheading finally accomplished the job.

E-XTRA

Legend dates Christopher back to the early third century. It is said he was a giant of a man, so large he was able to ferry people across a river in his arms or on his shoulder. On one trip, the legend goes, he nearly drowned carrying a child—who turned out to be Jesus.

St. Christopher no longer has a feast day, but the Church still recognizes that people venerate him as the patron saint of travelers, bus drivers, and porters. He is also invoked against tempests and plague.

St. Julian the Innkeeper (or Hospitaler)

His is a great story, so good it is possibly fiction.

Julian was a nobleman who lived in the Middle Ages (no dates for his life are known). One day while hunting he was told by a deer he was stalking that there would come a day when Julian would kill his mother and father. Impossible, thought Julian, but he moved to a faraway land to avoid any possibility of that happening.

E-FACT

Not only is the term "hagiography" used to refer to the genre that these stories of holy men and women fall into, but it is also sometimes used as a negative description of contemporary writings in which the author is uncritical and unscholarly.

He eventually married a wealthy widow and moved into her castle. One day while he was away, his parents came to visit. His wife gave them her bed. When Julian returned later that night rather than in the morning when he was expected, he saw a man and woman in his bed and assumed it was his wife and a lover. He killed them both. Imagine his surprise when he saw his wife walk in from church and realized his mistake. Overcome by guilt, he left the castle to do penance, accompanied by his spouse, who had apparently forgiven his mistrust. The two used their money to build an inn for travelers near a river and a hospital for the poor.

One day Julian found a dying man on the banks of the river and brought him home, putting him in his own bed. The man turned out to be an angel who assured Julian that God had forgiven him, adding that soon both Julian and his wife would be going to their reward. Both died within a few days.

It is thought that perhaps a clergyman made up this tale to show God's mercy and forgiveness no matter what the sin. But even that cannot be documented.

St. Julian's feast day of February 12 remains on some listings but not on the liturgical calendar. He is the patron saint of innkeepers and hotel workers and boatmen.

Figure 19-3: St. Philomena

St. Philomena

Philomena was a virgin and martyr in the early days of Christianity. A cult developed around her when bones of a young girl were found along with a small vial of what was thought to be blood. A tablet nearby carried an inscription that when translated read "Peace be with you, Philomena." All of this turned up in the St. Priscilla catacomb in Rome.

Early in the nineteenth century, miracles began to be reported at Philomena's tomb, which had been moved from the catacomb. Devotion to this saint grew to the point where Pope Gregory XVI legitimized her cult in 1837 and gave her the feast day of August 11. Philomena was a favorite saint of St. John-Baptiste Vianney, the Curé of Ars, known for his kindness as a confessor, who lived during her most popular years.

However, her name is no longer on the liturgical calendar. The church "suppressed" her feast day because there was so little known about her.

Chapter 20

Waiting to Be Tapped for Sainthood

Around the world there are numerous men and women at some stage of the canonization process, even if only at the grass-roots level. Some have already been beatified, while others are known only through the stories that are told about them. Those waiting to be tapped for sainthood come from a variety of ranks—popes and bishops, nuns and Eastern Orthodox priests' wives. This chapter will offer an introduction to these remarkable, often surprising, contemporary lives.

Mother Teresa of Calcutta (1910–1997)

Mother Teresa was born Agnes Gonxha Bojaxhiu in Skopje, Yugoslavia. At seventeen she left for Ireland to become a nun, and shortly after that, as Sr. Agnes, began teaching in India. When she was in her thirties she received what she described as "a call within a call." She believed that God was calling her to "be poor with the poor," she said, "and to love him in the distressing disguise of the poorest of the poor."

E-XTRA

Mother Teresa had a few critics who claimed she did not take full advantage of modern medical equipment that could have been made available. Others felt she did not "campaign" enough to change existing social structures, to which she replied, "We are not social workers."

With permission, Sr. Agnes left her convent, went to Calcutta, put on a white sari with blue trim and founded the religious order the Missionaries of Charity. Mother Teresa toiled for years with the homeless and the desperately sick, but she seemed to have a particular affinity for working with the poor who were dying. She wanted those who had lived so roughly to "die like angels."

Mother Teresa did not care for the administrative end of her job and was sometimes dismayed at the checks that came in from donors, because they required additional paperwork. The administrative tasks kept her from the ones who needed her, she said. The Missionaries of Charity eventually spread to eighty-two countries, doing, as their founder said, "small things with great love," which was the philosophy of the already canonized St. Thérèse of Lisieux, who fostered the "little way."

Figure 20-1: Mother Teresa

Figure 20-2: Pope John XXIII

Mother Teresa died peacefully in India on September 5, 1997. She was beatified in 2003 by Pope John Paul II, and she is expected to be canonized soon. The standard five-year waiting period before beginning the canonization process was waived for this remarkable woman who won the Nobel Peace Price in 1979 and was widely regarded as "A Living Saint."

Pope John XXIII (1881–1963)

He was pope from 1958 to 1963, a warm, friendly man, almost always smiling, in contrast to his predecessor, the usually serious-looking Pius XII. Pope John XXIII has since been called the most beloved pope of modern times, maybe of all time.

Born Angelo Giuseppe Roncalli, he served as a papal diplomat for twenty-five years in Bulgaria, France, and Turkey, then spent several years as patriarch of Venice. As Cardinal Roncalli, he was elected pope just before his seventy-seventh birthday. His was to be a transitional papacy, a few years sandwiched between the brilliant Pius XII and Giovanni Battista Montini, a younger cardinal who seemed likely to follow John.

E-XTRA

Pope John XXIII said that while he was drifting off to sleep at night, important thoughts would often come to him. "I must speak to the Pope about that," he would say to himself. Then, he explained, "I would be wide awake and remember, 'I am the Pope!'"

Vatican II

But Cardinal Roncalli surprised everyone. He had a brief papacy, but it certainly wasn't a quiet one. After six months in the office, he called Vatican Council II (the first council was held several centuries earlier). This was a meeting at St. Peter's Basilica of the world's cardinals and other high dignitaries. It opened in October 1962 and met in four separate sessions of a few months each, ending in December 1965.

The council did not convene to condemn errors or heresy. It concentrated on mercy, promotion of peace, and an ecumenical outreach, as well as returning the church to its earlier historical and biblical roots.

It was also the first council that made full use of electronics. There was no World Wide Web in 1962, but cameras, lights, television, and print media were present, bringing the council's work into millions of homes.

Change was whipping around the world in the 1960s and those winds blew through the Vatican as well. In an attempt to make church services more open and accessible, the mass was now to be said in the vernacular, or language of that country, instead of Latin.

The Roman Catholic Church has never been the same since Vatican II, although there are mixed opinions about the results of this council. While some feel that the changes were largely positive, others feel that many of the changes took away from the dignity and solemnity of the services.

"This Big Ship"

John XXIII himself, before and during the council, was a man of peace, struggling to reach out to secular and religious enemies of the Church. His manner was warm and disarming and many were eager to have an audience with him. Unfortunately, Pope John did not live to see the second year of the council or to conclude it. Diagnosed with stomach cancer, he died in June 1963. At that time he remarked to a friend: "At least I have launched this big ship—others will have to bring it into port." The second phase of the council opened in September 1963, headed by Cardinal Montini, who had become Pope Paul VI.

In February 2000, the pope beatified John XXIII, who is now known as "Blessed." At least one miracle has been attributed to him. After verification of a second, he will be formally canonized.

Pope Pius XII (1876–1958)

Pius XII, John XXIII's immediate predecessor, was the first pope to be heard widely on radio and seen on television. Opinions about his possible canonization vary, however, because of some his policies during World War II.

Pius XII was born Eugenio Pacelli. Ordained in 1899, his was not to be the path of the typical Italian parish priest. Just two years after his ordination he entered the papal service, teaching international law to papal diplomats in Rome. He became nuncio to Bavaria in 1917, then to the new German Republic in 1920, and finally, before his accession to the papacy, held the post of papal secretary of state. He admired the strength of German Catholicism. When he became pope on March 2, 1939, he chose Germans for his close advisers.

As Pope Pius XII, he promoted Marian devotion and declared a Marian year, defining the church dogma that is known as the Assumption. The number of dioceses during his papacy grew from 1,696 to 2,048. Pius XII also appointed many native bishops in Asia and Africa and bestowed a cardinal's hat on some bishops from those continents. He also struggled against the growing menace of Communism, which he strongly opposed, during those years. He served as pope until his death on October 9, 1958.

In recent years, however, there has been some controversy as Pius XII has been accused of appeasing Germany during World War II. The Vatican defends the silence from the papacy at that time as discretion: the pope could accomplish more by not facing down the Nazis. He was, after all, a trained diplomat.

But his opponents say the pope could have done much more to save Jews during the Holocaust—he could at least have spoken out against Hitler. On the other hand, some Jewish leaders support the pope, saying he did manage to save Jewish lives during the war, as well as sending financial help to those in need.

Pius XII's canonization is not likely to be soon, because of the controversies that surround him. It is difficult to know what was in the mind and heart of Pius XII during the war.

Did his affection for Germany keep him from recognizing evil in the rise of Hitler? Did it blind him from doing more? Or did he accomplish more than anyone has thought, but quietly? The issue is not likely to be resolved to the satisfaction of both sides in this continuing drama.

Dorothy Day (1897–1980)

Like many of the contemporary figures profiled in this book, Dorothy Day was not always a person of faith. She became a Roman Catholic as an adult, after struggling with many essential questions and sacrificing intimate relationships so that she could grow closer to God.

She was born in Brooklyn and baptized into the Episcopal Church. Her father claimed to be an atheist, and Dorothy had little to do with religion in her youth, although even as a child she was attracted to the stories of the saints.

She attended college for two years, and then worked for a socialist daily newspaper in Manhattan. When that newspaper folded, she worked for another one. She made many friends during her time in New York. Together, they frequented Greenwich Village cafes and discussed politics, socialism, and the war that America had just entered.

Figure 20-3: Dorothy Day

As her awareness of inequality increased, she decided to join a group headed to Washington, D.C., to stage a protest for women's suffrage.

Dorothy and her companions were arrested. While serving a ten-day prison sentence she asked a guard for a Bible. In writing about the incident later, she said that she convinced herself that she was not interested in religion, just in reading the Bible as literature.

Released from prison, Dorothy spent the next several years adrift. She wrote and even published a novel, *The Eleventh Virgin*. She enrolled in a nurses' training program. She had a lover, then a pregnancy that she aborted. She was haunted by the abortion for the rest of her life. She was also married for a short time and then divorced. During these years, her desire for religion increased, but she had no one to discuss it with: most of her friends were atheists.

Although Dorothy Day was attracted to Christianity, she struggled with this question: "Why was so much done in remedying the evil instead of avoiding it in the first place . . . Where were the saints to try to change the social order, not just to minister to the slaves but to do away with slavery?"

She fell in love again, and entered into what she called "a common-law marriage." At twenty-nine, Dorothy gave birth to a baby girl named Tamar, and she began to sense the presence of God in her life. Her partner had no use for her religious impulses, and he told her that should she become Catholic their relationship would end. Bravely, she decided to baptize the child and to join the Church.

By 1932 the country was in the midst of the Depression. She and Tamar were living in an apartment in Manhattan she shared with her younger brother and his wife. Dorothy was thirty-five and felt aimless.

Then one day she opened the door to find fifty-five-year-old Frenchman Peter Maurin on the other side, his pockets stuffed full of pamphlets. He had taught in France, but left to try his luck in Canada. In 1911 he moved to the United States, drifting from job to job and reading constantly. He talked to Dorothy about spiritual values and the materialism of the world. He told her he was convinced he should publish a newspaper, but he needed someone to work with him. Dorothy's training as a journalist came in handy, and a lifelong partnership began.

The Newspaper

Together, Dorothy and Peter started the *Catholic Worker*, a newspaper that sold for a penny a copy. It carried articles condemning racial inequality, the crime of child labor, the plight of West Virginia coal miners, the homeless, and other suffering groups of people. The paper was funded by contributions.

With the help of these donations, Dorothy was able to move to a home in Greenwich Village that became a "hospitality house." Anyone who knocked on that door looking for food or shelter was welcome, no matter how bedraggled or disruptive they were. "They are a member of the family in Christ," she would say.

Each day during the Depression hundreds of men came to the hospitality house for coffee and bread. By 1941 there were some thirty hospitality houses in this country and one in England.

In 1949 Peter Maurin died, but Dorothy continued with speaking engagements. Her last major trip was in August of 1973 when she flew to California to join a demonstration led by Cesar Chavez, for his United Farm Workers Union. Photographs at the time show her seated on a folding chair, protected from the sun by a large straw hat, and flanked by police and farm workers. She was arrested that day for violating an injunction limiting picketing. She was seventy-six.

On November 29, 1980, Dorothy Day died, with Tamar at her side. She was eighty-three years old.

The Movement Continues

By the mid-1990s there were more than 100 Catholic Worker houses of hospitality and farms across the United States and around the world. Each operates independently, although all conform to the vision Dorothy Day expressed in her talks and books. There is still a *Catholic Worker* newspaper, published in New York City, with a circulation of 90,000.

The Canonization Question

Although some saw her saintly qualities, others only saw the strikes against her: her out-of-wedlock child, her lovers, her abortion. Also, there did not seem to be any serious supporters for Day's canonization among those who knew her best and feared that canonization could reduce her to "a stained-glass window."

In March 2000, however, the Vatican announced that it had approved starting the canonization process on her behalf. The request came from Cardinal John O'Connor of the New York archdiocese. He wrote that he considered her a model for everyone, "but especially for women who have had or are considering abortion." He added, "She regretted it every day of her life."

Archbishop Fulton J. Sheen (1895–1979)

In the 1950s, there was a popular weekly half-hour television program called "Life Is Worth Living." In it, Archbishop Sheen (then a bishop in New York City) spoke to the viewing audience about various spiritual matters. His program was geared toward those both within and outside of the Roman Catholic Church. Although his only props were a blackboard and chalk, he attracted a viewing audience of nearly 30 million every Tuesday night. He once said, "If you believe the incredible you will do the impossible."

A native of El Paso, Illinois, Archbishop Sheen's first venture into the media was the radio, where he preached over the airwaves in the 1930s. He was also head of a national Catholic project known as the Propagation of the Faith, and he led a successful convert ministry.

E-XTRA

One of the most joyful moments of Archbishop Fulton Sheen's life occurred on October 3, 1979, when Pope John Paul II embraced him and said, "You have written and spoken well of the Lord Jesus. You are a loyal son of the Church!" Archbishop Fulton Sheen died just two months later.

Archbishop Fulton Sheen was most attracted to communications and the spoken and written word. Besides television, Archbishop Sheen wrote newspaper columns and was the author of many books, most of which are still in print and have been consistently reissued. He died in New York City in 1979.

In February 2000, New York City's Cardinal John O'Connor gave provisional approval to begin the archbishop's move toward sainthood. His cause has been taken up by the Archbishop Sheen Foundation in his hometown in Illinois. The foundation is looking for anyone who has letters, photos, film, or reports of physical or spiritual favors from the archbishop. On September 14, 2002, the Vatican officially opened up his cause for canonization.

Matushka Olga Michael (1916–1979)

Within the Eastern Orthodox context, the wives of priests are given honorary titles that reflect their role in the parish community. In the Russian tradition, priests' wives are called *Matushka*, which means "mother" in Russian. Just as the priest serves as a father to the community, his wife has a distinctive role as mother to the parish. This type of motherhood was certainly manifest in Matushka Olga, a native Eskimo who served with her husband, Archpriest Nikolai O. Michael, in the village of Kwethluk on the Kuskokwim River.

Matushka Olga may appear unremarkable at first glance, but through her seemingly ordinary life she was able to touch lives in extraordinary ways. She and her husband gave birth to thirteen children, although only eight of them survived to maturity. Matushka Olga gave birth to several of them without a midwife, and she served as a midwife to laboring mothers in her community, caring for them with compassion and gentleness.

She was graced with a special kind of intuition—she could often sense that a woman was pregnant long before anyone else knew. Likewise, she was able to discern which pregnancies might be difficult, and she was able to offer useful advice to pregnant women long before the challenges of their pregnancies became apparent to others.

Matushka Olga fulfilled many of the tasks that are traditionally associated with Orthodox priests' wives—she baked prosphera, the bread for communion, and she memorized many of the church hymns in her native tongue.

Her passion, however, was knitting. She devoted herself to making mittens, socks, and fur outerwear for those in need. She loved to send unsolicited gifts, including traditional Alaskan winter boots, or mukluks. All of the local (and not-so-local) clergy wore winter clothes crafted by her.

Matushka Olga was generous, despite her own financial limitations. Her family lived in a house with only three rooms, no sewer hookup, no furnace, and no running water. But her heart went to out to those in greater need. Her generosity may have occasionally caused some distress to her own children, as she was sometimes compelled to give away their clothes before they had a chance to outgrow them. She told her children that if they saw someone in the village wearing their clothes, they were to keep quiet about it.

According to one account, she asked one of her daughters to bring a child over who had been neglected. Matushka Olga cooked potato pancakes for the child, standing with her back to her. The child kept eating and eating, and Matushka Olga kept serving her more and more pancakes. Finally, her daughter reported that the little girl was "stealing" the pancakes. Matushka Olga instructed her daughter to keep quiet, to let the little girl take as much as she needed.

A Holy Death

Like many holy people, Matushka Olga's sanctity became more apparent after her death. After surviving one bout with cancer when she was younger, she had several years of remission, followed by a diagnosis that the cancer had returned. When she understood that death was inevitable, she began to prepare herself for the end. She died on November 8, 1979.

Although many people wished to attend her funeral, travel in Alaska is extremely difficult, especially to remote villages during the winter. But soon after she died, the weather shifted. The snow and ice melted suddenly and hundreds from miles around were able to attend her funeral on the unusually springlike day.

As the community processed out of the church with her body, a flock of birds joined the procession and followed her to her gravesite. This was an extremely unusual occurrence because by that time of the season, most birds have flown south.

The unseasonably warm weather had thawed the earth and made it soft and easy to dig. After the memorial meal, when all the guests had made it safely home, the winter winds howled again, ice covered the river, and the snows returned.

Dreams and Visions

Although Matushka Olga has departed this world, some believe that they have had encounters with her since her death. One woman, originally from Alaska but living in Arizona at the time, did not know that her mother, in Alaska, was sick. One night she had a dream in which Matushka Olga told her that her mother was to join Olga in a "bright and joyful place." The next day, the woman received news that her mother was seriously ill. She flew back to Alaska and was able to reassure her mother with Matushka Olga's words just before she died.

Another woman, who had suffered severe sexual abuse as a child, had an extraordinary encounter with Matushka Olga. The woman was awake and praying when she saw the Virgin Mary walking toward her. She soon realized that the Virgin Mary was not alone. When she asked who the Virgin Mary was with, she responded, "St. Olga."

The woman accompanied Matushka Olga to a little hill with a door on the side. Inside the house, everything was warm and dry. The woman was in pain, and she appeared to be five months pregnant. She began to go into labor, and Matushka Olga stood beside her, showing her how to breathe and helping her to push something out.

E-FACT

Matushka Olga was a Yup'ik Eskimo, and the house seen in the vision would have been traditional to her culture. The tea the women drank smelled of rose, violet, and pine—this would be Labrador tea, which grows abundantly on the tundra.

Matushka Olga then made some tea, and as the two women drank tea together, Olga became luminous. The woman reported that Olga "poured tenderness into her through her eyes." She believed that through Olga, she was experiencing deep healing.

Afterward, Olga explained to the woman that people can do evil things. She told her that the people who hurt her thought they could force her to carry their evil through rape, but that was not possible. She said, "Only God can carry evil away. The only thing they could put inside you was the seed of life which is a creation of God and cannot pollute anyone."

Afterward, the two women went outside the hut and saw a sky filled with shimmering stars. Matushka Olga may have said, or the two women may have just heard in their hearts, that "the moving curtain of light was to be for us a promise that God can create beauty from complete desolation and nothingness. For me, it was proof of the healing—great beauty where there had been nothing before but despair hidden by shame and great effort."

(Source material provided by an article by Fr. John Shimchick, "Matushka Olga Michael: A Helper in Restoring the World of God's Hands," published in *Portraits of the American Saints*, George A. Gray and Jan Bear, eds., from Diocese Council and Department of Missions Diocese of the West Orthodox Church in America, 1994.)

Contemporary Saints

Although the question of canonization remains open, these people continue to speak to contemporary times. They used the materials available to them to live faithfully in their own age and place—everything from television to newspaper to knitting needles. And ultimately, through their lives, others were able to glimpse the love of God. As Frederick Buechner wrote, "In his holy flirtation with the world, God sometimes drops a pocket handkerchief. Those handkerchiefs are called saints."

Appendix A

Saintly Lives in Historical Context

It is easy enough for most of us to recall major events that occurred in the world during the lifetime of Mother Teresa, a holy woman on the path to sainthood. But what was happening when Augustine of Hippo was writing his Confessions? When Ignatius of Loyola was founding the Jesuits?

Here is a chronology of historic events of varying importance that also shows the lifespan dates for notable people who affected those times. Interspersed with these listings are the birth and death dates of the saints who have figured most prominently in this book. This will help you put the saints' lives into the context of their times. The chronology only runs through the 1800s, since major events of the twentieth century are still within recent memory.

Date	Event
A.D. 33	Jesus crucified
c. 34	St. Stephen, a follower of Jesus, is stoned to death for his faith, becoming the first Christian martyr
c. 60	The term "Christian" comes into common use
c. 60–155	St. Polycarp
64	Emperor Nero blames Christians for the Great Fire of Rome; persecutions follow. Sts. Peter and Paul are martyred in that city at that time
1st century	Mary, Mother of Jesus
1st century	St. Andrew
1st century	St. Barnabas
1st century	St. Joseph
1st century	St. Joseph of Arimethea
1st century	St. John the Baptist
1st century	St. John the Evangelist
1st century	St. Jude
1st century	St. Luke
1st century	St. Mark
1st century	St. Mary Magdalene
1st century	St. Matthew
1st century	St. Paul
1st century	St. Peter

Date	Event
c. 177–312	Persecution of Christians continues in Rome under three emperors; growth of the cult of martyrs
c. 200–258	St. Cyprian
Died 203	Sts. Perpetua and Felicitas
Died c. 269	St. Valentine
Died c. 288	St. Sebastian
Died c. 303	St. Dorothy
Died c. 303	St. Lucy
Died c. 304	St. Agnes
311	Emperor Constantine converts to Christianity and signs an edict of religious tolerance throughout the Roman Empire
324	Constantine moves to the city of Byzantium and renames it Constantinople, making it the seat of the New Roman Empire
328–387	St. Monica
c. 340–420	St. Jerome
340–397	St. Ambrose
347–404	St. Paula
Died c. 350	St. Nicholas of Myra
354–430	St. Augustine of Hippo
381	Christianity becomes the legal and official religion of Rome when Emperor Theodosius I publishes a decree establishing the orthodoxy of Christian faith
389–461	St. Patrick
c. 390–459	St. Simeon Stylites
395	The Roman Empire divides into Eastern and Western
400	Entire world population estimated at just over 250 million
450–525	St. Brigid

Date	Event
476	The last western Roman emperor falls; Eastern Roman Empire will survive until 1453; during the Middle Ages the rift between the Roman church, headed by the pope, and Eastern Christianity, based in Constantinople and headed by the patriarch of Constantinople, widens
487–577	St. Brendan of Clonfert
540–604	St. Gregory I (the Great)
560–636	St. Isidore of Seville
Died c. 604	St. Augustine of Canterbury
c. 610	Mohammed starts a new religion, Islam, in Arabia
c. 618	St. Kevin of Glendalough
800	Charlemagne is crowned Holy Roman Emperor
1000–1001	Norse explorer Leif Ericson, sailing from Greenland, reaches North America
1054	After centuries of drifting apart, the Eastern Orthodox churches finally break from the Roman church over the issue of papal authority
1066	William of Norman defeats the Saxons and becomes king of England
1085	William the Conqueror orders a census in England that creates what has become known as the Domesday Book
1095	Papacy, under Urban II, launches the Crusades to reclaim holy sites from the Muslims
1098–1179	Hildegard of Bingen
1118–1170	St. Thomas à Becket
1150	University of Paris is founded
1167	Oxford University is founded
1181–1226	St. Francis of Assisi
c. 1185	Kyoto, Japan, is the world's largest city, with a population of 500,000
1194–1253	St. Clare of Assisi
1195–1231	St. Anthony of Padua

Date	Event
1206	Beginning of Genghis Khan's largest land empire in history, reaching from Mongolia west to eastern Europe
c. 1206–1280	St. Albert the Great (Albertus Magnus)
1207–1231	St. Elizabeth of Hungary
1209	Cambridge University is founded
1211	Construction of Rheims Cathedral, on the site of crowning of French kings, begins
1225–1274	St. Thomas Aquinas
1295	Marco Polo returns to Venice after twenty-five years in Asia and begins his memoirs
1309	Pope Clement V, a Frenchman, moves the papal seat from Rome to Avignon, France
1334–1351	Black Death (bubonic) plague kills one-third to one-half of Europe's population
1337–1453	Hundred Years' War (actually a few more) between English and French kings for the control of France
1347–1380	St. Catherine of Siena
1377	Papacy returns to Rome
1387	Geoffrey Chaucer writes *The Canterbury Tales*
1412–1431	St. Joan of Arc
1414–1476	The Medicis of Florence are bankers to the popes
c. 1438	The Incan Empire begins in Peru
c. 1440	Disintegration of the Mayan Empire
1446–1450	Johann Gutenberg invents moveable type for printing (it had been in use in the Far East, but Europeans didn't know that)
1453	After Turks conquer Constantinople, Byzantine Empire crumbles; new center of the Eastern Orthodox Church is Moscow
1469–1535	St. John Fisher
1475–1564	Michelangelo, architect of St. Peter's Basilica

Date	Event
1478–1535	St. Thomas More
1483	Spain's Inquisition under Tomás de Torquemada sees 2,000 "heretics" executed
1491–1556	St. Ignatius of Loyola
1492	Columbus sails from Spain to the New World
1499	Trade in African slaves begins in Lisbon, as Portugal explores the west coast of Africa
1500	World population is now about 400 million
1504–1572	St. Pius V
1506–1552	St. Francis Xavier
1510–1572	St. Francis Borgia
1515–1582	St. Teresa of Ávila
1517	Martin Luther nails his 95 Theses to a church door in Wittenberg, Germany, initiating the Protestant Reformation, which divides Western Christianity into the Roman Catholic Church and Protestantism
1519	Aztec Empire is at its height; the Spaniards arrive
1519–1522	Ferdinand Magellan circumnavigates the globe
1521–1597	St. Peter Canisius
1533–1554	King Henry VIII denies the pope's authority so he can marry Anne Boleyn; the next year he has Parliament declare him the head of the Church of England, marking the beginning of Anglican church
1541	Spanish conquistador Hernando de Soto becomes the first European to see the Mississippi River
1542–1591	St. John of the Cross
1555	The French physician and astrologer Nostradamus begins his prophecies of what the future holds
1564–1616	William Shakespeare, English playwright
1567–1622	St. Francis de Sales
1580–1660	St. Vincent de Paul

Date	Event
1582	Pope Gregory XIII introduces the Gregorian calendar, which no longer considers April 1 as New Year's Day; those who do not note this are known as "April fools"
1591–1660	St. Louise de Marillac
1599–1658	Oliver Cromwell, English Revolutionary soldier
c. 1600	Adherents to the philosophy of John Calvin, French-born Swiss Protestant thinker, break away from the English Puritans to form the Reformists
1605	Cervantes's *Don Quixote*, the first modern novel, is published
1607–1646	St. Isaac Jogues
1607	First permanent English colony on mainland America established at Jamestown, Virginia, by John Smith
1608	First permanent French colony in North America established in Quebec
1611	The King James version of the Bible is published in England
1613	Galileo Galilei says the earth revolves around the sun rather than being the fixed center of the universe; in 1633, the Inquisition finds Galileo, a Catholic, guilty of disobeying the church by publishing his thesis and calls for him to publicly recant; he does not and is sentenced to life imprisonment
1620	Pilgrims land at Plymouth, Massachusetts, to pursue religion freely
1636	Harvard College is founded in Cambridge, Massachusetts
1644–1718	William Penn, English Quaker, founds Pennsylvania as a colony of religious freedom
1682	Edmund Halley first notes the comet that will later bear his name, predicts its future appearances
1696–1787	St. Alphonsus Liguori
1700	Population of largest American city, Boston, is around 7,000; Native American population in all of what is now United States is 1 million
1723	First commercial valentines appear
1729	John Wesley, an English clergyman, begins a reform movement within the Church of England that leads to Methodism
1758–1843	Noah Webster, author of *An American Dictionary of the English Language*

Date	Event
1760	Industrial Revolution begins in England
1769–1852	St. Rose Philippine Duchesne
1770	James Cook claims Australia for Great Britain
1773	Boston Tea Party
1774–1821	St. Elizabeth Ann Seton
1775	Start of American Revolution
1776	Declaration of Independence is drafted
1781	Immanuel Kant writes *Critique of Pure Reason*, in which he establishes his theory of rational experience
1789	French Revolution begins
1801–1890	John Henry Newman
1804	Meriwether Lewis and William Clark set out to explore the new Louisiana Purchase and the land to the west, all the way to the Pacific
1811–1860	St. John Nepomucene Neumann
1815	Battle of Waterloo sees Napoleon defeated
1825	First regular train service begins in Great Britain
1837	Queen Victoria begins a lengthy reign in Great Britain that will last until 1901
1844–1879	St. Bernadette of Lourdes
1846	Famine hits Ireland as a result of potato crop failure and other factors; there are 1 million deaths
1848	Gold discovered in California; population of San Francisco soars from 1,000 to more than 25,000 in two years
1850–1917	St. Frances Xavier Cabrini
1858–1866	Laying of transatlantic cable
1861	U.S. Civil War begins
1864–1869	Leo Tolstoy writes *War and Peace*
1865	President Abraham Lincoln is assassinated

Date	Event
1867	Japan ends 675-year-old Shogun rule
1869–1948	Mohandas "Mahatma" Gandhi
1873–1897	St. Thérèse of Lisieux
1876	Alexander Graham Bell patents the telephone
1879	Thomas Alva Edison invents the electric light
1890–1902	St. Maria Goretti
1893	New Zealand becomes the first country to give women the vote
1894–1941	St. Maximilian Kolbe
1896	First modern Olympic games are held in Athens, Greece
1899–1900	World population at around l.5 billion
1999	World population hits 6 billion with great fanfare; 2 billion people call themselves Christians, and Christianity is the world's largest religion

Appendix B

Doctors of the Church

These are the thirty-three men and women who have been recognized by the church as pre-eminent theologians, those the faithful can learn from.

Albert the Great (Albertus Magnus) (c. 1206–1280): Dominican

Alphonsus Liguori (1696–1787): Redemptorist

Ambrose (c. 340–397): Bishop of Milan

Anselm (1033–1109): Archbishop of Canterbury

Anthony of Padua (1195–1231): Franciscan

Athanasius (c. 297–373): Bishop of Alexandria

Augustine (354–430): Bishop of Hippo

Basil the Great (329–379): Cappadocian

Bede the Venerable (c. 672–735): monk

Bernard of Clairvaux (1090–1153): Cistercian

Bonaventure (1221–1274): Franciscan

Catherine of Siena (1347–1380): Dominican

Cyril of Alexandria (c. 376–444): Patriarch of Alexandria

Cyril of Jerusalem (c. 315–386): Bishop of Jerusalem

Ephraem (c. 306–373): Deacon of Edessa

Francis de Sales (1567–1622): Bishop of Geneva

Gregory I (the Great) (c. 540–604): pope

Gregory Nazianzen (329–389): Cappadocian

Hilary of Poitiers (c. 315–368): Bishop of Poitiers

Isidore of Seville (560–636): Bishop of Seville

Jerome (c. 340–420): monastery head

John Chrysostom (347–407): Patriarch of Constantinople

John Damsacene (c. 675–749): monk

John of the Cross (1542–1591): Discalced Carmelite

Lawrence of Brindisi (1559–1619): Capuchin

Leo I (the Great) (c. 400–461): pope

Peter Canisius (1521–1597): Jesuit

Peter Chrysologus (c. 406–450): Bishop of Ravenna

Peter Damian (1001–1072): Benedictine

Robert Bellarmine (1542–1621): Jesuit

Teresa of Ávila (1515–1582): Discalced Carmelite

Thérèse of Lisieux (1873–1897): Carmelite

Thomas Aquinas (1225–1274): Dominican

Appendix C

Calendar of Saints' Feast Days

The Roman Catholic liturgical calendar denotes the Sundays of Advent and Lent, Easter, the Sundays from Easter to Pentecost, and other feasts that are celebrated annually (of course, exact dates change each year). Saints' feast days are listed only for dates not given over to what is known as the "temporal cycle"—the "official" annual celebrations.

What follows is not a liturgical calendar, but rather a calendar listing by month the feast days for the saints you have read about in these pages. Sometimes you'll see two or more saints sharing the same date. This is accurate, but not something you'll find in a liturgical calendar (unless the saints are paired and share a joint feast day, such as Anne and Joachim, Perpetua and Felicitas).

January	
1	Mary, Mother of Jesus
2	St. Adalhard, St. Basil the Great
3	St. Genevieve
4	St. Elizabeth Ann Seton
5	St. John Nepomucene Neumann, St. Simeon Stylites
15	St. Paul the Hermit
17	St. Devota, St. Anthony of Egypt
19	St. Canute, St. Henry of Uppsala
20	St. Sebastian
21	St. Agnes
22	St. Vincent of Saragossa
24	St. Francis de Sales
26	St. Paula
27	St. John Chrysostom
28	St. Thomas Aquinas
30	St. Aldegonda
31	St. John Bosco

February	
1	St. Brigid
3	St. Blaise, St. Ansgar
5	St. Agatha
6	St. Amand, St. Peter Baptist, St. Dorothy
9	St. Apollonia
10	St. Scholastica
12	St. Julian the Innkeeper
14	St. Valentine
21	John Henry Newman
23	St. Polycarp
25	St. Walburga

March	
1	St. David
3	St. Cunegund, St. Katharine Drexel
4	St. Casimir
7	Sts. Perpetua and Felicitas
8	St. John of God
9	St. Dominic Savio, St. Frances of Rome, St. Catherine of Bologna
13	St. Ansovinus
15	St. Louise de Marillac
17	St. Agricola of Avignon, St. Gertrude of Nivelles, St. Joseph of Arimethea, St. Patrick
19	St. Joseph
20	St. Cuthbert
21	St. Benedict
25	St. Dismas

April	
2	St. Francis of Paola
3	St. Adjutor
4	St. Isidore of Seville
7	St. Jean-Baptiste de la Salle
11	St. Gemma Galani, St. Stanislaus of Cracow
14	St. Peter González, St. Lidwina
16	St. Benedict Joseph Labre
23	St. George
25	St. Mark
27	St. Zita
30	St. Pius V

May	
1	St. Joseph the Worker
4	St. Florian
8	St. Plechelm
10	St. John of Ávila, St. Antonius of Florence, St. Catald, St. Isidore the Farmer
13	St. Julian of Norwich
15	St. Dymphna
16	St. John of Nepomuk, St. Honoratus, St. Brendan of Clonfert, St. Peregrine of Auxerre, St. John Nepomucene Neumann
19	St. Dunstan, St. Ivo, St. Celestine V
20	St. Bernardino of Siena
22	St. Rita, St. Julia of Corsica
27	St. Augustine of Canterbury
28	St. Bernard of Montjoux
29	St. Bona
30	St. Joan of Arc, St. Ferdinand

June	
1	St. Theobald
2	St. Elmo
3	St. Kevin of Glendalough, St. Morand
5	St. Boniface
8	St. Medard
9	St. Columba of Iona
11	St. Barnabas
13	St. Anthony of Padua
15	St. Vitus
21	St. Aloysius Gonzaga
22	St. Nicetas, St. John Fisher, St. Thomas More
23	St. Joseph Cafasso
24	St. John the Baptist
29	Sts. Peter and Paul

July	
3	St. Thomas
4	St. Elizabeth of Portugal
6	St. Maria Goretti
7	Sts. Cyril and Methodius
8	St. Kilian
11	St. Benedict II
12	St. John Gualbert
14	St. Camillus de Lellis
15	St. Swithun, St. Vladimir I of Kiev
19	Sts. Justa and Rufina
22	St. Mary Magdalene
23	St. Bridget of Sweden

July *(continued)*	
25	St. James the Greater
26	Sts. Anne and Joachim
27	St. Pantaleon
29	St. Olaf, St. Martha
31	St. Ignatius of Loyola

August	
1	St. Alphonsus Liguori, St. Friard
3	St. Hippolytus
4	St. John Vianney (Curé of Ars)
5	Sts. Addai and Mari
8	St. Dominic
10	St. Lawrence
14	St. Maximilian Kolbe
15	Feast of the Assumption
16	St. Roch
19	St. Sebald
20	St. Bernard of Clairvaux
23	St. Rose of Lima
24	St. Bartholomew, St. Ouen
25	St. Genesius the Actor
27	St. Monica
28	St. Augustine of Hippo, St. Moses the Black
31	St. Raymond Nonnatus

September	
1	St. Fiacre, St. Giles
3	St. Gregory I (the Great)
7	St. Gratis of Aosta
8	St. Hadrian
9	St. Peter Claver
10	St. Nicholas Tolentine
11	St. Hyacinth
16	St. Ludmilla, St. Cyprian
17	St. Hildegard of Bingen
18	St. Joseph of Cupertino
19	St. Januarius
21	St. Matthew
22	St. Phocas
23	St. Adamnan
26	Sts. Cosmas and Damian
27	St. Vincent de Paul
28	St. Wenceslas
29	Archangels Gabriel, Michael, and Raphael
30	St. Jerome, St. Gregory the Illuminator

October	
1	St. Thérèse of Lisieux
4	St. Francis of Assisi
6	St. Bruno
9	St. Denis, St. Louis Bertrand
10	St. Francis Borgia, St. Gereon
15	St. Teresa of Ávila
16	St. Gall, St. Gerard Majella

October *(continued)*	
18	St. Luke
19	St. Isaac Jogues and the North American Martyrs
20	Bl. Contardo Ferrini
22	St. Peter of Alcántara
23	St. John Capistrano
24	St. Anthony Claret
25	Sts. Crispin and Crispinian
27	St. Frumentius
28	St. Jude

November	
3	St. Hubert of Liège, St. Martin de Porres
4	St. Charles Borromeo
5	St. Kea
6	St. Leonard of Noblac
7	St. Willibrord
8	Four Crowned Martyrs
10	St. Aedh Mac Bricc, St. Gertrude the Great
11	St. Martin of Tours
13	St. Brice, St. Homobonus, St. Frances Xavier Cabrini, St. Stanislaus Kostka
15	St. Albert the Great (Albertus Magnus)
16	St. Margaret of Scotland
17	St. Elizabeth of Hungary, St. Gregory the Woodworker
18	St. Rose Philippine Duchesne, St. Odo of Cluny
22	St. Cecilia
26	St. Leonard Casanova, St. John Berchmans
30	St. Andrew

December	
1	St. Eligius
2	St. Bibiana
3	St. Francis Xavier
4	St. Osmund, St. Barbara
6	St. Nicholas of Myra
8	Feast of the Immaculate Conception
11	St. Damasus
13	St. Odilia, St. Lucy
14	St. John of the Cross
21	St. Peter Canisius
23	St. Thorlac, St. John Cantius
26	St. Stephen
27	St. John the Evangelist
29	St. Thomas à Becket

Appendix D

On the Job: Saints by Occupation

There are patron saints for almost every occupation. These saints won their role by association. Some of these associations were more pleasant than others. St. Lawrence, for example, a third-century martyr, was roasted on a grid and became the patron saint of cooks.

In the listing of patron saints that follows, the brief biography will note how the saint came to intercede in a particular career, life situation, or health problem. Naturally there was a good deal more to that holy person's life to make him or her merit canonization.

Sometimes a saint's biography, especially saints whose lives are little known, shows no evidence why that man or woman was chosen for patronage in a particular area. Perhaps the reasons are lost in the mists of history. Or maybe patronage was just divine inspiration on someone's part.

Accountants	St. Matthew
Actors	St. Genesius the Actor. Actor in Rome at the time of Emperor Diocletian. Killed for his faith by beheading.
	St. Vitus (June 15). His story dates back to 300, when Vitus, a Sicilian, was converted to Christianity at age twelve and became known for his conversions and miracles. In Rome he freed Emperor Diocletian's son from an evil spirit. His thanks was having the gesture taken as sorcery, and Vitus, his tutor, and servant were subjected to torture. In one account all three were boiled in oil. In a cheerier version, they were not harmed, and during a storm an angel led them back to their home. Some details of Vitus's story may be legend. The nervous disorder St. Vitus's Dance (chorea) was named after him, apparently after he was able to assist those suffering from it and from epilepsy.
Advertising workers	St. Bernardino of Siena (May 20). Preacher of fiery sermons, denouncing, among other things, gambling and witchcraft. This saint, who lived from 1380 to 1444, also rejuvenated and reformed the Friars of the Strict Observance, increasing their number from about 300 to more than 4,000 during his lifetime.
Agricultural workers	St. Phocas (September 22). A gardener at Paphlagonia in the Early Christian era, Phocas lived a pious life. When an army came to his house looking for him, he told them to wait and they would find Phocas in the morning. He then prepared spiritually for death, dug his grave, and told the soldiers who he was. They were hesitant to harm him—he had been a good host—but he urged them to behead him and they did.
Anesthetists	St. René Goupil
Apprentices	St. John Bosco, Italian saint (1815–1888) who established a refuge for boys, teaching them trades. Also published catechismal materials to instruct the youths in his care.

Archaeologists	St. Damasus (December 11). Fourth-century pope who restored catacombs, shrines, and tombs of martyrs.
Archers	St. Sebastian
Architects	St. Barbara
	St. Thomas (July 3). First-century apostle and saint who built many churches.
Artists	Fra Angelica
	St. Catherine of Bologna (March 9). A member of the Poor Clares, Catherine (1413–1463) is said to have experienced visions of Mary with the infant Jesus in her arms, later reproduced often in art.
	St. Luke
Astronauts, pilots	St. Joseph of Cupertino (September 18). Seventeenth-century Italian Franciscan (1603–1663) known as "the flying friar." His ecstasies and levitations had him "flying" over altars, at one time whipping through a church from one end to the other over the heads of the congregation.
Astronomers	St. Dominic (August 8). Founder of the Order of Preachers (Dominicans). A Spaniard, Dominic (1170–1221) took a new tack with his order. Rather than living in a monastery, Dominicans took the gospel message on the road, preaching as they traveled and living on very little. The Dominican order produced such theological giants as St. Thomas Aquinas; however, Torquemada, in charge of the Spanish Inquisition, was also a Dominican, taking the search for truth too far.
Athletes	St. Sebastian
Bakers	St. Elizabeth of Hungary
	St. Honoratus (May 16). Sixth-century French bishop noted for this miracle: while he was celebrating mass, the hand of God appeared above the chalice and held out bread.
	St. Nicholas
Bankers	St. Matthew
Blacksmiths	St. Dunstan. English bishop and great reformer (910–988) who was also a skilled metalworker and harpist.

Blacksmiths (*continued*)	St. John the Baptist
Boatmen	St. Julian the Hospitaler
Bookbinders	St. Celestine V (May 19). Thirteenth-century Italian-born Peter de Marrone became a hermit, a priest, and founder of the Celestine order. Against his better judgment, he accepted the papacy after political bickering left the seat vacant. A holy but simple man not meant for the demands of the papacy, he soon abdicated and returned to the monastery. Pope Boniface VIII, his successor, felt threatened by Celestine's popularity and put him in prison, where he died ten months later.
Bookkeepers	St. Matthew
Booksellers	St. John of God (March 8). Sixteenth-century Portuguese who did varied work before becoming a Christian, then built a hospital and cared for the sick.
Brewers	St. Augustine of Hippo
	St. Nicholas of Myra
Bricklayers	St. Stephen
Broadcasters	St. Gabriel the Archangel (September 29). In the Bible he brings news and is a heavenly intercessor. He was sent to Zachary's wife, Elizabeth, to tell her she would have a child—St. John the Baptist—who would prepare the way for the Savior. Gabriel also appeared to Mary to tell her she would be the mother of Jesus.
Builders	St. Barbara
	St. Vincent Ferrer (April 5). A Spanish Dominican priest, Vincent (1350–1419) is best known for preaching in Europe and for bringing unity to the church from the Great Schism, when first two and then three rival popes claimed authority.
Bus drivers	St. Christopher
Businesspeople	St. Homobonus (November 13). Twelfth-century Italian businessman; scrupulously honest, he also gave away a good deal of his profits. His name in Latin means "good man."

Butchers	St. Anthony of Egypt (January 17). An ascetic, Anthony (251–356) spent a good deal of his life living in the desert, practicing severe austerity, even living in a cemetery for a time. After twenty years he emerged to found a community of monks, then several branches of the monastery, fueled by the interest of men impressed by his holiness. He lived to be 105 and was remarked upon (favorably) by St. Augustine in his Confessions.
	St. Hadrian, a.k.a. Adrian (September 8). A third- or fourth-century martyr. Once a pagan military officer who converted to Christianity, he died being torn limb from limb.
	St. Luke
Cab drivers	St. Fiacre (September 1). Seventh-century Irish saint who built a refuge for the sick and poor. Patron saint of cab drivers of Paris, whose taxis are called fiacres. The first taxi rank there was located near the Hotel Saint-Fiacre.
Cabinetmakers	St. Anne
Candlemakers	St. Bernard of Clairvaux (August 20). An eleventh-century Burgundian nobleman, Bernard had poetic leanings but eventually became a Cistercian monk, a strict order. Beset by physical problems, no doubt exacerbated by his austere lifestyle, he founded his own monastery and wrote "sweetly" in his poetry and preaching, earning the title Doctor Mellifluous. Thus the connection from sweet to honey to bees, to wax and candles.
	St. John the Baptist
Carpenters	St. Joseph
Communications	St. Bernardino of Siena (see Advertising workers)
	St. Gabriel (see Broadcasters)
Cooks	St. Martha (July 29) First-century friend of Jesus, she was fussing in the kitchen while her sister, Mary, listened to Christ preach in the next room. Martha was mildly rebuked by Jesus for her choice.

Cooks (*continued*)	St. Lawrence (August 10). One of the seven deacons of Rome, this third-century saint was born in Spain and served as deacon to Pope Sixtus II, who was eventually condemned to death. When Sixtus told Lawrence that he would follow the pope to the grave in three days, Lawrence gave away money and many of the church's possessions to the needy. When the emperor asked for the return of the church's treasures, Lawrence collected the poor, sick, and other needy, presented them to the emperor, and told him they were the church's treasures. This was enough for the emperor. Lawrence was bound to a hot griddle. Apparently, in the middle of this agony, he managed to tell his tormentors that they should turn him over, he was quite done on that side. Later, historians agreed he was actually beheaded, but the link to cooks understandably persists. It is said his death led to the conversion of Rome.
Craftsmen	St. Catherine of Alexandria
Customs agents	St. Matthew
Dairy workers	St. Brigid of Ireland
Dancers	St. Vitus (see Actors)
Dentists	St. Apollonia (February 9). Third-century Alexandrian martyr. This elderly deaconess was beaten so severely that her teeth were either smashed or pulled out with pincers. Still refusing to denounce her faith, she flung herself into her captors' bonfire.
Dietitians	St. Martha (see Cooks)
Diplomats	St. Gabriel the Archangel (see Broadcasters)
Dockworkers	St. Nicholas
Domestic workers	St. Martha (see Cooks)
	St. Zita (April 27). Thirteenth-century Italian servant who took food from her wealthy household to give to the poor. When stopped once by her mistress, she opened the apron she had filled with food and rose petals spilled onto the floor.
Druggists	Sts. Cosmas and Damian (September 26). Fourth-century Arabian martyrs. These twin physicians took no money from their patients. They died by beheading. Their story could be legend, although miracles were attributed to them centuries after their death.

Ecologists	St. Francis of Assisi
Editors, publishers	St. John Bosco (see Apprentices)
Engineers	St. Ferdinand (May 30). Castilian king (Ferdinand III 1199–1252) who founded a university and a cathedral.
Farmers	St. George (April 23). A perhaps legendary knight who killed a dragon that had been terrifying the town of Sylene in Libya. Thought to be martyred under Emperor Diocletian, he became particularly popular in the Middle Ages, especially among the Crusaders.
	St. Isidore the Farmer (May 10). Twelfth-century Spanish hired hand who helped the needy.
Firefighters	St. Florian (May 4). Fourth-century officer of the Roman army. Some accounts say that when he declared his Christianity he was set on fire, others that he was scourged and cast into a river with a rock tied around him.
Fishermen	St. Andrew
	St. Peter
Flight attendants	St. Bona (May 29). Thirteenth-century religious zealot from Pisa who from age fourteen guided many on the journey from Pisa to Palestine, where she had first gone to visit her father.
Florists	St. Rose of Lima (August 23). First canonized saint of the Americas. Born in 1586 in Lima, Peru. Patronage comes from her name, and the fact that she loved tending her parents' garden. She died at thirty-one.
	St. Thérèse of Lisieux
Foresters	St. John Gualbert (July 12). Eleventh-century Florentine abbot who built a monastery from the wood of a nearby forest.
Funeral directors and undertakers	St. Dismas (March 25). Known as "the good thief," he was crucified next to Jesus.
	St. Joseph of Arimethea

Gardeners	St. Adalhard (January 2). A monk, Adalhard (753–827) was brought to court by his cousin, Charlemagne, and became one of his advisers. Presumably for supporting a revolt against Emperor Louis the Debonair, he was exiled to Aquitaine. Brought back by Louis, he was exiled again for some other transgression. A pious man who seemed to roll with the punches, Adalhard established two monasteries that became learning centers.
	St. Dorothy (303)
	St. Fiacre (see Cab Drivers)
	St. Phocas the Gardener (See Agricultural workers)
Glassworkers	St. Luke
Governors	St. Ferdinand (King Ferdinand III; see Engineers)
Gravediggers	St. Anthony of Egypt (see Cemetery workers)
Grocers and supermarket workers	St. Michael the Archangel (September 29). Leader of the heavenly army of angels who defeated Satan and his followers and hurled them from heaven. He metes out punishment but tempers it with divine justice. Usually he is represented with a sword, standing over a conquered dragon (that is, Satan). Since the sixth century, September 29 has also been known as Michaelmas Day, celebrated to honor the dedication of a basilica in Michael's honor in Rome. It is no longer commemorated, and today all three named archangels—Michael, Gabriel, and Raphael—have been given the feast day. It is still occasionally called Michaelmas Day.
Hairstylists	St. Martin de Porres (November 3). Born in 1579, this saint was a Peruvian whose father was a Spanish nobleman and mother a free black woman. He was a barber before becoming a Dominican lay brother. He did many good works, was extremely pious (given to self-flagellation), and, like Francis of Assisi, had an affinity for animals.
	St. Mary Magdalene
Homemakers	St. Anne

Hospital workers and administrators	St. Basil the Great (January 2). Born in Asia Minor (329–379) Basil taught and then became a hermit. He attracted disciples and founded the first monastery in Asia Minor. He was active in helping the poor and the sick, building what would today be called a hospital. A holy man, he was enormously effective in fighting heresy and issuing doctrinal writings. He is a Doctor of the Church.
	St. Frances Xavier Cabrini
Hotel workers and innkeepers	St. Amand (February 6). A French missionary, Amand (c. 584–679) lived as a hermit for fifteen years after his ordination, then became active in missionary work in Flanders, Ghent, and most likely Germany. He founded numerous monasteries in Belgium.
	St. Julian the Hospitaler
	St. Martha
Janitors and porters	St. Theobald (June 1). A twelfth-century Italian layman who worked as a janitor in a cathedral and gave most of his money to the poor.
Jewelers	St. Dunstan (see Blacksmiths)
	St. Eligius (December 1). French saint (588–660), also known as Eloi, was a metalworker who created two thrones for King Clotaire in Paris with gold and jewels. He used his wealth to found a monastery and a convent.
Journalists	St. Francis de Sales
Laborers	St. John Bosco (see Apprentices)
Lawyers	St. Catherine of Alexandria
	St. Ivo, also known as Yves Kermartin (May 19). A thirteenth-century Breton who studied law in Paris and practiced in Brittany, he defended the rich as well as destitute prostitutes. He became a fair, incorruptible judge and eventually a priest, helping parishioners with legal problems.
	St. Thomas More
Leatherworkers	St. John the Baptist
Librarians	St. Catherine of Alexandria
	St. Jerome

Locksmiths	St. Dunstan (see Blacksmiths)
Maids	St. Zita (see Domestic workers)
Manual laborers	St. Joseph
Medical technicians	St. Albert the Great
Merchants	St. Francis of Assisi
	St. Nicholas
Messengers	St. Gabriel the Archangel (see Broadcasters)
Metalworkers	St. Eligius (see Jewelers)
Midwives	St. Raymond Nonnatus (August 31). Thirteenth-century Spanish cardinal who was born by cesarean section after his mother died in labor. His surname means "not born"—an odd but interesting choice, since he obviously was.
Military	St. Joan of Arc
Military chaplains	St. John Capistrano (October 23). Fifteenth-century Italian nobleman ordained in 1420 and sent on frequent papal diplomatic missions; preached in Bavaria and Poland. When Turks captured Constantinople, he preached against them but was not successful. Led the Christian army in the Battle of Belgrade in 1456, which kept the Turks from taking that city and stemmed their overall progress.
Monks	St. John the Baptist
Musicians	St. Cecilia (November 22). Early Roman martyr. Legend is that she was unable to hear music played at her wedding because she was singing to God. She later converted her bridegroom to her faith. Both were martyred.
	St. Dunstan (see Blacksmiths)
	St. Gregory I (the Great)
	St. Odo of Cluny (November 18). French abbot (879–942); a musician who, among other talents, composed hymns.
Naval officers	St. Francis of Paola (April 2). Italian (1416–1507) who founded the Minims order. At one time he tossed his cloak on the water and sailed across the Straits of Messina on it.

Notaries	St. Luke
	St. Mark
Nurses	St. Agatha (February 5). Dates of her birth and death are unknown, but she is said to have been a wealthy Sicilian who dedicated her life to God and to chastity. When she refused the advances of a government official during a spate of Christian persecutions, he condemned her to a brothel, beat her, and then rolled her on a bed of hot coals until she died. St. Agatha is said to scold women who work on her feast day by appearing as an angry cat. She is known as Santo Gato (Saint Cat) in northern Spain.
	St. Camillus de Lellis (July 14). Hospital bursar in Italy who lived from 1550 to 1614. He was ordained and founded the Ministers of the Sick, a lay order that cared for patients in hospitals and at home. He pioneered such now-common nursing practices as isolating infected patients and a sensible diet.
	St. John of God (see Booksellers)
Nursing and nursing services	St. Catherine of Siena
	St. Elizabeth of Hungary
Obstetricians	St. Raymond Nonnatus (see Midwives)
Painters	St. Luke
Paratroopers	St. Michael the Archangel (see Grocers and supermarket workers)
Parish priests	St. John Vianney (August 4). French clergyman (1786–1859) best known as Curé of Ars. Named parish priest in 1818 in the village of Ars-en-Dombes, he spent his life with those 250 residents, doing good works. His fame as a confessor—he sometimes heard confessions eighteen hours a day and had a special talent for drawing out penitents—brought trainloads of pilgrims to Ars. He is considered the paradigm of a parish priest.
Pawnbrokers	St. Nicholas of Myra
Pencil makers	St. Thomas Aquinas
Pharmacists	Sts. Cosmas and Damian (see Druggists)

Pharmacists (*continued*)	St. Gemma Galani (April 11). Early twentieth-century Italian mystic whose father was a pharmacist. She experienced stigmata and died at twenty-five.
	St. Raphael the Archangel (September 29). The third of only three of the seven archangels mentioned by name. The name Raphael means "God hath healed," and he is patron saint of all those in the healing professions.
Physicians	Sts. Cosmas and Damian (see Druggists)
	St. Luke
	St. Pantaleon (July 27). Raised a Christian in the fourth century, became a doctor and then personal physician to the Roman emperor. He enjoyed court life perhaps a bit too much and lost his faith. Finding his way back, he offered his medical services to the poor at no charge. He suffered martyrdom during the reign of Diocletian. He was beheaded after six other methods were used to attempt unsuccessfully to kill him.
	St. Raphael (see Pharmacists)
Plasterers	St. Bartholomew (August 24). One of the twelve apostles. The little that is known about him may be apocryphal. He was to have founded a Christian community in India, where he is known to have preached. He also traveled to Armenia, where he was beheaded.
Poets	St. Cecilia (see Musicians)
	St. Columba
	St. David (March 1). Also known as St. Dewi. Sixth-century Welsh abbot and bishop of a monastery now called St. David's in Pembrokeshire. Many Welsh churches bear his name.
	St. John of the Cross
Police officers	St. Michael (see Grocers and supermarket workers)
Porters	St. Christopher
Postal workers	St. Gabriel (see Broadcasters)

Preachers	St. John Chrysostom (January 27). Patriarch of Constantinople who lived 347–407. He went from early life as a Christian ascetic to the bishopric (the office of bishop). He is remembered as one who wrote sermons that moved his congregation to tears. A prolific writer in explaining the faith, his brilliance led to being named a Doctor of the Church.
Printers	St. Augustine
	St. Genesius (see Actors)
Prostitutes, repentant	St. Mary Magdalene
Public relations	St. Bernardino of Siena (see Advertising workers)
Radio workers	St. Gabriel the Archangel (see Broadcasters)
Radiologists	St. Michael the Archangel (see Grocers and supermarket workers)
Road workers	St. Francis of Paola (see Naval officers)
	St. John the Baptist
Sailors	St. Cuthbert (March 20). Seventh-century Irish (or possibly Scottish) monk who became a hermit, then was brought out to take on the see at Hexham, and later Lindisfarne. At the end of his life, he cared for the sick and worked many miracles of healing.
	St. Elmo (June 2). Fourth-century bishop in Compagna, Italy, also known as Erasmus, who—another victim of Diocletian's persecution—was martyred. Some accounts say he was rolled in pitch and set on fire, which may account for his association with the phenomenon known as St. Elmo's fire, in which a blue light appears around a ship's mast during an electric storm.
	St. Nicholas
	St. Peter Gonzáles (April 14). Spanish-born Benedictine (1190–1246), he served as chaplain to King Ferdinand III (who was also later canonized). He preached a crusade against the Moors, then urged mercy for them. He was particularly concerned about sailors, hence this patronage.
Scholars	St. Brigid
Scientists	St. Albert the Great

Sculptors	Four Crowned Martyrs (November 8). These are either four Persian stonemasons, known by name, slain by Emperor Diocletian for not sacrificing to the gods, or they are four Roman soldiers martyred by the same emperor for the same reason. The Venerable Bede records that a seventh-century church in Canterbury was dedicated to them and contained their remains.
Security guards	St. Peter of Alcántara (October 22). A native of Spain, Peter (1499–1562) joined a religious order at sixteen, then founded a friary six years later. He preached, then lived as a hermit for a time. He founded an offshoot of the Order of the Conventuals that was more interested in penance and austerity, and eventually became the Alcatrines. He was also an adviser to St. Teresa of Ávila, helping her with her reform of the Carmelites.
Seminarians	St. Charles Borromeo (November 4). Sixteenth-century son of a count and the sister of a pope (who was a Medici), Charles, as you might expect with a pope uncle, moved along quickly in his career. Within a week of his elevation to pope, his uncle named him a cardinal and archbishop of Milan. At this point Charles was still a layman but he went on to become ordained and used his power and considerable intelligence to build schools and churches and hospitals, sometimes using his own money for projects. He also established seminaries for the clergy, and made many reforms. It was he who was finally able to bring the Council of Trent to a close in 1562. During the famine of 1570 in Milan, he managed to find food and feed 3,000 people a day.
Shepherds	St. Bernadette of Lourdes
Shoemakers	Sts. Crispin and Crispinian (October 25). Possibly legend, these two third-century Roman brothers went to Gaul to preach. At night they worked as shoemakers. Martyrs, they were beheaded by the order of Emperor Maximian.
Singers	St. Cecilia (see Musicians)
	St. Gregory I (the Great) (see Musicians)
Skaters	St. Lidwina (April 14). A Dutch holy woman (1380–1433) who was injured at sixteen while ice skating and became an invalid for the remainder of her life. She suffered a great deal, offering her pain for the reparation for sinners. Eventually she experienced visions, ate little or nothing, and became almost totally blind.

Skiers	St. Bernard of Montjoux (May 28). An Italian who lived c. 996–1081, he was a priest who spent most of his time doing missionary work in the Alps. He built schools and churches, but is best remembered for erecting hospices (in this context, these were inns, not services for the fatally ill) to aid lost travelers in mountain passes now named Great and Little Bernard after him. The St. Bernard dog is said to be named after him.
Social workers	St. Louise de Marillac
Soldiers	St. George (see Farmers)
	St. Ignatius of Loyola
	St. Joan of Arc
	St. Sebastian
Speleologists	St. Benedict (July 11). Sixth-century nobleman born in Norcia, Italy. After his first miracle as a youth, he took to an underground cave where he lived for three years, constantly tempted by the devil. On returning aboveground, he founded the Benedictine order, which made manual labor part of the day's schedule. He built a great monastery, Monte Cassino, affected monastic life for centuries, and went down in church history books as a founder of Western Monasticism. As recently as the 1970s, Pope Paul VI named him patron of all Europe.
Stonemasons	St. Stephen
Surgeons	Sts. Cosmas and Damian (see Druggists)
	St. Luke
Tailors	St. Homobonus (see Businesspeople)
Tapestry makers	St. Francis of Assisi
Tax collectors	St. Matthew
Teachers	St. Gregory I (the Great)
	St. John-Baptiste de la Salle (April 7). A French priest born in 1651, Jean-Baptiste founded the Brothers of the Christian Schools—or Christian Brothers, as they came to be known. He had avant-garde ideas about education, one of them grouping children in classes rather than receiving individual instruction.

Telecommunication	St. Gabriel (see Broadcasters)
Television workers	St. Gabriel (see Broadcasters)
Television writers	St. Clare of Assisi
Theologians	St. Alphonsus Liguori
	St. Augustine of Hippo
Watchmen	St. Matthew
Weavers	St. Paul the Hermit (January 15). Born in Egypt, Paul (c. 229–342), who is sometimes known as Paul the First Hermit to distinguish him from later Pauls, fled persecution from Emperor Decius, and fled again when he learned that his own brother-in-law planned to report him as a Christian. He became a hermit and liked the life—certainly safer than staying out in the world—and became a holy and admired man. St. Jerome visited him and wrote about his life, which ended, it is said, when he was 113.
Winegrowers	St. Martin of Tours (November 11). Martin (c. 316–397) is considered also a founder of Western monasticism, along with St. Benedict. Born to pagan parents, he was twelve when he began studying Christianity and eighteen when baptized. He became a monk in Milan, and then moved to Gaul, and established the first French monastic community south of Poitiers. He became bishop of Tours for a while, living at the cathedral, then returned to the monastic life he preferred. Many miracles were attributed to him.
	St. Morand (June 3). Twelfth-century nobleman born in Germany who became a Benedictine monk and later confidant to a count in Lower Alsace. He was known for his holiness, his kindness to the people, and his miracles. It is said that he fasted through Lent eating nothing but a bunch of grapes.
Wine merchants	St. Amand (see Hotel workers and innkeepers)
Wool workers	St. John the Baptist
Workers	St. Joseph
Writers, authors	St. Francis de Sales
	St. Lucy

Index

Everything® Quilting Book
Everything® Scrapbooking Book
Everything® Sewing Book
Everything® Soapmaking Book, 2nd Ed.
Everything® Woodworking Book

HOME IMPROVEMENT

Everything® Feng Shui Book
Everything® Feng Shui Decluttering Book, $9.95
Everything® Fix-It Book
Everything® Home Decorating Book
Everything® Home Storage Solutions Book
Everything® Homebuilding Book
Everything® Organize Your Home Book

KIDS' BOOKS

All titles are $7.95

Everything® Kids' Animal Puzzle & Activity Book
Everything® Kids' Baseball Book, 4th Ed.
Everything® Kids' Bible Trivia Book
Everything® Kids' Bugs Book
Everything® Kids' Cars and Trucks Puzzle & Activity Book
Everything® Kids' Christmas Puzzle & Activity Book
Everything® Kids' Cookbook
Everything® Kids' Crazy Puzzles Book
Everything® Kids' Dinosaurs Book
Everything® Kids' First Spanish Puzzle and Activity Book
Everything® Kids' Gross Cookbook
Everything® Kids' Gross Hidden Pictures Book
Everything® Kids' Gross Jokes Book
Everything® Kids' Gross Mazes Book
Everything® Kids' Gross Puzzle and Activity Book
Everything® Kids' Halloween Puzzle & Activity Book
Everything® Kids' Hidden Pictures Book
Everything® Kids' Horses Book
Everything® Kids' Joke Book
Everything® Kids' Knock Knock Book
Everything® Kids' Learning Spanish Book
Everything® Kids' Math Puzzles Book
Everything® Kids' Mazes Book
Everything® Kids' Money Book
Everything® Kids' Nature Book
Everything® Kids' Pirates Puzzle and Activity Book
Everything® Kids' Presidents Book
Everything® Kids' Princess Puzzle and Activity Book
Everything® Kids' Puzzle Book
Everything® Kids' Riddles & Brain Teasers Book
Everything® Kids' Science Experiments Book
Everything® Kids' Sharks Book
Everything® Kids' Soccer Book
Everything® Kids' States Book
Everything® Kids' Travel Activity Book

KIDS' STORY BOOKS

Everything® Fairy Tales Book

LANGUAGE

Everything® Conversational Japanese Book with CD, $19.95
Everything® French Grammar Book
Everything® French Phrase Book, $9.95
Everything® French Verb Book, $9.95
Everything® German Practice Book with CD, $19.95
Everything® Inglés Book
Everything® Intermediate Spanish Book with CD, $19.95
Everything® Learning Brazilian Portuguese Book with CD, $19.95
Everything® Learning French Book
Everything® Learning German Book
Everything® Learning Italian Book
Everything® Learning Latin Book
Everything® Learning Spanish Book with CD, 2nd Edition, $19.95
Everything® Russian Practice Book with CD, $19.95
Everything® Sign Language Book
Everything® Spanish Grammar Book
Everything® Spanish Phrase Book, $9.95
Everything® Spanish Practice Book with CD, $19.95
Everything® Spanish Verb Book, $9.95
Everything® Speaking Mandarin Chinese Book with CD, $19.95

MUSIC

Everything® Drums Book with CD, $19.95
Everything® Guitar Book with CD, 2nd Edition, $19.95
Everything® Guitar Chords Book with CD, $19.95
Everything® Home Recording Book
Everything® Music Theory Book with CD, $19.95
Everything® Reading Music Book with CD, $19.95
Everything® Rock & Blues Guitar Book with CD, $19.95
Everything® Rock and Blues Piano Book with CD, $19.95
Everything® Songwriting Book

NEW AGE

Everything® Astrology Book, 2nd Ed.
Everything® Birthday Personology Book
Everything® Dreams Book, 2nd Ed.
Everything® Love Signs Book, $9.95
Everything® Numerology Book
Everything® Paganism Book
Everything® Palmistry Book
Everything® Psychic Book
Everything® Reiki Book
Everything® Sex Signs Book, $9.95
Everything® Tarot Book, 2nd Ed.
Everything® Toltec Wisdom Book
Everything® Wicca and Witchcraft Book

PARENTING

Everything® Baby Names Book, 2nd Ed.
Everything® Baby Shower Book
Everything® Baby's First Year Book
Everything® Birthing Book
Everything® Breastfeeding Book
Everything® Father-to-Be Book
Everything® Father's First Year Book
Everything® Get Ready for Baby Book
Everything® Get Your Baby to Sleep Book, $9.95
Everything® Getting Pregnant Book
Everything® Guide to Raising a One-Year-Old
Everything® Guide to Raising a Two-Year-Old
Everything® Homeschooling Book
Everything® Mother's First Year Book
Everything® Parent's Guide to Childhood Illnesses
Everything® Parent's Guide to Children and Divorce
Everything® Parent's Guide to Children with ADD/ADHD
Everything® Parent's Guide to Children with Asperger's Syndrome
Everything® Parent's Guide to Children with Autism
Everything® Parent's Guide to Children with Bipolar Disorder
Everything® Parent's Guide to Children with Depression
Everything® Parent's Guide to Children with Dyslexia
Everything® Parent's Guide to Children with Juvenile Diabetes
Everything® Parent's Guide to Positive Discipline
Everything® Parent's Guide to Raising a Successful Child
Everything® Parent's Guide to Raising Boys
Everything® Parent's Guide to Raising Girls
Everything® Parent's Guide to Raising Siblings
Everything® Parent's Guide to Sensory Integration Disorder
Everything® Parent's Guide to Tantrums
Everything® Parent's Guide to the Strong-Willed Child
Everything® Parenting a Teenager Book
Everything® Potty Training Book, $9.95
Everything® Pregnancy Book, 3rd Ed.
Everything® Pregnancy Fitness Book
Everything® Pregnancy Nutrition Book
Everything® Pregnancy Organizer, 2nd Ed., $16.95
Everything® Toddler Activities Book
Everything® Toddler Book